THE
MOTORCARAVAN
MANUAL

John Wickersham

Haynes

THE BOOK ®

Author: John Wickersham

Editor: Jill Gough

Cover design: David Hermelin

Photographs: John Wickersham

Illustrations: Geoff Denney

© John Wickersham 1998

First published 1998
Reprinted 1999

Published by: Haynes Publishing, Sparkford, nr Yeovil, Somerset, England BA22 7JJ

A catalogue record for this book is available from the British Library

ISBN 1 85960 322 X

Printed in Great Britain by J. H. Haynes & Co. Ltd.

Gas Regulations

Gas Regulations and the way in which appliance manufacturers interpret them regarding the installation of their products are subject to continuing change. It is *strongly recommended* that anyone contemplating the installation of a gas appliance should consult the appliance manufacturer's customer service department before undertaking any work themselves. This may reveal different recommendations from those stated here, in which it is suggested that a competent amateur could consider tackling the preliminary carpentry and fitting work in accordance with the installation instructions. However, it is suggested in the chapters concerned with gas systems and appliances that work on the gas connection(s), flues and the final testing of an installation should always be entrusted to a competent and appropriately qualified gas engineer as defined on page 57.

Cover photograph: **The Bessacarr on location in the Lake District.** *(Courtesy of Bessacarr Motorhomes, East Yorkshire)*

Previous page, left: Fixed roof Meteor from Murvi Motor Caravans. *Right:* Low Profile Stimson Provence from Design Developments.

Contents

Foreword

The Camping and Caravanning Club understands that the key to enjoyable and safe use of any kind of camping equipment is education, that's why we welcome this major contribution to camping literature which we are sure will be of great use to our 60,000 Camping and Caravanning Club members who use motorcaravans.

Peter Frost
The Camping and Caravanning Club

With nearly 35,000 motorcaravanning members, The Caravan Club warmly welcomes the publication of the Haynes *Motorcaravan Manual.* This readable, yet highly detailed Manual is clearly presented and contains a wealth of useful information, much of it not available from other sources. There are very few such comprehensive guides available to the public, and the information here is presented in an easy-to-follow style with excellent illustrations. The *Motorcaravan Manual* will prove invaluable reading for all motorcaravanners, both for general information and DIY instructions.

Trevor Watson
The Caravan Club

The manual goes into enough depth on the topics it covers to give a clear understanding of the function and workings of the many aspects of the motor caravan without creating a technical minefield that leaves the reader confused and uncertain. As a specialist club for motor caravanners, I feel the manual will be an instant hit with our members and will certainly become part of the Club's merchandise for re-sale to its members and also part of the Club's reference library when dealing with the many questions relating to motor caravanning that are directed to the Club Office by both members and non-members. Congratulations on an excellent publication and I hope it generates the success it deserves.

Colin Reay
The Motor Caravanners' Club

Introduction

In a listing of new motorcaravans, one of this month's magazines provides specifications on 232 models built in Britain and 194 imported models for home market sale. This means there is data on no less than 426 motorcaravans in total, taking into account variations on the base vehicle, the choice of engine and the interior layout.

Add to this all the pre-owned motorcaravans standing on dealer forecourts or described in classified advertisements and you are presented with a stunning array of vehicles. Anyone interested in motorcaravanning certainly has a wonderful opportunity to find a model to suit his or her requirements.

The fact there are so many different types of motorcaravan is wonderful news. On the other hand, it is this prodigious array of so many dissimilar vehicles that causes problems when you decide to write a book about them. This was clearly my concern when trying to decide what to include in this manual.

Truthfully I would have happily provided three times as many words and pictures. But a wise and experienced publisher knows perfectly well that if a manual's cover price is three times greater, few people would want to buy it!

Then there's another issue. In spite of the wonderful array of high quality models on the market, some indefatigable enthusiasts still prefer to design and build their own motorcaravan. Quite often the results are notable and it would be a sad day if regulations and legal constraints stifled such entrepreneurial endeavour. After all, many prominent companies can be traced back to the efforts of a lone enthusiast. Siddle Cook and his Elddis DIY caravan, Colin Chapman and his DIY Lotus sports cars, John Haynes and his first Austin 7 car repair manual are such examples.

So the final chapter is addressed to self-build enthusiasts. My only warning is this: never underestimate the challenges ahead. Having built several boats and three cars, I was under the illusion that building a motorcaravan would be fairly straightforward. Wrong! Dare I confess that it took longer to complete my motorcaravan and to iron out its nasty little problems than it took to complete a substantial self-build house?

With this caveat, I sincerely hope the material that follows meets the needs of a wide audience, whatever your choice of motorcaravan. Certainly the manual couldn't have been completed without the help of many people in the industry. Not only was much advice given so freely; many technical staff also proof-read my manuscripts with meticulous care.

When the work was complete, to receive such kind encouragement from the technical specialists at the Clubs has made all the efforts worthwhile.

John Wickersham
August, 1998

Motorcaravan designs

Although we use the word 'motorcaravan', there are many products which fall under this description. In this opening chapter, we compare contrasting designs and draw attention to strengths and weaknesses of different models – both on the road and on site.

Motorhomes, campervans, coachbuilts, van conversions and high-tops are all particular types of motorcaravan. There are other types too, and different vehicles meet different needs. It is therefore helpful to highlight their distinguishing features.

Driving characteristics

The 'perfect' motorcaravan would offer the driving characteristics of a car while providing spacious comfort in the living area. In reality, there is always a situation of compromise; whereas some motorcaravans have been based on cars, the majority use a commercial vehicle as the base unit. Modern commercial products are undoubtedly very comfortable, but none are completely 'car-like'.

This has prompted some manufacturers to modify multi-purpose vehicles, substituting some of the seats with a kitchen unit and creating a fold-down bed arrangement. On the road, acceleration, economy and cornering characteristics are retained, although the living area is inevitably cramped. Setting up a bed can also be an awkward exercise as it occupies a significant part of the interior.

In contrast, larger motorcaravans offer remarkably spacious accommodation. Their habitation area occupies a coachbuilt living space that has been grafted on to a commercial cab; but although life is unquestionably fine on site, on the road many coachbuilt motorcaravans are slow off the mark and corner with disconcerting body roll. Some models struggle to attain speeds in excess of 60mph and there is the added problem that small country lanes may be too narrow for this type of motorcaravan. The design itself thus affects driving characteristics, but so too does the power unit.

Engine options

A key element for any buyer or builder to consider is the engine. Some models can be slow, and although speed isn't everything, bear in mind that when travelling on continental motorways, an inability to keep up with the flow of traffic is disconcerting, if not a little dangerous.

Another key issue is whether to opt for a vehicle with a petrol engine, a diesel engine, or a turbo diesel engine. Fuel prices should help to shape your decision, remembering that diesel fuel in France is far cheaper than petrol. In the UK, however, the pump price for diesel is not much cheaper than the price of petrol. Furthermore, savings on diesel fuel may disappear when the higher costs of servicing a diesel engine are taken into account, and in spite of recent refinements, the noise level of a diesel engine can be intrusive.

It is interesting that many motoring writers and motorcaravan testers reveal a preference for petrol engines – they certainly provide a livelier performance. However, if you like the low-rev pulling power of a diesel engine, a turbo adds a little more sparkle. At the same time, this component is sometimes claimed to shorten the life of a diesel engine.

Choosing the most suitable engine is important and much depends on your driving style. This is why it would be unwise to buy an expensive motorcaravan without first arranging a test drive on a variety of roads. Hire before you buy schemes are discussed in Chapter Two, as a useful way of ensuring your choice of engine is the right one.

Chassis type

Another important element is the chassis which is discussed under *Motorcaravan Types*, and also in Chapter Nine.

6

How large?

When purchasing a motorcaravan remember that size isn't everything! Decide what is the smallest living space that would provide you with comfort and convenience. Having compared models in light of this decision, your chosen motorcaravan is likely to offer much more versatility than one which is unnecessarily large.

Many potential purchasers overlook this element but when buying a coachbuilt motorcaravan, it is a critical design feature. The type of chassis used by the manufacturer has implications for driving characteristics, access to the living area, and interior headroom.

Daily use

Another factor to consider is whether a motorcaravan has to be used for routine transport such as driving to work. Van conversions can fulfil this role whereas coachbuilt models are far less versatile. Height is often a handicap and many public car parks have a barrier at the point of entry which limits access.

Where funds permit it is best to run a second vehicle for routine transport. At the same time, a motorcaravan needs to be used regularly, so putting it into store for prolonged periods is best avoided. It is not just a battery that suffers when a vehicle is parked for a long spell; mechanical components can seize up, tyre sidewalls deteriorate and so on.

Motorcaravan types

Recognising that different owners need a motorcaravan for different reasons, it is under-standable that there are various designs, although in essence there are two categories:

- models which use the original metal shell of a panel van or multi-purpose vehicle;
- coachbuilt models where a shell is purpose-built and mounted on a suitable chassis.

This is a broad simplification but it distinguishes the two main routes in design and construction that characterise motorcaravans. Within these groups are a number of variations – not to mention vehicles – that defy classification.

Articulated units are a case in point. In the United States, 'fifth-wheel' recreational vehicles are relatively common and while their overall size is usually too large for Britain's smaller roads, the flexibility they offer is attractive. Smaller versions have been built in Britain but are seldom seen.

Fifth-wheel vehicles aside, the following classification groups of motorcaravan are recognised, three of which are variations on the van conversion theme and three of which are coachbuilt models:

FIXED ROOF

Using a panel van as a base is a logical way to create a motorcaravan. The process is often described as a 'conversion' although some manufacturers dislike this term. To the DIY builder, a van conversion is more straightforward than self-building a coachbuilt motorcaravan from scratch.

A problem with most fixed roof base vehicles is that many are too low to permit full standing room. The Murvi Morello and the La Strada Regent are exceptions since their base vehicle offers more headroom than most commercial vans. Width is another limiting factor. If you want a bed which permits sleeping *across* the vehicle, a coachbuilt construction is normally needed.

Motorcaravans based on MPVs are growing in popularity and represent a special example of a fixed roof conversion. This assures 'car-like' driving but the relatively high price of the base vehicle leads to an expensive end product.

Plus points
- Good driving characteristics.
- Many models are easy to park – in terms of height as well as width.
- Some models can be garaged.
- Wide access to the interior, via a sliding door or double rear doors, can be useful.
- Some models can be used as temporary load carriers on account of access, e.g. to shift furniture.
- Good access makes this type of motorcaravan especially appropriate for wheelchair users.

Minus points
- Heat loss due to single-glazed windows.
- Lack of standing room means disciplined living e.g. cooking from a seated position.
- Storage space is usually restricted.

Recent examples
There are several fixed roof van-based motorcaravans including models from Reimo, Bilbo's, and Murvi. Motorcaravans based on MPVs are available from Wheelhome.

A fixed roof motorcaravan like this Murvi Meteor doesn't provide standing room inside.

Motorcaravan designs

Good headroom is achieved in the La Strada Regent which is built on a Mercedes Sprinter panel van.

ELEVATING (RISING) ROOF

This type of motorcaravan is an improved version of the fixed roof type because there is headroom inside. However, the installation of an elevating roof is not a new idea – Type 2 Volkswagen 'Campervans' achieved great popularity in the 1970s with strong sales throughout Europe and the United States. At present these 'Vee Dubs' have cult status and many young people run them, renovate them and revere them. Beautifully restored models abound on both sides of the Atlantic and reference is made to a VW renovation project in Chapter Eleven.

Currently the elevating roof motorcaravan has achieved renewed interest and numerous models are available on a variety of base vehicles. Normally the elevating roof section deploys an attached fabric panel as it rises; other models have sometimes used hinged solid sides e.g. the Holdsworth Villa 3 (1987) and the Auto-Sleeper Trooper, which is still in production.

Some conversions use an ultra compact vehicle like the Daihatsu Hijetta or the Citroën Berlingo. The result is a tiny motorcaravan and

Plus points

- As with fixed roof conversions, good driving, parking and garaging are key features.
- Good access to the interior enables the vehicle to be used as a temporary load carrier and provides wheelchair access.

Minus points

- Heat loss occurs from single-glazed windows and the fabric sides of an elevating roof structure.
- Interior storage space is limited.

Recent examples

There are several examples based on light vans including models from Auto-Sleepers, Bilbo's, Devon, Drivelodge, Johns Cross Conversions and Reimo. Motorcaravans with elevating roofs based on MPVs are available from Wheelhome.

Some micro motorcaravans like the Daihatsu Hijetta from Johns Cross employ a rising roof system to increase headroom.

Setting up beds

When comparing high-top motorcaravans, look closely at the method of erecting the bed (or beds). In some instances the base is created using a multitude of cushion sections; the resulting mattress may lack the integrity you need for a good night's sleep. The Murvi Meteor and Morello feature 'rock and roll' fold back bench seating which produces a more successful bed base.

these 'micro motorcaravans', as they are sometimes called, are suitable for a single person.

While the chief function of an elevating system is to afford headroom, many rising roof systems incorporate a high level bed. This may be little more than a stretcher-style structure to sleep a young child. On the other hand, some designers have cleverly incorporated an adult-sized double bed within the rising roof structure.

HIGH-TOPS

Some panel vans offer good headroom and reference has already been made to the Murvi Morello and La Strada motorcaravans under the heading *Fixed roof* on page 8. However, another way to achieve headroom is to fit a 'high-top' roof.

Replacing the original roof on a panel van using a moulded extension unit is a popular ploy. High-top motorcaravans are justifiably popular and the use of glass reinforced plastic (GRP) prevents the structure from being top heavy. Road-holding characteristics when cornering are scarcely affected.

When you step inside this type of motorcaravan, the interior may seem surprisingly spacious. Side or ceiling-mounted glass panels help to create this impression and the overall effect hides the product's panel van parentage.

Many specialists include high-tops in their product range but ownership opportunities don't stop there. Advertisements in motorcaravan magazines include independent roof section manufacturers who will install their GRP roof moulding onto a van supplied by the customer. With this modification complete, many aspiring

self-build enthusiasts then fit out the interior to meet their personal needs.

With regard to the cost of conversion, professionally-built motorcaravans are often surprisingly expensive. In fact a considerably larger coachbuilt model might be available at a lower price. This is because adding thermal insulation and fitting out a panel van, with all its composite angles, is a time-consuming exercise. A slab-sided coachbuilt box constructed from pre-fabricated insulated panels presents a far easier base on which to work.

Interior space is dependent on the base vehicle. Motor manufacturers offer short, medium and long wheelbase vehicles and the choice of model ultimately determines interior size. Some

Plus points
- Driving characteristics are usually good.
- A sliding side door and double rear doors afford good access and load-carrying potential.
- Some models incorporate a separate bathroom.
- There is a feeling of space inside.

Minus points
- Heat loss occurs from single-glazed windows.
- Some models are surprisingly expensive.

Recent examples

This is a competitive market with products from Autocruise, Auto-Sleepers, Bessacarr, Bilbo's, Reimo, Swift as well as many small volume converters like Devon and Drivelodge.

High-top models sometimes include a toilet/shower room; the Auto-Sleepers Symphony is an example.

professional conversions, like the Auto-Sleepers Symphony and the Swift Mondial, include a generous sized washroom and toilet.

Smaller models lack this provision and toilet facilities are rather rudimentary. Typically a portable toilet has to be lifted from a locker and a make-shift curtain enclosure is prepared to provide privacy.

Once detached from its pick-up truck, this dismountable unit offers generous living space.

DISMOUNTABLES

Sometimes called a 'demountable', this design is particularly popular in the United States where pick-up trucks are comparatively common. Crew cab pick-ups, in which there is a double line of seating, are especially suitable base vehicles – but they are rarely seen in Britain.

The concept is simple; a purpose-made living compartment is carried 'piggy-back' style on the pick-up and can be detached when necessary. This enables a site pitch to be secured, after which time the vehicle can be driven independently.

The same advantage is offered on arriving home and detached 'living capsules' are a common sight in many American back yards.

The versatility of dismountable units is attractive and they are currently imported into Britain on a small scale. More recently, the British-built Apollo has also appeared. In theory the idea seems sound but in practice there are several weaknesses.

Even supposing you own a suitable pick-up truck, the mounted compartment produces a top-heavy configuration although folding roof models resolve this. Driving a dismountable motorcaravan

on twisty roads can be disconcerting; also the matter of projection beyond the sides of a base vehicle is strictly regulated within European legislation.

Plus points
- Being able to detach and park the living accommodation releases the base vehicle for independent use.
- The living accommodation can be surprisingly well organised with the benefit of an overcab bed.

Minus points
- A suitable pick-up truck is needed.
- Cab space is not utilised as part of the living accommodation.
- On the road, some dismountables roll badly when cornering; the overall rig is unavoidably top-heavy.

Recent examples
Dismountables are manufactured by Apollo and Island Plastics. American products, including folding roof models, are imported by Niche Marketing.

Models made in Britain by Apollo are often exhibited at outdoor shows.

11

COACHBUILT

Using a base vehicle cab unit, a coachbuilt construction can offer spacious accommodation. Sometimes the vehicle manufacturer's chassis is used (on an Auto-Sleeper model); alternatively a replacement AL-KO Kober lightweight chassis is grafted on to the cab (on a Swift Kon-Tiki). The latter approach produces a lower floor with fewer steps to climb when making your entry. Equally it achieves a lower centre of gravity which is favourable when cornering.

An over-cab design – often referred to as a 'Luton' – is either used for storage or sleeping accommodation. In many cases, however, over-cab compartments are a clumsy configuration which affect the aerodynamic design of the vehicle – with likely implications for fuel economy.

Recognising that many users never use an over-cab bed, designers have also produced low profile coachbuilts which have a cleaner line, lower overall height and more likelihood of achieving better fuel economy. Models from Bessacarr and Machzone are examples although low-line models are more prolific on

The Bessacarr Esprit is a luxury two-berth low profile coachbuilt motorcaravan.

the Continent than in the United Kingdom.

As regards constructional detail, different materials are used by different manufacturers. An explanation of coach-building methods is explained in Chapter Three, and the construction has implications for general maintenance and repair work.

Living accommodation can incorporate a wide variety of facilities, layouts and beds depending on the size of the vehicle. However, driving performance in a large coachbuilt is compromised and should be taken into account. Such models would hardly be appropriate for day-to-day utility transport.

Plus points
• Many occupants can be accommodated in a large motorcaravan.
• Living accommodation can be surprisingly well organised with the benefit of an over-cab bed.
• Several smaller coachbuilts offer a generous amount of space for the money.

Minus points
• Parking a large coachbuilt model may be difficult.
• Versatility in road performance falls short of smaller van conversions.
• Hardly suitable for day-to-day utility transport.
• In some models, the ladder to reach an over-cab bunk cannot be erected when a double bed is made-up beneath it.

Recent examples
Over-cab coachbuilt manufacturers include: Autohomes, Auto-Sleepers, Auto-Trail, Bessacarr, Buccaneer, Ci, Compass, Elddis, Granduca, Herald, Hymer, Machzone, Mobilvetta, Pilote, and Swift.

Low profile manufacturers include: Autocruise, Bessacarr, Elnagh, Laika and Machzone.

A-CLASS

The construction of this kind of motorcaravan starts with a commercial chassis, running gear, power unit, seating, instrumentation – but no cab. In consequence the entire body is constructed as an integral unit.

Not only are the external looks striking, but the internal layout of an A-class is equally impressive. When parked, the vehicle's high-backed swivel seats in the cab are rotated to form part of the living area.

Building the entire body from scratch is a major task and this is reflected in the price. A European A-class motorcaravan is often as costly as a larger American motorhome, but it is more suited to our smaller roads and for many people an A-class model is their ultimate choice.

The Hymer, manufactured in Germany, exemplifies the smart appearance of an A-class design.

Motorcaravan designs

Only the Swift Bel-Air and models from Machzone and Suntor are made in Britain. Many more examples are manufactured in other European countries, some of which are imported into the United Kingdom.

Plus points

- All the features of a coachbuilt model are applicable with the added bonus that cab space is integrated with the living area.
- A drop-down bed over the cab seats is often fitted and is a great asset; a pre-made bed can be accessed in seconds.
- Several A-class models have excellent shower rooms.

Minus points

- Parking an A-class motorcaravan may be difficult.
- There is a disappointingly small kitchen in many of the German models.
- The price of an A-class model is considerable.

Recent examples

A-class manufacturers include: Hymer, Laika, Machzone, Mobilvetta, Niesmann, Pilote, and Swift.

Like many A-class motorcaravans, the Pilote Galaxy has a drop-down double bed located over the driver and passenger seats.

The lowered bed is soon ready for occupation; if preferred it can be put away with the bedding in place.

AMERICAN MOTORHOMES

Calculated on price per square metre of living space, the American motorhome represents incredible value for money. For instance a Georgie Boy Maverick 29QB Custom is currently on sale for around £58,000 (1998 Price). The vehicle has a large number of robust external lockers, a built-in generator with dashboard control switch, a permanent double bed, a bath, a large screen over-cab TV set, a powerful Ford 7.3 turbo diesel engine with automatic transmission, and a multitude of extras.

These fine kings of the road have a keen following of owners and are notably appropriate as recreational vehicles in their country of origin. Whether they are suited to Britain's roads is left for the reader to decide. It really depends where you like to take your holidays.

Plus points

- Remarkable value for money when measured on floor space and fittings.
- Ideal for large groups of people – some models sleep up to eight people.

Minus points

- Maintenance costs likely to be high and relatively few specialists are able to carry out mechanical work.
- Obtaining spare parts might present problems.
- Some sites are unable to take American motorhomes.
- High fuel and general maintenance costs.
- Parking and general access problems limit use.
- Furniture is sometimes poorly built.
- Many non-standard parts fitted.

Recent examples

Georgie Boy, imported by Midland International; Damon, imported by Westcroft American Motorhomes; Fleetwood, imported by Brownhills; Monaco, imported by Travelworld American; and Winnebago, imported by Dudleys.

American motorhomes are well suited to venues with wide roads and large open spaces.

Buying and using a motorcaravan

Once you have decided to buy a motorcaravan, new or used, the next task is to draw together as much information about different models as possible. Help can be obtained from a number of sources.

Manufacturers promote their products with vigour, so it helps to know how to get impartial advice. With that in mind, this chapter looks at ways of building up a clearer picture of different models.

In addition to this, a potential owner should remember there are matters such as insurance, breakdown schemes and storage to consider. These points will be covered towards the end of the chapter.

Motorcaravan publications

In Britain, most newsagents carry a remarkable selection of magazines, of which motorcaravan periodicals are a good example. Currently there are four monthly magazines specifically devoted to motorcaravanning, and two other titles cover related topics such as trailer caravanning and touring in conjunction with motorcaravanning. Beyond this there are three periodicals distributed to members of caravan and motorcaravan clubs, giving a total of nine magazines.

These publications contain invaluable articles and advertisements which draw attention to a range of products and services. Information for a potential owner includes:

Data listings of models, specifications and prices

Most magazines carry full data listings of current models with information on base vehicles, carrying capacity (payload), external dimensions, number of beds, price and so on.

The magazine titled *Motorcaravan Motorhome Monthly* (MMM) publishes a five-part guide to second-hand prices, which appears in successive issues under the following headings:

Part One: Panel van conversions with fixed and rising roofs;
Part Two: Panel van conversions with high-tops;
Part Three: Coachbuilts based on the Fiat/Talbot and Fiat/Peugeot chassis;
Part Four: Coachbuilts (other chassis), A-class models and dismountables;
Part Five: American motorhomes.

Test reports

Illustrated reports compiled by experienced testers provide further insight and photographs show the 'test motorcaravan' in use. In most magazines, test reports are conducted on both new and used vehicles and sometimes there are comparative evaluations where two or three similar models are compared on a back-to-back basis.

Thoroughness is a feature of most test reports although the degree of objectivity and critical evaluation is variable. Moreover, poor constructional details and design weaknesses may only become apparent during long-term ownership.

Normally a manufacturer only makes a test vehicle available for a brief period. In a few instances, however, critical appraisals are conducted over several months and then it becomes possible to assess the performance of a motorcaravan in a wide variety of conditions. A test that embraces both summer and winter weather can certainly provide a deeper insight into the merits of a vehicle.

Overall, test reports provide helpful information. Both *Motor Caravan Monthly* (MCM) and *Motorcaravan Motorhome Monthly* (MMM) operate a service which enables readers to obtain copies of past reports. All the leading publications offer a 'back issues service', through which magazines are available for long periods

14

after publication. Another useful buyers' guide is an annual publication from *Which Motorcaravan* and *MMM* in which an abridged version of 50 tests published in their magazines during the previous two years are re-presented in a *Road Test Yearbook*.

Calendar of exhibitions and outdoor show dates

While manufacturer brochures and road test reports will extend your knowledge about motorcaravans, it always helps to see a product for yourself. One way to do this is to attend a major indoor exhibition; another is to visit one of the outside shows staged during the warmer months of the year. Outdoor shows are usually held at either a major racecourse or an agricultural showground. Not only are local dealers in attendance displaying the latest models, but there is also the opportunity to talk to other motorcaravan owners.

All magazines publish a list of forthcoming exhibitions and shows, which are staged at venues throughout the country.

Address lists of Owners' Clubs

Some motorcaravanners are members of a club specially devoted to particular marques. At present there are over thirty Owners' Clubs. In addition there are two clubs catering for owners of American motorhomes. The addresses of club secretaries are published in motorcaravan magazines and most clubs hold weekend rallies.

Once you feel clear about which models meet your requirements, talking to owners is one of the best ways to find out what a conversion is really like. In practice, some members show great manufacturer loyalty and defend their choice of motorcaravan with eager enthusiasm. Others are more willing to divulge problems they have encountered during ownership, passing on

practical advice with enthusiasm. Owners' clubs are an important source of guidance – particularly if you're interested in a pre-owned model that is no longer in production.

National caravan and motorcaravan clubs

More than half a million owners are members of the two national clubs concerned with caravanning and motorcaravanning. Both have a significant number of motorcaravanners in membership and the historical development of the two clubs has led to distinctive and separate characteristics. The Camping and Caravanning Club welcomes campers in all kinds of units including motorcaravans whereas The Caravan Club is more specifically run for caravan and motorcaravan owners.

Notwithstanding their differences, both clubs provide members with holiday booking services, insurance schemes, instructional courses in driving techniques and a technical advice service, supported by worksheets and introductory video programmes.

A third club, The Motor Caravanners' Club, is more specific in purpose, as the title indicates. Although membership is comparatively small, advice on technical matters is again available. For example, one of its publications titled *The Private Conversions Manual*, is written for self-builders; further publications offering guidance when choosing a motorcaravan are mentioned in the box below.

The Motor Caravan Information Service

If you plan to purchase a *new* motorcaravan, this information service can provide general guidance on behalf of the member manufacturers. Literature

Outdoor shows offer opportunities to meet owners and to discuss the merits of many different models.

Technical literature

The Motor Caravanners' Club publishes a 36-page booklet entitled *Motor Caravans – Choosing and Using* which is available to members.

The Camping and Caravanning Club publishes technical leaflets for members; one of its separate groups – The Motor Caravan Section – has members with experience of owning a wide range of models.

The Caravan Club publishes the pamphlet, *Tips for Motorcaravanners*, which is available to members and non-members alike. In addition, members can request a free leaflet titled *Choice of Motor Caravan* and a number of other technical leaflets.

covers a number of motorcaravanning issues; there are also publications which list companies who operate motorcaravan hire schemes.

Guidance on construction legislation is published periodically and the Information Service staff attend major events like The Motor Show to exhibit recent products and developments.

Annual design awards

Examples of good practice in design and construction are given recognition at two award schemes conducted during two major indoor exhibitions. At the annual Caravan and Outdoor Leisure Show at Earls Court a competition has been running for a number of years under the auspices of *Caravan Industry*, a trade journal. This includes both individual awards and categories for elements like 'The Best Washroom' and 'The Best Kitchen'.

Recently The Caravan Club introduced the Motor Caravan Design Awards, which are judged at The National Boat, Caravan & Leisure Show held at the National Exhibition Centre, Birmingham. This entails a painstaking analysis of design elements and many key features are subjected to close scrutiny. The work is carried out over five days by a judging panel supported by a team of technical experts who investigate matters like payloads and conformance with dimensional requirements.

The evaluation is conducted with notable thoroughness. Since the inception of the contest in 1996, winners in different price and type groupings have included these models:

1996: Compass Calypso 2.0 petrol, Elddis Eclipse 2.2 petrol, Murvi Morello 2.5 turbo diesel

1997: Murvi Meteor 2 litre petrol, Swift Mondial 2.0 litre petrol, Auto-Sleeper Executive 2.5 turbo diesel, and Auto-Sleeper Medallion 2.5 turbo diesel
1998: Elddis Autostratus LS 2.0 petrol, Murvi Morello 2.5 turbo diesel, Swift Kon-Tiki 650 2.5 turbo diesel.

These award schemes are very important within the industry, though it should be acknowledged that some of the smaller manufacturers are unable to participate on account of the high costs of exhibiting products at major shows.

The base vehicle

In the opening chapter, reference was made to different engine options and the importance of choosing a vehicle whose power and economy meet your requirements. In addition to the engine, the ride quality, transmission, and availability of options like power assisted steering (PAS) are also important to consider.

As a rule, most British-built motorcaravans are fitted with a manual gearbox. Few base vehicles offer automatic transmission since this is seldom needed on what is essentially a commercial van. An exception comes with some Mercedes Benz, Ford and Volkswagen base vehicles, but the choice is limited.

The subject of towing is another contentious issue and the number of motorcaravans that can be fitted with a towbar is rather disappointing. If you plan to purchase a van conversion, it is worth contacting independent towbar manufacturers as well as franchise dealers to confirm that a towing kit is available. Potential purchasers of a coachbuilt motorcaravan should

Power assisted steering (PAS)

Almost all current base vehicles include power assisted steering as a standard feature. However, this was not the case until quite recently. When buying a second-hand vehicle, this is a feature to check.

In the Caravan Club Design Awards competition 1997, the overall winner was the Auto-Sleeper Medallion 2.5 turbo diesel.

enquire with the manufacturer about the feasibility of towing.

As regards optional accessories on modern vehicles, if you decide at a later date that a key item is needed, there are several specialists who may be able to help. To give some examples:

• A normally aspirated diesel engine can be fitted with a turbocharger and intercooler by specialists like TB Turbo.
• Power-assisted steering can be fitted to some vehicles by specialists like Somar Transtec.
• Improved radiator cooling and automatic transmission oil cooling units are available from Kenlowe.
• A cruise control can be fitted using an Ultimate Design kit or the Adroit Services Cruise 2000.

When considering the base vehicles normally used for modern motorcaravans, five different models are prominent. These are: Fiat Ducato, Ford Transit, Mercedes Sprinter, Peugeot Boxer and VW Transporter T4.

The Fiat Ducato and Peugeot Boxer were collaboratively developed and are virtually identical; however, sales are conducted independently and competitively.

Others appear in lesser numbers, like the

Citroën Berlingo, C15 and Synergie, Daihatsu Hijet, Fiat Scudo, LDV Pilot and Convoy, Mercedes Vito, Nissan Serena, Powervan, Renault Trafic, Toyota Hiace Urvan and Vanette models.

A more detailed list of base vehicles is frequently published in motorcaravan magazines and the lists of specifications and options given in *Which Motorcaravan* and *Motorcaravan Motorhome Monthly* are especially detailed. In 1998 *Which Motorcaravan* produced a supplement on base vehicles.

If you're looking at second-hand motorcaravans, older base vehicles include the Talbot Express (forerunner of the Fiat Ducato/Peugeot Boxer), earlier models of Ford Transit, Renault Trafic, Volkswagen Transporter, Bedford CF and the Leyland Sherpa.

Recognising the options available and acknowledging the differences from one model to another, it is again strongly recommended that a prospective purchaser arranges a test drive. In this connection the 'hire before you buy' idea mentioned later is worthy of consideration.

It is only on the road that more subtle aspects of performance are identified. For instance suspension is important, especially when riding in the back of a motorcaravan. On recent models it is generally felt that the all-independent springing on the latest VW Transporters gives a softer ride than is achievable with the more common rear leaf springs that are fitted to many vehicles e.g. the Ford Transit, but it really depends on personal preferences. The AL-KO AMC system uses torsion bar suspension and is described in Chapter Nine.

Base vehicle engine options

NOTE: *The information here is accurate at the time of writing. Manufacturers, however, are making frequent changes and you should check the current options with a franchise dealer.*

FIAT DUCATO	2 litre petrol, 1.9 litre diesel, 1.9 litre turbo diesel, 2.8 litre diesel, 2.8 litre turbo diesel.
FORD TRANSIT	2 litre petrol, 2.5 litre diesel, 2.5 litre turbo diesel.
MERCEDES SPRINTER	2.3 litre petrol, 2.3 litre diesel, 2.9 litre turbo diesel.
PEUGEOT BOXER	2 litre petrol, 1.9 litre diesel, 1.9 litre turbo diesel, 2.5 litre diesel, 2.5 litre turbo diesel. (A direct injection 2.5 turbo diesel which raises power output from 103 bhp to 107 bhp was announced towards the end of 1997.)
VW TRANSPORTER T4	2 litre petrol, 1.9 litre turbo diesel, 2.4 litre diesel, 2.5 litre petrol.
VW LT	2.5 litre turbo diesel.

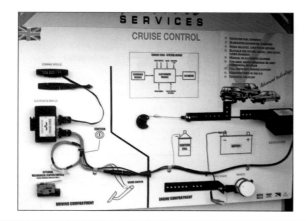

Conversion elements

Strictly speaking, a monocoque (single section) van shell is not built on a chassis in the traditional sense. Instead there are strengthened box sections welded to the floor base – referred to as the 'floor pan'. On the other hand, a chassis cab base unit is different because a substantial chassis structure extends to the rear of the cab. Many coachbuilt motorcaravans, e.g. models from Auto-Sleepers, are built on these original chassis and suspension units.

While strength and torsional rigidity are beyond question, the floor level in these models is high above the ground. This means there is a considerable step-up when entering the living quarters. It also means the overall height of the motorcaravan is greater, with implications for fuel consumption and an increased likelihood of roll when cornering.

In response to this, some manufacturers have the original chassis replaced with AL-KO Kober's low line chassis. This conversion can be achieved on front-wheel-drive vehicles like the Fiat Ducato and Peugeot Boxer, but not rear-wheel-drive vehicles like the Ford Transit. The original wheels and brake assemblies are transferred to the new lightweight chassis by AL-KO Kober who carry out the conversion. The final product, described more fully in Chapter Nine, will thus be lower and motorcaravans constructed on this base include the Swift Kon-Tiki and the Bessacarr Esprit.

Curiously, chassis details are not mentioned in most motorcaravan magazine data listings – though it is an important design element.

When comparing more general features in a conversion, look at the following:

Layout and sleeping arrangements

Personal taste is usually involved here. Check the conversion from day- to night-time use. If there's an over-cab bed for instance, is it easily accessible with good lighting, a shelf for your watch, jewellery and storage for your clothing? Look at beds that have to be specially erected. Is a jigsaw of interlocking cushions needed to form the base, and is the surface flat? Enquire where specially shaped seat backs will be stowed when beds are made-up.

Travelling safety

Check how many rear seats have a seat belt and relate this to the number of berths. Several models have more berths than belted travel seats and there's a growing feeling that this is unsatisfactory. Try the belts – are they comfortable when fastened?

Kitchen

Look at the usable worktop space. Is there adequate food storage? Is there an oven – do you intend using an oven? Some imported models do not have a grill, and many British motorcaravanners regard this as a

Manufacturer approval

Ford and Volkswagen operate schemes whereby the expertise of certain motorcaravan manufacturers is given official recognition. For instance Volkswagen used to list *Recognised Converters* (usually larger manufacturers) and *Design Compatible Converters* (many of whom were small volume builders). By 1999, Volkswagen will have implemented a replacement scheme in which motorcaravan manufacturers whose products are of approved quality will be designated as *Accredited Converters*. This is a formal confirmation that the motorcaravan manufacturer's additions are not in conflict with the design and construction of the base vehicle.

When built on the base vehicle manufacturer's chassis, the living space is usually quite high above the ground. On this Swift Royale the pronounced step is clearly apparent.

Many coachbuilt motorcaravans are built using the original cab, suspension and chassis unit designed for commercial vehicles.

Many kitchens have smart appliances but worktop space is often poor.

Virtually no British motorcaravans provide a kitchen waste facility. This door bin on a Laika Ecovia is a welcome solution.

serious omission. Consider where kitchen rubbish will be collected. With the exception of the Murvi Morello, virtually no British motorcaravans incorporate a kitchen waste facility. Italian models such as the Laika and Mobilvetta Euroyacht are much better in this provision.

Storage

Look at storage potential, including inside and outside lockers. Is there a tall locker for skis or

fishing rods? Check roof racks and rear ladders, too. Some racks have side rails but no cross bars on which to carry the luggage. Tie points are often lacking too.

Spare wheel

Check how easy it is to remove the spare wheel. Some locations are abundantly easy to reach; others involve lying on your back under the chassis. Confirm corner steady operation – these can easily get damaged.

Loading capacity

Establish the loading capacity and consider this in relationship to the number of people you intend to take on holiday.

This Pilote A-class motorcaravan is one of a small number which have tall lockers for items like snow skis or fishing rods.

Large external capacity lockers are important for owners embarking on activity holidays.

Roof racks vary in quality. If there's only a perimeter rail, smaller items are especially difficult to tie down.

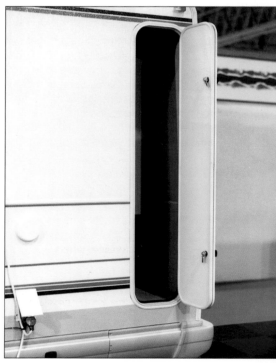

Handbooks

Ask to see the handbooks – there should be one for the base vehicle and one for the living facilities. Many handbooks for the latter element are surprisingly poor and a few converters include no documentation material at all.

Price and hidden costs

Check the total price, ensuring that delivery charges and all 'hidden costs' are included. Some new models e.g. the Murvi Morello come with a complete on-the-road package including gas, regulator, cutlery, crockery and leisure battery – but this is unusual. Most motorcaravans lack some of these items.

Health and safety compliance

Consider whether you want a motorcaravan with living accommodation that complies with Code of Practice 201 defined by the Society of Motor Manufacturers and Traders (SMMT) and the National Caravan Council (NCC). **Note:** *This will become EN 1646-1 in respect of 1999 models as stated in the Appendix.* Stringent requirements related to health and safety have to be met and the badge which confirms compliance is mounted on the exterior. The merit of achieving this mark of assurance in respect of Health and Safety goes

Loading terms

Current practice is to express weights in kilograms (1kg = 2.2lbs)

Maximum Technically Permissible Laden Mass (MTPLM): This refers to a vehicle's gross weight, as defined by the base vehicle manufacturer. Note: It has previously been called 'Maximum Laden Weight' (MLW). Also used are 'Maximum Authorised Mass' (MAM), Gross Vehicle Weight (GVW) and Maximum Authorised Weight (MAW).

Mass in running order: This is the unladen weight of a vehicle taking into account the maximum fuel weight and a weight allowance for the driver taken as 75kg.

Maximum user payload: The payload is a vehicle's maximum carrying capacity and is calculated by deducting a vehicle's mass in running order from its maximum technically permissible laden mass.

Maximum axle weights: Both front and rear axles have maximum weights, too, and these figures must not be exceeded by the load.

Information plates: Data related to weights is usually displayed on a metal plate. Typically this is permanently fixed in the engine bay (see below).

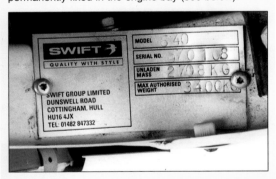

Weighbridge: To confirm a vehicle doesn't exceed its MTPLM, it is necessary to put a fully laden vehicle with full petrol tank and its full complement of passengers on a weighbridge.

NOTE: *Sometimes there are minor discrepancies in the way a motorcaravan manufacturer expresses the data. A payload figure, for example, will vary according to the base vehicle option. To give an example, Auto-Sleepers currently express the unladen mass weight with the addition of coolants, (oil and water), maximum fuel capacity, washer fluid, driver (75kg), spare wheel, crockery, fire extinguisher and tools. So it is important to check details most carefully prior to making a purchase to ensure the actual loading potential meets your particular needs.*
New motorcaravans from 1999 will have to comply with BSEN 1646-2, which defines how weights and payloads must be expressed.

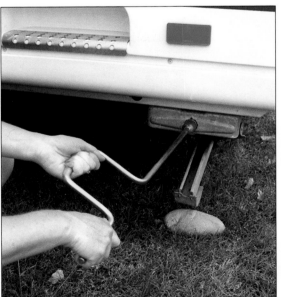

Buyers are advised to check how easy it is to reach a spare wheel.

When purchasing a pre-owned coachbuilt motorcaravan, if there are corner steadies, check their operation.

without question. At the same time there are a number of fine models which are not thus accredited – many imported motorcaravans are an example. This is a matter you need to consider.

Nature of use

The previous chapter recognises that some owners use a motorcaravan for day-to-day driving as well as holidays, so reflect on the motorcaravan's intended uses.

Winter use

If you intend to use your motorcaravan all year round, remember that if water tanks are mounted externally, problems can occur when the vehicle is used in cold temperatures. For instance, some models in the ranges from Auto-Sleepers, Auto-Trail

If a model has under-floor tanks, a winter user can have an alternative on-board water supply fitted.

Specialists are able to adapt motorcaravans so they are suitable for disabled users.

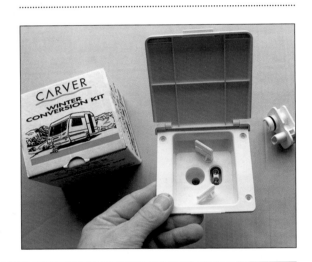

and Compass have external tanks as standard. Adaptations can be made, of course, and there are also conversion kits, which are discussed in Chapter Six.

Some motorcaravans are especially designed for year-round use, such as the 1998 Laika Ecovip range. High level of insulation and features like blown air heating outlets directed under bed mattresses enhance comfort; special heating units ensure water tanks are not affected by frost.

Wheelchair access

Adaptations are possible on a number of models and supplements on the subject of adapted vehicles are often published in motorcaravan magazines.

With regard to disabled use, Public Notice 701/7 published by Customs and Excise explains in Section 8 that the supply of motor vehicles to disabled people may carry a zero rated Value-Added Tax status. This usually applies to a motorcaravan designed or adapted for a disabled person in a wheelchair – provided its design is not intended to include more than five other persons. Both new and second-hand motorcaravans normally gain this concession.

A Customs & Excise Office can provide further information on this subject.

As regards modifications to a vehicle, it is often wiser to specify adaptations to a current model rather than having a motorcaravan specially built. It is far easier achieving resale at a later date of a conventional model with adaptations.

Purchasing considerations

Recognising the cost of a new motorcaravan, a first-time purchaser might be advised to start with a pre-owned model in order to confirm that

When buying a pre-owned motorcaravan, items like crockery and cutlery are often included in the sale.

motorcaravanning comes up to expectation. Sometimes a pre-owned model will be sold with a full complement of items like a fitted roller awning, cutlery, crockery, levelling devices and so on. If you buy a new motorcaravan, many of these items will not be included in the sale.

Pre-owned purchases

Starting with the classified advertisements in motorcaravan magazines, it is soon clear there are plenty of purchases to consider. Vehicles with modest recorded mileages in immaculate condition are often in evidence. It is acknowledged that most motorcaravanners look after their vehicles very carefully.

Dealers will also have stocks of pre-owned vehicles and a warranty should be included. Moreover a full forecourt provides opportunity to compare models.

Lastly there are auctions. Some are held at local level, often using a storage depot as the venue. On a national scale there's a caravan and motorcaravan division of British Car Auctions (BCA). Periodic sales are programmed around the country; centres at Brighouse and Measham usually offer a good range of stock for bidders. Information on a motorcaravan's history is affixed to the screen of each lot in the sale and the process of buying is not the 'gamble' that many people imagine. To assist a prospective bidder, there is a guidebook on buying and selling procedures available from BCA's head office.

Obviously anyone making a purchase of a pre-owned vehicle will accept the meaning of 'caveat emptor', or 'buyer beware'. A 'sold as seen' disclaimer emphasises more than ever the importance of checking the product. This involves the two elements already discussed – base vehicle and habitation provision. As regards the base vehicle:

- Check there is an MoT and service vouchers to verify mileage.
- Look at the tyres – irregular wear on the front may indicate steering misalignment.
- Look for worn foot pedals in the cab – a sure sign of a higher mileage.
- Check for dirty oil on the dipstick.
- Look for damp under the cab carpets – which may originate from a faulty screen seal or even a leaking heater radiator matrix.
- Insist the owner takes you on a test drive; better still, drive the vehicle yourself if all documents are in order.

The list could go on and for anyone for whom mechanical matters are anathema, it is prudent to pay one of the motoring organisations or better still, a specialist company like Autovan Services, for an engineer's inspection and report.

As regards the living area, there are several simple checks to carry out. These include:

- turning on the hob and other cooking appliances;
- confirming the heating system is working;

British Car Auctions hold a number of caravan and motorcaravan sales at some of their venues.

- trying the fridge – though it takes time for cooling to commence;
- looking at cushions, seat backs and bases;
- checking most carefully for signs of damp on the walls or inside internal lockers.

On some coachbuilt models, the ingress of rain causes serious deterioration – though leaks sometimes develop in van conversions, too. If there's an unpleasant 'musty' smell when you step inside, this is the give-away. It would be wise to arrange for a damp test to be carried out by a caravan service engineer before completing a purchase – this subject is discussed more fully in Chapter Three.

Buying new

Buying a new motorcaravan doesn't involve the uncertainty that surrounds the purchase of a used model. However, look at the scope of the warranty

Auctions for caravans and motorcaravans are sometimes conducted locally.

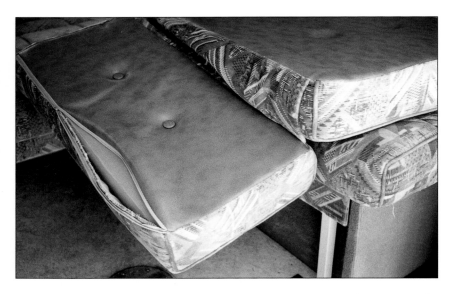

In a pre-owned model, check the upholstery – replacements can be costly.

Unlike the larger manufacturers, specialists like Young Conversions can build a motorcaravan to suit an individual's requirements.

and check procedure in the event of an early problem. For instance if you accept an attractive sales offer from a dealer situated a long way from your home, ask what procedure has to be followed if a gas leak develops in a supply pipe. Similarly, enquire what procedure has to be followed if there's a problem with the base vehicle.

Buying a motorcaravan can be done in a number of ways:

• Purchase is usually possible at a major exhibition. For instance a manufacturer's stand is staffed by sales representatives from approved dealers around the country as well as by personnel from the factory (or importing agency).
• Alternatively you can make the purchase at the premises of a dealer. There are a number of long

established specialists and in many cases these are family concerns where the owners are enthusiastic motorcaravanners.
• Buying direct from a manufacturer is a procedure followed in the case of low volume specialists who may not have a network of dealers.

Whichever route you take, insist on a road test. Sometimes there is diffidence on the part of sellers to sanction this. However, parting with a large sum of money without confirming a vehicle's driving characteristics and ride quality is ill-advised.

Bespoke models

A rather different route to ownership is to buy a 'made-to-order' motorcaravan. Small converters like Young Conversions pride themselves on the fact that no two motorcaravans leave their factory the same. This might be surprising because in magazine buyers' guides, the company currently has a number of models listed. However, these are normally adapted to meet a customer's individual requirements. Adaptations may be relatively minor – perhaps a particular upholstery fabric is required. On the other hand, a purchaser might want more major alterations like a radical change in layout.

Other specialists like Nu Venture are similar in their service, even allowing a customer to supply their own base vehicle for fitting out. This may be either a new or second-hand vehicle and work can be a partial or complete conversion.

Another converter is EMC (Euro Motor Campers) whose Huntsman, Stag and Tupelo are listed models. The company also manufactures high-top roof sections, modular furniture kits, and stocks a prodigious array of components. Like Nu Venture and Young, the company has a flexibility in supply that high volume manufacturers are seldom able to achieve.

Self-building and renovating

Completely different strategies adopted by many motorcaravan enthusiasts are:

• to renovate a second-hand vehicle,
• to convert a van or
• to build a motorcaravan from scratch.

Some notable vehicles have been constructed by DIY enthusiasts and some of today's manufacturers grew from simple beginnings where a determined constructor tackled a self-build conversion.

Much can be learnt from the self-build approach and even an 'armchair builder' who ultimately buys a new motorcaravan can be helpfully informed by seeing what is involved. Accordingly Chapter Eleven is devoted to self-build case studies, each of which is radically different.

Hiring prior to buying

Hiring as a prelude to buying has much to commend it. Over twenty companies around the country run hiring schemes and the Motor Caravan Information Service can supply a list of hirers. There are also advertisements placed by hirers in motorcaravan magazines.

Some hirers are small specialists, often run on a private basis. Other operations form part of a dealership and after a year of hiring, vehicles are then sold second-hand. In some cases there are special offers linked with purchasing. For instance Marquis Motorhomes informs hirers that if they purchase a motorcaravan within twelve months of a hire, one week of the fee will be deducted from its price. This offer extends to other vehicles – not just the model hired.

When contemplating hiring, it will be noted that fees are considerably different in winter as opposed to summer. There are also surcharges for continental travel – mainly dictated by greater insurance costs – and some hirers limit use to mainland Britain.

As a rule, the services offered are very complete. For instance the Marquis Motorhome branch near Southampton will store your car in a security compound during the hire and the service provides:

• Comprehensive insurance
• Collision damage waiver
• A campsite guidebook
• Maps and a foreign road atlas
• Cutlery, crockery and cooking pans
• Two full Camping Gaz cylinders
• Cab radio cassette player
• Toilet starter pack with chemicals sufficient for a fortnight
• GB plate for use abroad.
There is no limit on mileage.

As a rule, Marquis hire fleet vehicles are from the Swift and Compass ranges. It is necessary to telephone around hirers nationwide to find what vehicles they have available. Without question, here is a good way to appraise a motorcaravan before embarking on a purchase.

Realities of ownership

Choosing and buying is one thing; owning is another. There are certain matters to bear in mind, such as safe driving, insurance, and breakdown matters.

Driving courses are run by the caravan clubs using venues like old airfields. These are well-run and well-attended – so early bookings are needed.

Insurance schemes are often the subject of magazine reviews and there are more than fifteen specialists involved. In general, motorcaravan owners represent a 'good risk' and premiums are not normally high.

Some brokers like Bakers of Cheltenham are able to offer cover if you drive a self-built model. However, many DIY builders use kit car insurance specialists who advertise in component car magazines. Gibson Insurance Consultants provide an 'agreed value' scheme for older vehicles; a number of brokers also include RAC breakdown cover. Some insurers charge extra for left hand drive vehicles. One thing is clear when making comparisons, there are surprising differences between the schemes.

Breakdown assistance is a service worth considering, though it is important to confirm that a scheme covers larger vehicles. For instance 'get you home' extensions may be good on paper but not on the roadside. Personal experience has shown that motorcaravans can get damaged when being pulled on to a low loading transporter, and larger motorcaravans may need a commercial collection rescue vehicle.

Parking at home is sometimes raised as a problem and prospective owners need to decide whether a vehicle would need parking at a storage specialist. Several well-equipped centres include indoor accommodation and the clientele includes local as well as overseas owners. Parking at home depends where you live and the amount of space in your drive.

There is also the matter of covenants which determine what may and may not be parked adjacent to your home. These can be vague, imprecise and needful of clarification.

Servicing is another fundamental feature of ownership and there are habitation elements to check as well as mechanical matters. But this is a topic in its own right and detailed guidance is given in Chapter Three.

The branch of Marquis Motorhomes near Winchester offers a 'hire before you buy' service.

3

Contents

General maintenance and repair

Looking after a motorcaravan amounts to more than keeping the engine tuned – appliances in the living area also need to be cleaned, serviced and kept in a good state of repair. The exterior bodywork needs regular attention too.

Like any vehicle, a motorcaravan needs regular mechanical servicing. Most owners arrange for this work to be carried out at a garage. However, the 'habitation' element of a motorcaravan requires periodic attention as well and whereas few owners neglect mechanical matters, servicing work in the living area and on the exterior bodywork sometimes gets overlooked.

The first part of this chapter outlines different types of body construction, cleaning techniques and repair work. The later part then turns attention to the living area and looks at the 'habitation service'.

Body construction

Recognising that there are many different types of motorcaravan, it is not surprising that construction methods are widely dissimilar. On a van conversion, for example, its steel structure and the retention of the original single-glazed windows means the outer shell has broad similarities with a car. Methods of cleaning are similar in both cases; so too, are the strategies for repair work and repainting.

More fundamental differences are apparent in respect of coachbuilt motorcaravans. A large number of models are classified as 'coachbuilts' but this hides the fact that a number of different constructional techniques are employed. Moreover, different materials are used and this has implications for both repair and maintenance work.

A traditional approach to coachbuilding is to construct the living quarters *in situ*, starting with a timber framework. A thermal insulant such as rigid foam is then cut and fixed between these structural members. The interior is finished next by affixing decorative-faced plywood sheeting to the wooden framework, and on the outside, a cladding material like pre-painted sheet aluminium is added.

This approach is employed by Buccaneer whose quality products are well-known.

A different coachbuilding technique is to build the floor and walls of the living compartment using pre-fabricated composite panels. These are manufactured using three separate components:

• decorative plywood,
• block foam,
• an aluminium skin.

Individually, none of these components are particularly strong, but when coated with a high specification adhesive and bonded together in a large press, the resulting composite panel assumes noteworthy strength; it also remains remarkably light. Apertures for the door and windows are prepared at this initial construction stage and these are lined with a timber frame to achieve rigidity. The timber surround also provides a sound fixing point for hinges and catches.

The use of bonded sandwich construction is popular and coachbuilding specialists like Auto-Trail, Compass and Elddis have employed this technique for some time. However, a variation on the theme – which is growing in popularity – is to clad the exterior using a thin layer of pre-coloured glass fibre sheet instead of aluminium. This approach is used on models from the Swift Group such as the current Royale and Kon-Tiki. In addition, coachbuilt models bearing the Bessacarr badge have an outer skin of glass fibre sheet. The Ravenna, Pescara and Pollensa from Auto-Sleepers use this alternative cladding as well. In the event of a minor accident, this material is much easier to repair than aluminium sheet.

Yet another approach is to commence the conversion using a rigid glass reinforced plastic (GRP) shell which is fixed to the vehicle chassis. The shell has to have an insulating material installed on the inside before the internal decorative wall panels are finally added. This

26

Prefabricated panels used in many coachbuilt motorcaravans comprise a bonded sandwich of cladding material, insulant and internal decorative ply.

Recent coachbuilt models from Swift are finished with a thin GRP outer skin instead of aluminium cladding.

method of construction is labour-intensive but it permits the use of attractive external contours which are an agreeable alternative to more prosaic 'slab-sided' vehicles. It is an approach that has been used for a number of years by Auto-Sleepers and Island Plastics. In addition, the Starcraft and Rancher self-build motorcaravans, featured in Chapter Eleven, are both built in this way.

These various approaches to construction emphasise the point that the bodywork on each motorcaravan is often different. It might be painted steel panels, moulded GRP, ABS moulded plastic, pre-coloured smooth-faced aluminium sheet, decorative faced aluminium sheet or a pigmented layer of thin GRP sheet. Add plastic ventilators, moulded bumpers, acrylic windows, and sections of safety glass and the sheer diversity of products suddenly becomes apparent. This explains why such a variety of cleaning agents is sold to deal with all the different materials.

Cleaning

Keeping your caravan clean and tidy, both inside and out, will not only keep appliances functioning efficiently, but will help in the event of a re-sale.

Cleaning products

Many proprietary car cleaning products can be used for motorcaravans but some components need a specially-formulated treatment. The acrylic material used for windows is an example.

Recognising the specific characteristics of certain materials, several specialists have paid close attention to the needs of caravanners and motorcaravanners. For instance Auto Glym, already well-known in the automotive industry, has

developed a full working knowledge of motorcaravanners' particular requirements. Laboratory research has underpinned product development and samples taken from every batch produced are kept in extensive storage rooms. If a product fails to perform to a customer's expectation, samples from the original batch can then be subjected to further analysis.

The need for specific cleaning compounds for specific materials is self-evident, but professional training courses conducted at the Auto Glym factory enhance knowledge and understanding even further. Many of the guidelines presented here are based on recommendations from the company's technical specialists.

Having this technical knowledge is useful but how can the motorcaravanner find out what are the best products? Unfortunately the business of conducting exacting and impartial tests on cleaning compounds is not easy and in many instances the owner only finds out through experience what appears to produce a long-lasting effect. Ease of application is another issue which undoubtedly influences choice. Price may play a part, too.

So although the Auto Glym product range is much-liked by classic car owners, caravanners and motorcaravanners, two imported product ranges have also made their mark at motorcaravan exhibitions and rallies.

One example is the Crystal Glo range – the Acrylic Wash and Acrylic Vehicle Polish products are especially successful. The polish can be used on a variety of materials including: painted surfaces, polished aluminium, GRP, chrome, plastic and Perspex. Once applied, this Canadian product will normally last for around six months.

The range of treatments from Mer is also notable. In particular, Mer Car Polish, manufactured in Germany, is easy to apply and

A long-handled cranked radiator brush is ideal for cleaning round awkward body fittings.

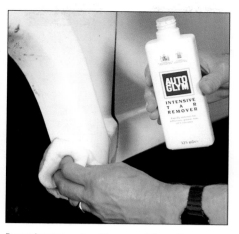
Removing tar spots with a proprietary cleaner should precede washing.

A special wheel cleaning brush is available from Auto Glym.

versatile in use. For instance, it can be used neat as a polish or diluted in water to produce a 'wash 'n shine' effect. It also removes algae and moss from motorcaravans with ease, and of course there are other products in the Mer range to consider as well.

When considering all the materials on the market, it is only by personal experiment that you can make up your mind which cleaners you prefer.

Cleaning techniques

The following guidance, based on techniques employed by valet specialists, is concerned with a full cleaning regime.

Tools

A strong bristled brush – for agitating the cleaner when removing resistant brake deposits from the wheels. A traditional brush sold in hardware stores for cleaning large saucepans achieves this function, although purpose-made wheel brushes have now been introduced by Auto Glym.

A cranked radiator paint brush – when applying a cleaning compound to remove moss and algae from recesses, the long-handled brush designed for painting the back of radiators is an excellent tool.

Soft nylon floor brush – this is useful for agitating dust when upholstery cleaner has been applied to a fabric cover.

Hard compound sponge – upholstery cleaner is often good on interior surfaces like decorative faced ply. However, a car cleaning sponge is too soft – a hard sponge used by interior decorators can be better for shifting resistant marks.

Kitchen roll paper – this is used in conjunction with some acrylic window cleaners instead of a conventional rag.

Cotton polishing cloth – A cleaning cloth should not contain lint – old T-shirts and similar garments include lint along with other synthetics.

Open weave cloth which is 100% cotton stock is strongly recommended.

In a complete valet operation, the strategy is to start with really dirty jobs and then to move to more refined tasks and finishing operations. The procedure here describes a full schedule – though sections will sometimes be omitted.

The recommended order is:

1. Engine
2. Wheels and tyres
3. Door shuts
4. Body shampoo
5. Interior cleaning
6. Tar spots
7. Body polishing
8. Glass
9. Tyre dressing.

If the engine compartment is on the cleaning schedule it should be tackled first. Take full note of instructions accompanying engine cleaners and remember to tie a plastic bag over key electrical items like a central electronic alarm. It is also important that the engine is cold and switched off. The cleaning procedure involves: applying the cleaner, agitation with a brush, and then gentle and judicious flooding with fresh water. Experts use

Once a tyre cleaner and grease remover has been applied to the tyres, the compound should be hosed off.

Stain removal

The black carbon trickles that stain bodywork directly under ventilators, door stays and similar attachments can be effectively removed using Auto Glym Engine Cleaner. This is a versatile product which, in addition to engine cleaning, is good for removing grease from tyres, cleaning plastic covers, discoloured vents, fuel stains (especially diesel), exhaust marks, door shuts, ovens and even saucepans stained on the outside.

A product like Fast Glass is applied and removed while wet, using kitchen roll paper.

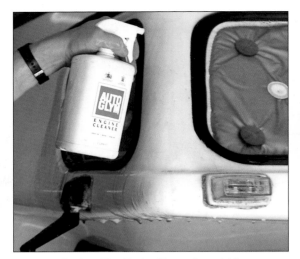

A product like Auto Glym Engine Cleaner is useful for removing algae and embedded grease.

After application, the engine cleaner should be agitated with a brush before rinsing off.

pressure hoses but it is important to operate with caution so that no temporary damage is done to ignition items.

Attention then turns to the wheels, but make sure they are cold – hot brake discs can create reactions with some chemicals. Most cleaners should be removed promptly and not allowed to dry; so it is best to complete one wheel at a time.

After cleaning the wheel rims or cover, the tyres should be tackled next. Grease should be removed and engine cleaner applied to the tyres, agitated with a brush and hosed off. The final application of a tyre renovation treatment should be left until the end of the cleaning operation.

A grease remover should next be used on door shuts and wheel arches – some engine cleaners are especially effective here.

Turning attention to the main body, a shampoo conditioner is recommended – but use a product locally like Auto Glym Engine Cleaner to remove stubborn stains. When agitated with a radiator brush, this treatment quickly removes carbon stains, bird deposits, algae and moss.

Subsequently the shampoo should be rinsed off, but don't use a high pressure hose. This has the effect of 'bouncing off' the conditioning film that most shampoos leave after application. Gentle flooding on a metal panel enables some conditioners to electrostatically bond to the surface thus affording protection.

Attention now turns to the interior. As regards a motorcaravan's upholstery, a number of manufacturers sell treatments that are suitable on cushion fabrics as well as vehicle seat covers. Of course, it is always wise to try a product on a small test area first. As a rule, never use a scrubbing action, especially on fabrics like velour. It is better to employ a stippling action using a nylon brush which has medium strength bristles. When the surface is subsequently wiped with a clean, damp cotton cloth, the amount of dirt pulled away often comes as a surprise.

After completing work in the living quarters, stubborn tar spots should be removed from the body. Several proprietary products are specifically made to tackle these marks.

The subsequent application of body treatments is then determined by the materials. If your motorcaravan is clad with patterned aluminium, such as a stucco surface finish, it is wise to leave this alone. Some of the paints used on aluminium sheet can be lifted by polishes and it is better to be content with the sheen left by a shampoo.

However, on painted steel and GRP, a good coat of polish will achieve protection that may last for six months or more. Take note of the product instructions and when applying a polish, be careful to keep it from black plastic components like motorcaravan door handles and bumpers. These should be coated later with a purpose-made treatment.

Windows should be tackled next. The point must be emphasised that acrylic and other artificial windows are easily scratched and a completely different treatment is needed from a safety glass window. There are many cleaning compounds sold

General maintenance and repair

Ordinary polish can discolour black plastic fittings so a bumper treatment should be used.

Once applied, some upholstery cleaners should be stippled cautiously before removal with a clean cloth.

for safety glass but products suitable for motorcaravan windows are far harder to find.

One product that can be used on a clean and dust-free window is Crystal Glo Acrylic Vehicle Polish. Another is Auto Glym Fast Glass which is sprayed on to the window and then promptly spread across the surface with a piece of paper kitchen roll. In equal haste it should be removed with another piece of clean kitchen roll.

At this stage, finish jobs like the application of plastic treatments is carried out. Several products are available for black fittings – bumper treatments, for example, can effectively revive a sheen on a motorcaravan door handle or an external mirror housing.

To finish the operation, a final application of a tyre dressing treatment completes the valet in style. Notice that rubber-based paints are less popular nowadays. Products like Auto Glym Instant Tyre Dressing are much better – as long as you follow the application instructions. When tyre conditioner is sprayed on to the rubber it forms white streaks which initially look unpleasant – but don't touch the tyre. Leave the dressing to dry for ten to fifteen minutes, after which the effect is most surprising – the revived surface makes the tyres look new again.

Leaks and damp problems

On the road, a motorcaravan is subjected to considerable forces. A bumpy surface subjects the body to flexion, tension and relentless impact. Thankfully a good design can sustain this kind of treatment, but over a long period it is one reason why adjacent panels develop weak spots.

Hardening sealant is another problem. Flexible mastic that waterproofs the junctions between joining materials eventually loses its resilience. The effects of direct sunshine and the extremes of

seasonal temperatures help to hasten the demise of this all-important weatherproofing material; problems are accentuated further if there's a different rate of expansion between two adjacent materials.

Puncture points constitute a further weakness. For instance, screws that hold a length of decorative aluminium strip in place puncture the base material in a number of places. Even components like lamp clusters are notorious weak spots in driving rain, especially if a rubber mounting gasket loses its resilience. One well-respected marque had problems when the mitred joints on the corners of the window frames started to leak.

Any type of motorcaravan can develop a leak but it is the coachbuilt that seems especially prone to problems. Logically it might seem that walls constructed from prefabricated bonded panels might not suffer from seepage as much as traditionally-built non-bonded sections. But this isn't necessarily the case. Rainwater penetrates many insulating products used in the core, whether the components are bonded or not. The ingress of

Leaks often start when mastic loses its resilience and becomes brittle.

Sealants

Many of the mastic sealants and adhesives used in motorcaravan construction are only available to manufacturers in large batches. However, some specialists like Carafax will supply small quantities by mail order. Sika, another prominent company in the industry, sells its sealants in car repair shops. The ribbon sealant from W4 is also sold through Motorcaravan accessory shops.

If seepage isn't identified early, the damage to a coachbuilt motorcaravan can be serious.

Damp testing is done with a meter on the inside panels, especially around openings.

rainwater might not be evident on the interior ply for some time – even though damage below the surface could be quite severe.

As always, prevention is better than cure and all motorcaravan owners should get a dealer to carry out a damp test every year. The device normally used employs an electrical current that will track along zones of moisture and record a reading. Inexpensive damp testers are available from DIY stores but skill and experience are needed to ensure they are used correctly.

Working on the inside, a service engineer will take readings around the perimeters of windows, doors, roof lights as well as the junction points between wall and ceiling panels. If a zone of damp is identified, the next task is to ascertain the origin of the moisture. This isn't always easy.

In a bad case of damp, major re-construction work may be necessary and this is something to entrust to an expert. Companies like Crossley Coachcraft in Leyland and Autovan Services at Wimborne are examples of specialists whose reputation for tackling major re-building work is well-known in the industry.

A less demanding remedial measure that some owners tackle involves the removal and reinstatement of decorative strips, awning rails, and components like roof lights. Weather-resistance is greatly improved by re-fixing these fittings on a new bed of flexible sealant.

Where decorative strips are concerned, the job necessitates removal of a plastic cover strip to reveal the screw heads. When the screws which hold the aluminium extrusion strip in place are removed, check to see if any of them are rusty. If the thread is in bad shape, this is a certain sign that water has crept behind the trim strip and seeped into the sub structure via this particular puncture point. A new screw and new flexible sealant are urgently needed.

Sealants

The importance of retaining plasticity is a key feature of a motorcaravan sealant. However, there are different types and these can be classified in the following groups:

After removing a plastic insert, a trim strip can be detached by removing the screws.

The backing paper is removed from ribbon sealant before the trim strip is re-bedded on fresh mastic.

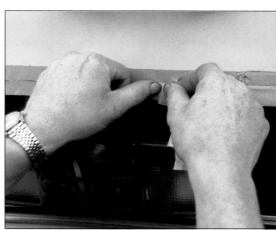

- Butyl rubber-based sealants purchased in a cartridge and injected from a dispenser gun.
- Butyl rubber sealant in tape form, supplied with a backing strip for easier handling.
- Silicone-based sealant purchased in a cartridge. This is applied by dispenser gun and many DIY enthusiasts will have applied this type of product at home to seal around a bath.

There are also sealants which act as adhesives; however, a guiding principle is that the higher the strength of a product in terms of its bonding capacity, the lower the likelihood of it having flexibility. Conversely high flexibility is usually off-set by a lower level of bonding strength.

Needless to say, performance characteristics are complex. As far as the DIY enthusiast is concerned a key issue is to decide which product to use. Whilst cartridge butyl sealants are used with enviable skill by motorcaravan builders, butyl ribbon sealant is often more suitable for the amateur repairer.

Ribbon sealant is manufactured in different widths and its working characteristics differ from product to product. The sealant from W4 Accessories – regularly stocked in accessory shops – is easy to use and can be cut to size with a woodworking knife; but its 'pull effect' is modest. In contrast, Caraseal 303 butyl strip from Carafax is very sticky to the touch and achieves a notable bond as soon as the surfaces make contact. The trouble is, if you position the strip inaccurately, it can be a tough job to remove it.

If you decide to re-mount a length of aluminium guttering, a trim strip, or a component like a roof light, ribbon sealant is excellent. However, if screws are needed to hold the component in place, make puncture points in the strip with a bradawl otherwise the turning screws will wind the sealant round their shaft when they're tightened up.

Once excess sealant is removed, the task is complete – though some owners go one step further and apply a bead of silicone sealant around the perimeter of the fitting. There's nothing wrong with this 'belt and braces approach' but applying a bead of silicone neatly demands patience. To produce a tidy finish, the applied sealant should be wiped with a finger dipped in methylated spirits to produce a bevel edge. Excess will be pulled away in the process but careful workmanship will be rewarded.

Body repairs

Before accident damage can be tackled, it is necessary to establish what type of material needs attention; for instance, steel panels that form part of the base vehicle are tackled in the same way as a similar damaged section on a car.

Guidance on body repairs and painting procedures are given in *The Car Bodywork Repair Manual* by Lindsay Porter, published by Haynes. This manual also has a chapter dealing specifically with glass fibre repair work.

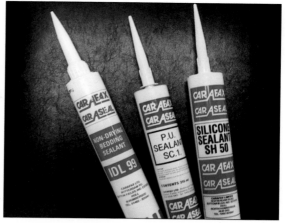

Some sealant compounds are supplied in cartridges and application is done using a dispenser gun.

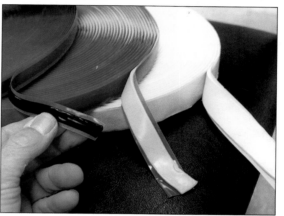

The ribbon sealants from Carafax are supplied in a variety of grades, colours and widths.

On the other hand, many motorcaravans are clad in aluminium or embellished with acrylic-capped ABS mouldings. Repair work here is rather different, as it is necessary to identify the damaged material before proceeding with the remedial work.

Identifying ABS and GRP panels

The main feature of glass reinforced plastic (GRP) is that the panel has been laminated in a mould, usually by hand. The finished product is shiny on one side and rough on the reverse; in fact the glass matting that reinforces the polyester resin is soon recognised.

The great feature of GRP is that it is relatively easy to repair. Surface damage to the outer layer – called the 'gel coat' – can even be remedied using a body filler bought from an automotive supplier. Structural damage, however, necessitates a repair of any cracked or missing sections using chopped strand glass fibre mat; this has to be impregnated with polyester resin, stippled with a brush and rolled with a washer roller. Further guidance on GRP products and their use is available from Trylon, a specialist supplier.

Panels in GRP can also be repainted irrespective of whether the original product may have been moulded with a coloured pigment mixed into the polyester resin. Specialist automotive paint suppliers will mix paint to the exact tint and supply the prepared product in an aerosol spray can. You

Matching paint

Specialist automotive paint suppliers will mix paint to the exact tint you require, and supply it in an aerosol spray can.

33

The roughened rear face of this body skirt indicates it is made from GRP, which is easy to repair.

The surface gel coat on this Kon Tiki rear panel was damaged on a kerbstone – again, easy to repair as it is made from GRP.

A smooth finish on both surfaces indicates this is an ABS plastic panel; if damaged it would have to be replaced.

would also need an etching primer to ensure the paint adheres to a GRP panel.

Body sections made from acrylic capped ABS are far less satisfactory. The material is shiny on both sides and is used for components like wheel spats and underskirts. Motorcaravans like some of the Granduca coachbuilt models have large sections of ABS embellishment panels on the rear of the bodywork.

Although the material is light, it cannot be repaired like GRP if it gets damaged in an accident. Usually it is necessary to replace the entire panel.

Similar problems occur if an aluminium panel gets damaged. Aluminium stretches and dents cannot be beaten out. A depressed section can be filled with a polyester resin filling compound; but it is virtually impossible to re-create an authentic match if the original aluminium sheet has a stucco or reeded finish.

The professional coachbuilder will repair a damaged section by fixing a complete replacement aluminium panel on top of the old one, but special adhesive is used to affix this new sheet. Trim strips and awning rails all help to disguise the fact that

an additional section has been fitted on top of the original one. But when the job is done by an expert the repair is impossible to recognise.

Delamination

Notwithstanding the merits of pre-fabricated floor and wall panels, problems occur if a section delaminates from the foam in the core. This is especially prevalent in trailer caravans where torsional stresses during towing are particularly acute. However, there are instances where problems are reported in coachbuilt motorcaravans, too.

If a section of a floor panel delaminates, the flexing ply creates a creaking sound. Sometimes a large 'blister' is evident where the bonding has failed. On wall panels, a similar blister on the outside indicates that the aluminium cladding is pulling away from the foam core.

A floor repair is effected by drilling a series of holes around the faulty area. On a wall, deep drilling from the interior opens up a throughway to the blister itself. An epoxy resin two-part adhesive is

Special repair kits from Apollo enable a skilful owner to repair a delaminating wall or floor panel.

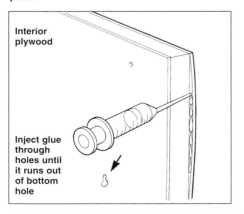

Interior plywood

Inject glue through holes until it runs out of bottom hole

Injecting a re-bonding agent is normally done from the inside; Apollo can supply a complete repair kit.

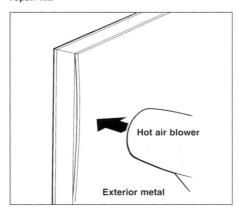

Hot air blower

Exterior metal

By parking close to a building, an injected area of delaminating wall cladding can be wedged back into place.

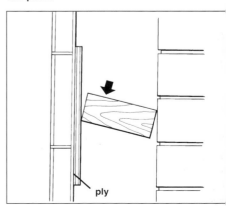

ply

then injected into the blistered area using a purpose-made syringe.

When the syringe is withdrawn, screws are then temporarily driven into the holes to contain the liquid; any surplus must be removed quickly as the adhesive sets 'rock hard'. Then the delaminated area is pressed back into place and clamped until the adhesive is set. On a floor panel, a board is used to cover the blistered area and is held down with heavy objects like house bricks. In the case of delaminated aluminium on an outside wall, the motorcaravan should be parked close to a building so that wedges can be positioned to press against the injected blistered section.

Most owners would have this work carried out by a specialist but some DIY enthusiasts have completed repairs successfully themselves. Chemicals, syringes and instructions are supplied by Apollo Chemicals.

Servicing work in the living area

Although motorcaravan owners recognise the importance of servicing a base vehicle, the living area sometimes gets overlooked. However, this is a serious omission as personal safety could be at stake.

Carrying out a routine pressure check of the gas supply system, for example, is an important task. If leaks are detected, faulty couplings will be repaired by the service engineer since a fault could lead to fatality. Cases of carbon monoxide poisoning through faulty gas appliances have *also* occurred and accidents could have been avoided if routine servicing work had been carried out.

Handbook advice

Handbooks might advise on items that have to be checked and serviced, but the information is variable – both in quality and detail. In some instances, motorcaravans from smaller volume converters are supplied without a handbook.

It is for this reason that the SMMT and NCC looked particularly closely at the subject.

The SMMT/NCC Annual Habitation Check

The Society of Motor Manufacturers and Traders (SMMT), working in conjunction with the National Caravan Council (NCC), have published a booklet entitled the *Recommended Annual Habitation Service Check*. A copy should be included in the document wallet supplied with a new motorcaravan. Alternatively it can often be obtained from a dealer; or direct from the SMMT.

This SMMT/NCC guide makes reference to eleven areas of attention. These include:

• The integrity of the body mounting points
• Windows
• Doors
• Attachments to chassis
• Attachments to body exterior
• Internal components
• Rising roof mechanisms
• Gas system
• Water system
• Electrical system
• Ventilation.

Within these eleven areas of attention are further subdivisions that deal with specific items. For example, one important servicing check is the damp test. This is critical, especially in respect of coachbuilt motorcaravans, where leaks are frequently reported. Water ingress can also be a problem with van conversions – leaks sometimes develop around external ventilators, roof lights and similar fittings.

Not surprisingly the wide range of motorcaravan designs means that some checking areas are not universally relevant. The rising roof inspection listed in the SMMT/NCC booklet is one example.

Appliance servicing

Carrying out checks on appliances is a safety-critical matter – especially those that operate on gas. When left unused for an extended period, these appliances often start to perform poorly. The accumulation of dust is one contributor to inefficient operation but spiders and insects can also create problems. Even a spider's web can upset the shape of a flame, and it is this obstruction that often prevents a pilot flame from igniting the main burner on a space heater, so cleaning the burners with the help of an air line forms part of the service work.

In addition, the shape of a gas flame has to be checked by a qualified service engineer, as does its colour. Tips of yellow on the hob burners, for example, may indicate an incorrect gas/air mixture. This will result in sooty deposits being left on pots and pans. More serious is the fact that an incorrect air mixture might lead to a carbon monoxide problem. This is why an expert's attention is crucial; altering a gas/air mixture should never be attempted by the owner.

The fridge is another gas-operated appliance that needs periodic attention. Electrolux makes it perfectly clear that a refrigerator should be

A gas engineer often uses a pressure tester to confirm a supply system is free of leaks.

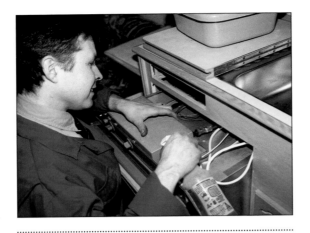

serviced annually and this means removing it from the motorcaravan so that work can be carried out on a bench. Further description of the servicing procedure is shown in Chapter Seven.

One warning is that a normal habitation service usually only checks to see if a refrigerator achieves cooling. A full service as recommended by Electrolux is generally regarded as an additional job. Don't be misled into thinking that the 'service check' is the same as a full fridge service.

DIY servicing

Owners who have experience and competence in practical skills are able to carry out many of the tasks involved in servicing themselves. Checking window catches, lubricating door hinges and tightening the spring mechanism on a roller blind are scarcely taxing.

At the same time, there are some service operations like pressure testing a gas system, which must only be undertaken by a qualified gas engineer. Similarly the tests needed on a 230v mains supply system are best carried out by a qualified electrician. In both instances, you should ask the service engineer to supply a written, dated confirmation sheet to be certain that the gas and mains electrical systems have been tested and found in order. Being able to pass on service records like this is especially helpful when selling a motorcaravan at a later date.

Whereas some jobs are successfully

undertaken by DIY owners, many motorcaravanners would prefer to put the entire task in the hands of an approved service centre. Needless to say, during a warranty period, failure to do this usually invalidates a manufacturer's guarantee.

What really needs to be done?

The facing page sets out a typical Service Schedule. It has been drawn up using recommendations given in the SMMT/NCC booklet and the recommendations from appliance manufacturers. It also takes note of advice and practical guidance given at service engineers' training courses.

Some repair workshops do not provide the customer with documentation in respect of 'servicing work' they have carried out, but this is unsatisfactory. The position should be checked at the time of making an appointment – it is very important to know what is included in the service. Written confirmation should always be provided afterwards about the condition of key items like the habitation section's structural integrity, the gas system, and the electricity systems.

It should also be confirmed what the dealer will do if something is found to be faulty during the course of the inspection. In some service centres, minor faults like an inoperative interior light will be repaired within the time allotted for the service. Spare parts, of course, will be charged separately. It is the matter of repairing more significant faults that needs prior discussion. Whilst it often makes sense for a repair to be carried out there and then, it is normal for a dealer to seek 'instruction to proceed' authorisation from an owner if an expensive replacement part is needed.

As a rough guide, a habitation service – excluding work on a fridge – is likely to involve 3–4 hours work. The cost varies from dealer to dealer depending on the hourly rate for labour. Parts will be charged separately.

With regard to the accreditation of service centres, the Automobile Association in conjunction with the National Caravan Council and The Caravan Club have published details of a network of approved workshops. These are well equipped and rigorously checked. Although their main focus may be on trailer caravans, many service the habitation area of motorcaravans as well. Nearly a hundred centres have been approved and further details are available from The Caravan Club.

These elements relate to a standard service. Further items may be added in a 'standard plus service'. These could include:

- Service refrigerator in accordance with Electrolux instructions
- Check operation of all road lights
- Check rising roof mechanisms, if fitted
- Check operation/mounting of all seat belts

36

Standard service schedule

Make: **Model:**   **Year:**   **Registration number:**   **Vehicle Identification no:**

Section 1: Undergear

Comments

1. Check body mounting fixings ☐ ....
2. Check cab-to-body junction ☐ ....
3. Check mounting of underfloor tanks ☐ ....
4. Check spare wheel cradle operation/tyre ☐ ....
5. Examine wheel boxes for corrosion/damage ☐ ....
6. Check and lubricate corner steadies (if fitted) ☐ ....
7. Check step operation (if fitted) and lubricate ☐ ....

General comments on Undergear: ....
....
....
....

Section 2: Gas/gas appliances

Comments

1. Carry out pressure test on system ☐ ....
2. Replace washer on butane regulator ☐ ....
3. Replace flexible hose; use new hoseclips ☐ ....
4. Fridge: Light and test for cooling ☐ ....
5. Light and verify operation of cooking appliances ☐ ....
6. Check space heater operation, clean burners ☐ ....
7. Check water heater operation, clean burners ☐ ....

General comments on gas appliances: ....
....
....

Section 3: Electrical

Comments

1. Check RCD and MCBs on central unit ☐ ....
2. Test 13 amp mains sockets ☐ ....
3. Test 12v sockets ☐ ....
4. Check integrity of all wiring and fuses ☐ ....
5. Check operation of all interior lights ☐ ....
6. Check awning lamp/outside pump socket ☐ ....
7. Check auxiliary battery ☐ ....

General comments on electrical appliances: ....
....
....

Section 4: Water systems

Comments

1. Check operation of water pump, clean grit filter ☐ ....
2. Check waste & fresh water systems for leaks ☐ ....
3. Flush through with purifying cleaner ☐ ....
4. Inspect tanks/emptying system ☐ ....
5. Change charcoal water filter, if fitted ☐ ....
6. Check toilet flush and blade operation ☐ ....

General comments on water systems: ....
....
....

Section 5: External Bodywork & General Condition

Comments

1. Look for poor sealant and potential leak points ☐ ....
2. Check/oil door locks; oil hinges ☐ ....
3. Check body attachments, vents, roof lights, racks ☐ ....
4. Confirm window operation, lubricate hinges/stays ☐ ....

Comments on bodywork/general: ....
....
....

Section 6: Internal elements

Comments

1. Carry out a damp and seepage test ☐ ....
2. Verify cab seat operation and adjustments ☐ ....
3. Check furniture; lubricate catches & hinges ☐ ....
4. Confirm blind and curtain operation ☐ ....
5. Check vents (high and low) & drop-out holes ☐ ....

Comments in general: ....
....
....

Section 7: Fire warning systems

Comments

1. Check fire alarm operation ☐ ....
2. Check expiry date on extinguisher and notices ☐ ....
3. Check fire blanket location/fixing ☐ ....

Comments in general: ....
....
....

Work completed on:

Work completed by:

4

Electrical systems

The electrical provision in a motorcaravan is more complicated than the electrical system in the home. Not only is there a mains system, there is also a low voltage supply; and although both are completely separate, there is a degree of inter-relationship.

The focus in this chapter is on electricity in the living quarters. This comprises a 230v AC system, known as the **mains supply**; and a 12v DC provision, described as the **low voltage system**.

The system which serves the base vehicle is separate yet again, and is not covered here as there is already a textbook dealing with automotive wiring, ignition, vehicle accessories, engine management systems and so on. This is a Haynes Manual entitled *Automobile Electrical & Electronic Systems*, by Tony Tranter.

As regards provision in the living quarters, a 230v supply on a busy site sometimes drops below 200v. Similarly, a 12v provision is another misnomer. For instance, if the vehicle or leisure batteries read 12v across their terminals, it means they are in a discharged condition. This is explained more thoroughly under the heading *Checking condition* on page 44.

The subject of electricity in motorcaravans is wide-ranging so it helps to break it down into six sections:

1. Low voltage systems (12v DC)
2. Leisure batteries
3. Charging
4. Mains systems (230v AC)
5. Portable Generators
6. Inverters.

Low voltage systems

A safe and efficient 12v system is dependent on a number of elements. A well-designed circuit is one feature; a dependable supply is another.

The circuit

Nearly all motorcaravans use a battery to supply the low voltage system. On the other hand, transformer/rectifiers *are* available for motorcaravans – the Ranger Power Pack, for example, will convert a 230v AC supply to 12v DC. Some continental motorcaravans employ this arrangement exclusively – but in Britain, we usually prefer to use a battery.

To be more accurate, we actually use *two* batteries. The normal source is a leisure battery (auxiliary battery) which is exclusively designed to run lights and appliances in a living space. If this fails, the vehicle battery can then be switched into use as an alternative. However, this should only be regarded as a temporary arrangement – if the charge level drops too low, vehicle starting might be affected.

Recognising the diversity of appliances that run on a low voltage supply, a circuit designer now follows a practice which is adopted in the mains supply in our homes. This is where the original feed is sub-divided into separate routes which, in turn, branch out to supply distinct groups of appliances.

Each branch is independently protected by a fuse, the rating of which is appropriate for the appliances being served. For instance a radio cassette player has a particularly low consumption, so it is normally protected by a 5 amp fuse. On the other hand, a water pump has a higher consumption, and a 10 amp fuse is usually fitted.

Quite often the separate branches are also fitted with a switch, so if you needed to look at a troublesome water pump on a dark evening, you could switch off its supply without having to interrupt the supply to the interior lights. This is very convenient, though some motorcaravan control units don't incorporate switches. In this instance, to isolate a particular supply you have to take out the appropriate fuse from the control panel instead.

The device which divides a supply into individually protected branches is called a fused distribution unit. In Britain, the units fitted are usually made either by Zig Electronics of Stroud or Plug-In-Systems of Hull. Some are conspicuous in location: others are more discreet and may be mounted behind a hinged cover.

Two other features commonly fitted are:

• a battery selection switch,
• a battery condition indicator.

The selection switch enables you to choose whether the supply is drawn from your auxiliary

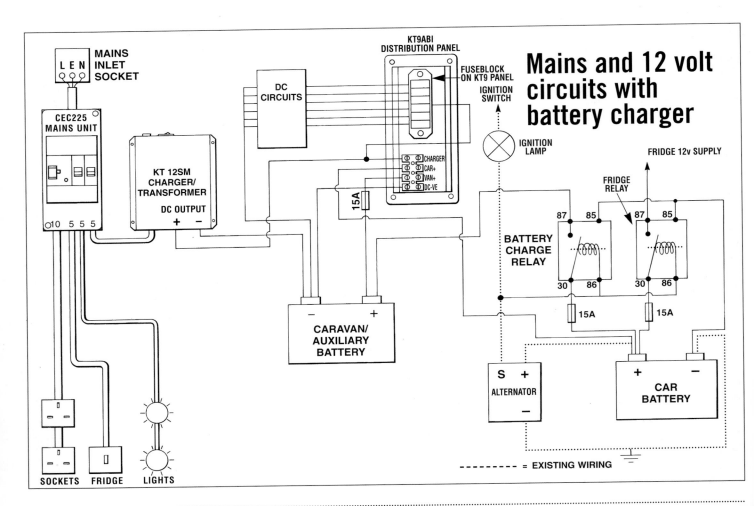

Mains and 12 volt circuits with battery charger

MAINS INLET SOCKET — L E N

CEC225 MAINS UNIT — 10 5 5 5

KT 12SM CHARGER/TRANSFORMER — DC OUTPUT + −

SOCKETS FRIDGE LIGHTS

DC CIRCUITS

KT9ABI DISTRIBUTION PANEL

FUSEBLOCK ON KT9 PANEL

IGNITION SWITCH

CHARGER
CAR+
VAN+
DC-VE

15A

IGNITION LAMP

CARAVAN/ AUXILIARY BATTERY — − +

FRIDGE 12v SUPPLY

FRIDGE RELAY

BATTERY CHARGE RELAY

87 85   87 85
30 86   30 86

15A   15A

S + ALTERNATOR −

CAR BATTERY — + −

- - - - - - - - = EXISTING WIRING

Wiring diagram of mains and low voltage supplies in a motorcaravan.

Safety

• The supply cable to a low voltage circuit *must* be protected by an in-line fuse connected to the feed coming from the battery's positive terminal. It should also be close to the source. However, since a leisure battery is usually installed in a ventilated locker, the fuse should be positioned *outside* this enclosure. This is because a battery sometimes gives off an inflammable gas (hydrogen) while being charged. A fuse often sparks when it fails, so the wisdom of situating it *outside* a battery compartment is clear.

• The rating of a battery supply fuse varies. Plug-In-Systems recommend that for most motorcaravans, a 15 amp fuse is appropriate. However, in a large model full of electrical appliances, if everything were to be operated at once, the full complement of 12v appliances would draw a total current of 15–20 amps; but this is unlikely and circuit designers usually consider 60% of total demand as a realistic maximum.

A 12v distribution unit divides a low voltage supply into separate fuse-protected feeds.

The rear connections on this low voltage distribution unit are clearly marked.

battery or the vehicle battery. Sometimes the switches fitted have three positions, the centre of which isolates the circuit and draws from *neither* supply.

As regards the battery condition indicator, this provides warning when re-charging is needed. Usually a meter is fitted to monitor a battery's condition because it gives a greater degree of indication. However, some distribution units are still fitted with two light-emitting diodes. A green light on the panel shows the battery is in good condition; a red light warns that recharging is needed. These warning systems are also useful for other reasons; for instance if the automatic shut down on a water heater comes into operation, you might presume that the gas cylinder is empty. On the other hand, if the battery warning light is on, it might mean there is insufficient power to operate the water heater's electronic circuits – hence the triggering of the automatic shut-down mechanism.

To show motorcaravanners a typical wiring layout, Plug-In-Systems has a large display board which is taken to selected rallies. This clearly shows how everything is connected up; in addition, their wiring diagram clarifies the system even further. The accompanying illustration reproduces Plug-In-Systems' visual aid and readers intending to carry out a self-build conversion or re-fit will find the guidance invaluable. So, too, will a motorcaravan owner whose handbook lacks detailed guidance on the low voltage provision.

A clear wiring diagram is extremely useful. However, it only conveys part of the picture. It is important to recognise that there are different types of cable used in circuits. The following section explains this further.

Cable rating

Whilst the layman often talks about 'wire', an electrician usually prefers the term 'cable'. It is also helpful to understand some other terminology too. The panel on the right explains some key words.

When coupling up appliances, both the thickness of the connecting cable and its length are significant; for instance, thick cable is needed to ensure there's a good flow of current. If the cable is too thin, there's a resistance to current flow – a situation that might cause the plastic insulation around the wire to get warm – or even hot.

The length of a cable run also needs consideration; the longer the run, the greater the drop in volts. So if your leisure battery is situated a long distance from the base vehicle alternator, a significant voltage loss is inevitable when charging the battery while driving. The shorter the connecting cable, the better the charge rate. Voltage loss is less pronounced, however, if a thicker cable is fitted.

As regards the type of cable needed, a motorcaravan low voltage system should be wired using automotive cable. This has good flexibility because it is made from separate strands or 'filaments' and these have a standard thickness of $0.33mm^2$.

A low consumption appliance like a fluorescent light only needs a thin cable whereas a high consumption appliance, like a refrigerator, needs thicker cable. But this is a simplification and a more precise specification is needed.

Cable rating is indicated on the packaging and

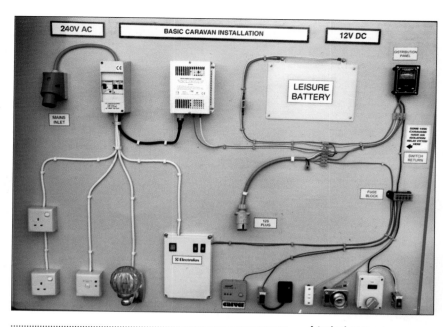

A typical caravan or motorcaravan wiring layout.

information is sometimes expressed in respect of its cross sectional area in mm^2. Alternatively the label might quote an *Approximate continuous current rating* in amps. On a practical note, if a label is missing, you can confirm cable rating by carefully counting the filaments, presuming the strands are of standard size. The table overleaf relates the ratings to typical motorcaravan applications.

Terminology

A practical comparison often helps a beginner to understand a theoretical issue. For example, to be hit by a fast-moving lead shot might be very unpleasant. The pressure it imposes at the time of impact wouldn't pass unnoticed. But speed isn't everything. To be hit by a much slower object – like a double-decker bus – could be worse since the size of the object now comes into play. Now combine the two elements and the result is infinitely more potent. These mental pictures help to illustrate the difference between volts, amps and watts.

Volts – This unit of measurement is concerned with *pressure*. However, in a practical situation, a cable offers a resistance that can lead to a loss of pressure. The longer the cable, the greater the drop in voltage.

Amps – Amperes or 'amps' refers to the *amount* of electricity. In practical terms, a motorcaravan fridge needs a large amount of electricity to work properly (8 amps), and requires a relatively thick connecting cable. In contrast, an interior strip light only needs a small amount of electricity (0.7 amps), and works quite successfully with a much thinner connecting cable.

Watts – This is the *rate* at which electrical energy is used and some appliances are more greedy than others. Watts are a combination of both the pressure of flow (volts) and the amount of current (amps). The formula to remember is:

Watts = Volts x Amps

41

No of strands	Cross sectional area in mm²	Current rating in amps	Application in motorcaravans
14	1.00	8.75	Interior lights
21	1.50	12.75	Wire to extractor fans, but check the model
28	2.00	17.50	Feed to fridge (minimum) See note
36	2.50	21.75	Feed to battery from the charger Feed to a diaphragm water pump e.g. Whale Evenflow

• A cable that is too thin for a high consumption appliance may start to get warm as a result of the cable's resistance. If the rise in temperature then starts to cause the insulation to melt, there's a serious problem ahead. If several cables are strapped together, for example, melting insulation could lead to a short circuit.

• A low voltage supply doesn't pose the threat of electrocution like a mains supply, but if you've seen the powerful spark that is caused when there's a short circuit, you'll appreciate the acute fire risk that accompanies a 12v system. Melting insulation is sometimes the cause of short circuits. Fuses in a circuit are intended to overcome this risk but they have to be of the correct rating and appropriately located in a supply system.

NOTE: *For a number of years, Electrolux installation manuals stated that if 2.0mm² cable is fitted, the cable run must not exceed 8 metres. Longer cable runs – between 8 and 10.5 metres – need 2.5mm² cable to avoid an unacceptable drop in voltage. However, Electrolux now recommends that only 2.5mm² cable should be fitted.*

To confirm that an installation is satisfactory, a voltmeter should be used to take a reading at the low voltage connector block on top of the appliance. This should be done when the engine is running. If the reading falls below 12v, a cable of higher rating is needed.

Making connections

Sometimes additions are needed in a motorcaravan. It's not unusual to find that an extra spotlight or a 12v socket would prove useful. If you're competent in electrical work, the job isn't difficult provided the appropriate cable is chosen and the appliance is coupled into the existing circuit correctly.

For instance, if you wanted to fit a 12v socket for a colour TV – large models may be rated up to 100 watts – it would be quite wrong to take the feed from a supply cable serving the lights. A fluorescent light draws around 8 watts, so the manufacturer would probably have connected this up using 1.00mm² cable (as shown in the table); a colour TV would be more appropriately served by a cable of 2.00mm².

Where possible, it is best to route the cable for a proposed socket back to the distribution unit; however, visible cable pinned to the surface looks unattractive and could be obstructive, so time should be spent finding a route that keeps it out of sight.

Coupling up a spotlight is less of a problem because there's likely to be a feed to another light fitting not too far away. Forming the join is the next

An existing light unit can provide a point of connection for additional lighting.

A connecting block provides opportunity for adding extra lights.

Additional spotlights are not difficult to add to a low voltage supply.

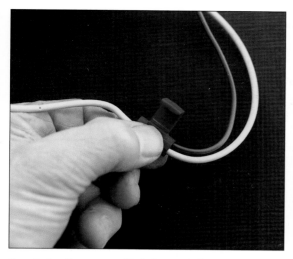

Snap locks allow a new cable to be coupled into an existing feed wire.

Crimp connectors are easy to fit.

consideration and sometimes a connecting block is used.

Another product often used for making a connection is the 'snap lock', sometimes referred to as a Scotchlock. This connector creates an electrical connection with an existing cable by means of a small metal tag which slices its way through the insulation sleeve on both feeds. Using a snap lock means that you don't have to cut the original cable.

Notwithstanding the simplicity of the snap lock system, some electricians prefer the use of crimp connectors. If you have never used these products, it is a good idea to buy a starter kit. This includes the crimping tool, together with a selection of different crimp couplings. The photograph at the top of the next column shows how a typical fitting is pressed on to the prepared end of the cable.

The use of soft solder is less common although some auto electricians favour its use in particular circumstances.

Electro-magnetic compatability

Purchasers of recent motorcaravans have found that electrical appliances in the living quarters, with the exception of the refrigerator, will not operate while the engine is running; for example, all lights are disabled. This can be a hindrance – but there is a good reason for this latest feature.

The new wiring practice is related to a phenomenon referred to as 'electro-magnetic compatibility' or EMC for short. Installers recognise that modern vehicles now employ electronic control systems. Two key items are ABS braking and sophisticated engine management computers.

Regrettably the operation of these control devices might be influenced when other electrical equipment is used while a vehicle is being driven. Malfunction in a safety-critical aid like ABS braking could have serious consequences, so the response is to fit an automatic isolation switch into the wiring system – a component more commonly called a 'relay'. This detects when the engine is running and switches off the supply of electricity to the living area.

Owners of older motorcaravans might not need such a system; sophisticated electronics in motor vehicles are comparatively recent. However, an attempt to by-pass this control on a newer model could conceivably lead to a serious accident e.g. interference with brake operation. This matter has raised problems and the concession to keep a fridge running on a 12v supply has been questioned by manufacturers whose fan operated heaters are approved for operation during driving. In truth, the debate may have only just started.

Leisure batteries

Neither the base vehicle battery, nor an auxiliary leisure battery should be seen as 'fit and forget' accessories. On the contrary, they need regular attention and special measures have to be taken if the vehicle is likely to remain unused for an extended period.

Isolation and battery charging relays ready for installation in a production motorcaravan.

43

Construction and use

In both construction and use, vehicle and leisure batteries are different.

A vehicle battery is designed to produce a surge of power to operate a starter motor. This is a demanding task, but once the engine is running, the battery gains an immediate re-charge from the vehicle's alternator.

In contrast, a leisure battery has to provide current over an extended period – and time might elapse before recharging is possible. However, a recharge mustn't be delayed too long; battery manufacturers advise strongly against discharging a battery completely because this can cause permanent damage.

The continued pattern of charge/discharge (referred to as deep cycling) is something that a vehicle battery can't endure for long. The lead plates sustain damage quickly and the all-important paste held within them can fall away. In a leisure battery, however, the plates are constructed with separators so that their paste is held *in situ* more effectively. This is reflected in the higher cost of the product – though in respect of its working life, a leisure battery would normally provide longer service.

In Elecsol leisure batteries, carbon fibre is used in the plate construction. This is an unusual development and early indications suggest that Elecsol batteries will give notably long service. Without doubt, the inclusion of a five-year warranty is proof of the manufacturer's confidence in the product.

Notwithstanding the cautionary advice about avoiding a total discharge, it is worth stating that a leisure battery installed in a motorcaravan is more likely to receive a periodic 'top-up' than a battery in a touring caravan. This is because a tourer is often left on a pitch for a long period and if there's no mains hook-up, re-charging the leisure battery might pose problems. The fact that most motorcaravans are driven off-site regularly means there's a periodic recharge from the alternator.

Guidance on use

To get the best from a leisure battery, the following recommendations are put forward by manufacturers:

• The terminals should be smeared with grease, like Triflow, or petroleum jelly (Vaseline).
• Check the electrolyte periodically and if the level falls below the top of the plates, top up with de-ionised water. This is available from car accessory shops.
• A battery must not be left in a discharged state; this is often the reason why a battery is irreparably damaged.
• If your motorcaravan is parked for an extended period, make provision for keeping the leisure battery in a charged condition. This might involve transferring it to a bench for charging; alternatively some owners use a trickle charger like the Airflow which is left permanently connected.
• Completely sealed non-spill gel electrolyte batteries like the Varta Drymobil, are less common and you should seek the manufacturer's advice about care and maintenance.
• When removing a battery, disconnect the negative terminal first; when installing a battery, connect the negative terminal last.

Checking condition

To check battery condition it is usual to make the test with a meter, although specific gravity testing is an alternative.

Obviously it's best to take a voltage reading directly from the battery terminals, but several points need to be borne in mind.

• The use of a digital voltmeter is recommended since these are easy to read and the level of accuracy is usually good. A voltmeter of this kind

Triflow grease is a moisture-resisting product suitable for battery pillars.

If the electrolyte drops low in a cell, de-ionised water should be added.

Checking the specific gravity of the electrolyte confirms battery condition.

A digital multimeter is used to take voltage readings.

can be purchased from electrical specialists like Tandy.

• Make sure all appliances are disconnected – even a permanently connected clock can falsify the reading.

• If a battery has just been disconnected from a charger, or you've recently been driving your motorcaravan, the reading will not be a true indication of battery condition. It is necessary for the battery to settle before being tested with a voltmeter, which means waiting for at least four hours. The reason for this is that an elderly battery has a problem holding its charge; if you can wait even longer the voltmeter will provide an even better indication of battery condition.

• While a battery is described as providing a 12v power supply, the description is misleading. In fact a reading of 12v indicates the battery is completely discharged. The state of charge is often interpreted as follows:

Voltmeter reading	Approx. charge state
12.7v or over	100%
12.5v	75%
12.4v	50%
12.2v	25%
12v or under	Discharged

Battery life between charges

The capacity of a battery is expressed in amp-hours (Ah) and this indicates how long it can provide an output before needing a re-charge. As a rule, the external dimensions of a leisure battery

are related to its Ah capacity and whilst a 90Ah battery product needs a re-charge less frequently than a 60Ah version, there isn't always sufficient stowage space. The purpose-made battery boxes fitted in many motorcaravans will only accept 60 or 75Ah versions.

In practice, this may not present a problem. Motorcaravanners who are constantly on the move are unlikely to be affected. It is only when you park a vehicle for an extended period – perhaps because you're travelling out of the site by means of other transport – that a 90Ah battery would be better. But what does this capacity rating mean in practical terms?

To assess how long a battery will provide power between charges, a simple calculation has to be made. This only provides a rough estimation, but it is still a helpful indicator.

1. Establish the wattage of appliances. Typical examples: a single tube strip light – 8 watts; a spotlight – 10 watts; a water pump – 50 watts; a colour TV – 50 watts.
NOTE: *The wattage of portable colour TVs can vary, so check your appliance. Some models like the Goodmans Compact 510 are as low as 21w max.*

The external dimensions of a 90Ah battery are greater than those of a 75Ah battery.

Battery performance

Variations in battery performance between charges:

• The stated capacity of a battery, expressed in amp hours, presumes the temperature is 25°C (77°F).

For approximately every 1° drop in temperature, there's a 1% fall in battery capacity, so when a battery which is nominally rated as 60Ah is operating in a temperature of 15°C (60°F) it effectively becomes a 54Ah battery.

Problems are even more acute for winter motorcaravanners. Not only will a battery work harder to provide lighting and fan-assisted heating on long, dark evenings; the actual capacity of the battery is considerably less than its Ah rating might suggest.

• Performance between charges deteriorates as a battery gets older.

• If a variety of appliances are used at the same time, thereby creating a more rapid discharge rate, battery performance characteristics are affected detrimentally.

If there's space in an engine compartment for a leisure battery, this assures good charging from the alternator.

2. Work out how many hours (or fractions of an hour) they will be used in a 24-hour period.
3. Calculate watt hours for each appliance by multiplying wattage by hours in use.
4. Add together the total of Watt hours.

This is shown in the following table:

Equipment	Rating in watts	Hours in use	Watt hours
Two 8 watt lights	16	5	80
Two 10 watt spot lights	20	1	20
Water pump	50	0.2	10
Colour TV	50	5	250
Total watt hours			**360**

Divide watt hours by volts to get ampere hours:

$$360 \div 12 = 30Ah$$

So if your motorcaravan is fitted with a 60Ah battery, at this rate of use (30Ah consumed in 24 hours) it will last for two days before a re-charge is needed. This is only a rough guide, however, and the point was made earlier that running a battery to the point of total discharge is a bad practice. Newcomers to motorcaravanning are often surprised at how quickly a leisure battery loses its charge. The above guidance clarifies the position and also confirms the merit of fitting a larger capacity 90Ah battery where there's space.

Leisure battery location

The closer a leisure battery is to the alternator, the better the charge rate, and provided there's ventilation and adequate space, the engine compartment undoubtedly meets this requirement. In practice, there isn't always space under the bonnet; an alternative therefore, is under a cab seat – presuming that the base vehicle has its power unit at the front.

The reason for this, as discussed earlier, is that a long run of connecting cable leads to a fall-off in voltage and a poorer charge rate as a result.

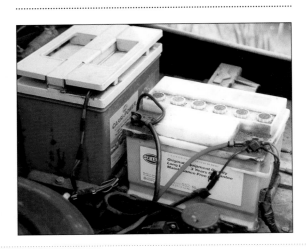

Fitting a leisure battery in a wardrobe which is a long way from an alternator means alternator charging is less efficient.

Clamp clips are ideal for connecting up to a leisure battery.

Admittedly a thicker gauge of cable helps to reduce voltage loss on long cable runs, but putting a leisure battery in a locker at the rear of a vehicle or in a distant wardrobe is not advantageous from an electrical standpoint.

Other points regarding location are as follows:

• A battery must not share a locker with gas cylinders. (A spark from a battery terminal next to a leaking gas cylinder could cause an explosion!) The ideal location is in a separate locker vented to the outside of the vehicle.

• Avoid using crocodile clips on battery terminals. A clip might become dislodged and a spark across a poor connection can be powerful. Traditional bolt-on clamps sold in auto shops are recommended, although clamping clips sold at motorcaravan accessory shops are better still.

• A battery location must have ventilation. The reason for this is given in the Safety panel on the opposite page.

An elbow coupling is designed to accept a venting tube.

Tubing from the battery can be passed through a hole in the floor.

During charging, a battery sometimes gives off hydrogen. This gas is lighter than air, explosive, and has a distinctive odour. Should the gas accidentally ignite – and a cigarette can cause this – the casing of a battery may be blown apart and corrosive acid forcibly ejected. Eye injury and flesh burns are likely.

There are two ways of venting hydrogen to the outside. If a battery is housed in a purpose-made locker, an outlet vent is needed which has been installed above the top of the battery because hydrogen rises. The alternative is to couple up a venting tube – most leisure batteries have a connector nozzle that accepts flexible tubing. Provided this joint is perfectly sound, the plastic tubing can be led through a hole in a side wall or floor, dispersing the hydrogen to the outside. If dispersal is done this way as opposed to a wall vent, the outlet can now be at a low level since the gas is contained within the plastic tube and forced downwards.

Charging

A leisure battery can be charged using any of the following:

• a portable or fixed mains charger
• the engine alternator
• a petrol generator
• a wind or solar system

Mains chargers

As regards mains chargers, the following points are worth noting:

• The amp output of a charger influences how quickly a battery is revived. Too high an amperage, however, is not good for a battery in the long term.
• A leisure battery needs a different charging regime compared to a vehicle battery. This is why an inexpensive portable car battery charger isn't recommended. On the other hand, some of the better types incorporate a selection switch; this provides the appropriate regime for either an auto or a leisure battery.

• A battery can be 'over-charged' and when this occurs, the electrolyte (the diluted sulphuric acid in the casing) may start to evaporate. If this happens, top up the battery using ionised water.
• Periodic checking of the electrolyte level is important; it should just cover the plates in each cell.
• There are several separate cells in a battery, each of which has its own top-up point. Sometimes a cell can fail and this upsets an automatic charger's sensing system. Instead of switching off automatically when the other cells are re-charged, it maintains its full output on account of the failed cell.
• When on a mains hook-up, some people keep a built-in motorcaravan charger constantly running. This was acceptable with older chargers that incorporated a transformer. Manufacturers of 'switched mode' electronic chargers now

Fixed chargers from Zig, like the T45 unit, have been fitted to many motorcaravans.

Some portable chargers have a switch setting to provide the charging regime appropriate for a leisure battery.

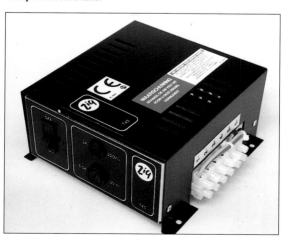

Vehicle battery charging

Although a motorcaravan built-in charger looks after the leisure battery, it may not be switchable to charge the vehicle battery. To achieve this, some motorcaravanners carry a conventional portable charger.

Another solution is to fit the Vanguard Battery Mate which provides a trickle charge to the vehicle battery using the motorcaravan's built-in charger. It is completely automatic in operation. Installation involves coupling the positive terminals of both the vehicle and leisure batteries via the Battery Mate control relay product. When connected to a mains hook-up, the motorcaravan's batteries can now both derive benefits from the fixed charger.

recommend that a charger is turned off when the battery level indicator shows a satisfactory condition.

• 12v should not be drawn direct from a mains operated charger *without* having a battery in place. This is because the output will fluctuate and some appliances in a motorcaravan *must* have a stable supply. Having a battery in circuit smooths out irregularities and prevents damage to appliances.

• The charge rate on a gel-type battery (as opposed to one containing diluted sulphuric acid) should not exceed 13.8v.

• In spite of warnings, some motorcaravanners still attempt to use a 12v supply without a leisure battery in circuit (i.e. by drawing directly from a charger as if it were a transformer/rectifier). Recognising this, many manufacturers of chargers installed in motorcaravans limit their output to 13.8v as a safety measure. This introduces a problem with dilute sulphuric acid batteries as the next point emphasises.

• To start the charging process where a battery is in low condition, a number of manufacturers specify that a start-up output from the charger of 14.2 to 14.4v is essential. When the battery's voltage reaches a certain level, charger output should then fall back to a 13.8 'float' voltage. Some battery manufacturers assert that a discharged battery might never re-achieve its peak condition if a 14.2 to 14.4 start-up voltage cannot be delivered by the charger.

Taking the above points into account, the best type of charger is one offering 'stage charging'. This commences with an output around 14.4v, then dropping to 13.8v, and subsequently switching off automatically when the battery achieves a full charge. Two products achieving this are the LabCraft BC126 and BC1210 variable output chargers that are made to fit in the company's TP2 battery carrying box. The TP2 is a product long-established with trailer caravanners.

Another useful product is the Airflow Battery Conditioner. This compact unit indicates battery condition via light emitting diodes (LEDs) and provides charging when connected to the mains.

Electronic circuits monitor battery condition and activate the Airflow Conditioner automatically when charging is needed. In consequence it can be left connected for an extended period.

The engine alternator

Enabling a leisure battery to receive a charge from the alternator while the engine is running isn't merely a matter of linking the vehicle batteries together in parallel (parallel is where the positive terminals are connected; and the negative terminals are similarly linked). Were this to be done, current would be pulled from *both* batteries when starting the vehicle. This could damage the leisure battery and sometimes a fuse would be 'blown' in the process.

The connection between the batteries has to be severed by fitting a relay (an electrically operated switch). When wired up correctly, the two batteries are thus kept separate until the engine is actually running. Incidentally, a similar relay is also fitted to the 12v supply feeding a refrigerator.

Several manufacturers specialise in these relays, including Hella, Lucas and Ring, and kits are made for both motor and trailer caravans. Wiring diagrams are provided and the diagram opposite from Plug-In-Systems shows how a fridge relay, a battery charging relay and the isolation relay for the low voltage supply in the living quarters are all connected up.

Triggering the fridge and charging relays is done by connecting into the ignition light feed from the alternator. In practice, this is not easy in some vehicles and an auto electrician at a franchise dealer should be consulted. Taking an alternative supply from an ignition-controlled accessory on the base vehicle may not be acceptable either – some accessories are activated when the starter is being operated, hence the leisure battery is inappropriately brought into the starting procedure.

Finally, a number of auto electricians suggest it is better to fit two separate relays for charging and fridge operation. Whereas combination relays *are* available, if faults occur, it's undoubtedly easier to identify a problem if both functions are kept independent.

Petrol generators

With the widespread use of 'switched-mode' battery chargers in motorcaravans, the fluctuating supply that often comes from a petrol generator can present problems. Difficulties occur if you plug the 230v output from the generator into your motorcaravan mains system and then operate the built-in leisure battery charger. It is much better to charge the battery directly by coupling up to the separate 12v terminals fitted to most generators.

Whilst problems are less evident in the older built-in chargers that have a transformer, component damage in electronic switched-mode models is periodically reported.

The LabCraft BC1210 variable output charger fits within a purpose-designed battery carrrying box.

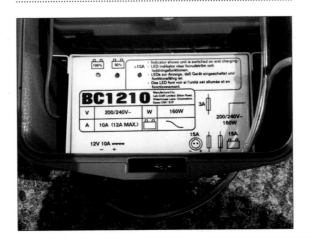

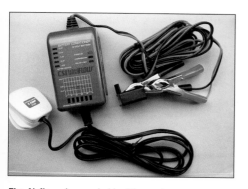

The Airflow charger is ideal for motorcaravans placed in storage because it can be left permanently connected up.

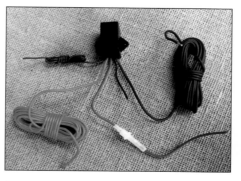

A relay for refrigerator 12v operation and leisure battery charging.

Separate Hella relays for fridge and battery charging are notably reliable.

Solar and wind generators

The idea of getting 'something for nothing' is very attractive. On the other hand, these types of generator will only provide a trickle charge for a battery.

Strictly speaking, the term 'solar' is inaccurate because photo-voltaic cells (which produce power from light) also produce some electricity in cloudy weather; they don't depend on sunshine. Solar panels are popular products and are often on sale at outdoor motorcaravan exhibitions.

With both products a regulator is needed to ensure a battery isn't over-charged. For example, damage might otherwise occur through an abnormally high output produced by a wind generator during a gale.

Several products are available, complete with installation kits, but cost is undoubtedly a disincentive.

Wiring for fridge, battery charging and isolating relays in a motorcaravan.

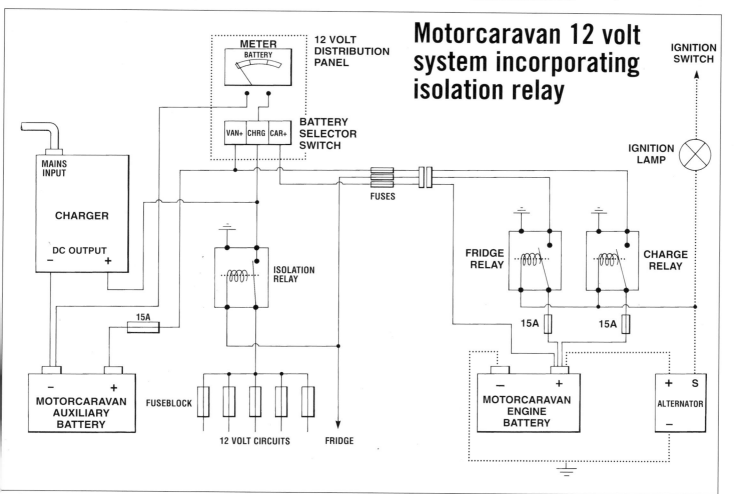

Motorcaravan 12 volt system incorporating isolation relay

Mains systems

This section describes the components used in a mains supply and provides general safety guidance, including procedures for coupling-up on site.

As regards owner installation, some very good kits are available and enable a competent and careful practitioner to install a mains supply where one hasn't already been fitted. Most people would entrust this work to a qualified electrician, but some DIY enthusiasts undoubtedly have the knowledge and ability to fit one of these kits themselves. The work involved is shown in Chapter Eleven where a VW Campervan is fitted with a mains system.

Note: *DIY installations must be tested by a qualified electrician and should have a signed test certificate to verify compliance with the current IEE regulations. Contact the NICEIC or ECA for details of approved inspectors in your area.*

As regards the provision itself, it should comprise:

• A supply circuit wired to IEE standards. This means 2.5mm² flexible cable will connect from the Input Socket to the RCD; 1.5mm² flexible cable is required for all other circuits from the MCBs.
• A mains consumer unit manufactured with a Residual Current Device (RCD); this immediately cuts off the supply if anyone accidentally touches a live wire. It also includes Miniature Circuit Breakers (MCBs) to protect individual circuits – there is usually one for the fridge and one for the sockets.

NOTE:
1. An MCB is a trip switch – a modern equivalent of the old fashioned rewirable fuse. The MCBs now have to incorporate double-pole switching, or single pole and switched neutral operation.
2. The RCD used to be called an 'Earth Leakage Circuit Breaker' or a 'Residual Current Circuit Breaker'.
3. Most consumer units deal solely with 230v electricity but the Plug-In-Systems PMS3 product embraces mains, charging and 12v systems in a single control box.
• An earth wire covered with a green and yellow sheathing, must be connected from the earth bar in the consumer unit and bolted to the chassis. A warning plate should be attached to the bolt.
• 'Three-pin' 13 amp sockets in the motorcaravan –

....

The Powerpart Mains wiring kit is supplied with full fitting instructions.

The PMS 3H from Plug-In Systems incorporates low voltage, mains supply and battery charging facilities in a single unit.

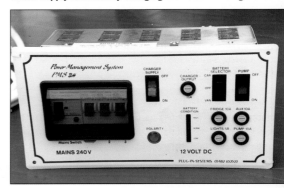

An earth cable bolted to the chassis must be clearly labelled.

Safety

• It is strongly recommended that a mains system should be checked annually by a qualified electrician and a written certificate issued to verify the installation is safe.
• If you buy a second-hand motorcaravan fitted with a DIY supply that doesn't meet with the standards, have it removed and replaced with an approved system. Periodically check your RCD operation by pressing the test button. This should switch off the system instantly – just as it should if anyone accidentally touched a live wire.
• The RCD operates by monitoring the balance in live and neutral cables. If you accidentally touch a live supply, the current runs through your body taking a short cut to earth. This imbalance is detected, whereupon the RCD cut-off switch operates and the flow is immediately disconnected. It all happens in milliseconds, but you'll still receive a very brief shock.
• It is best to use only double insulated appliances in your motorcaravan. The BEAB approval sign is affixed to appliances fulfilling this safety requirement.

An adaptor is needed before a hook-up cable can draw electricity from a 13 amp domestic socket.

preferably the latest types which feature double pole switching.
• An input socket which complies with BS4343.
• A connecting cable complying with BS6500 – Ref 3184Y. This must not exceed 25 metres. It contains three flexible cores for positive, negative and earth connections, each of which has a cross section area of 2.5mm². You are NOT recommended to link up more than one extension lead to reach a distant hook-up point.

The system fitted in a motorcaravan is designed to connect with site 'hook-up' pillars in the UK which are fitted with an industrial socket. If you want to connect the supply lead to a 13 amp socket at home – perhaps to pre-cool a fridge prior to departure – you'll need an adaptor. Similarly an adaptor is needed to connect into many hook-up pillars on the Continent.

Motorcaravanners travelling abroad need to take an adaptor to couple up with a continental mains supply although some foreign sites are now using the British-style socket.

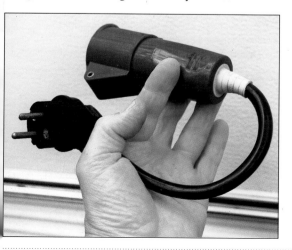

Connecting up to a site supply

When you've gained a warden's approval to have a mains supply, always follow this hook-up routine:

1. Switch off the motorcaravan's isolation switch on the consumer unit.
2. Uncoil the hook-up lead. Never leave it coiled on a drum because this can lead to overheating.
3. Insert the end with recessed tubes (female) into your motorcaravan input socket.
4. Insert the opposite end with pins (male) into the site supply point. On some sites you have to rotate the connector clockwise until it locks.
5. Turn on the main switch of the consumer unit to put the system into operation.
6. Having coupled up, it's wise to check polarity – there may be a warning light on your consumer unit. Failing this, it's worth buying a socket tester from a dealer or electrical factor.

Disconnection follows a reverse order. In the case of the twist socket fitted on several sites, you need to depress a red button to release the connector. Similarly the inlet sockets on some motorcaravans are fitted with a plug release button.

Polarity

In the UK, it is traditional for a switch to create a break in the live feed serving an appliance or lamp fitting. In other words if a light is switched off, no current reaches the bulb or its socket.

On the Continent, switches operate on both live *and* neutral connections, a system known as double pole switching. This is undoubtedly very safe, but less care is given abroad when contractors install campsite hook-ups. Live and neutral feeds are often reversed and the situation, called 'reverse polarity', is not really significant if the continental practice of using double pole switches is followed.

Unfortunately it can be very dangerous for the UK tourist whose motorcaravan is normally only fitted with single pole switches. When you switch off an appliance it's true that it ceases to function, but if we take a light as an example – *the light fitting remains live* because switching is now on the cable leading *out* of the unit.

The advice is to cease using a supply with reversed polarity – just in case you accidentally touch a live connection. However, some owners create their own polarity changeover device and perhaps the best solution is to intentionally wire up a second continental adaptor with reversed connections. This effectively remedies the problem at source and by carrying both adaptors when ever touring abroad, together with a polarity tester plug, the situation is solved.

Motorcaravans manufactured since 1993 now have double pole switched MCBs so the problem is less acute. But regrettably, single pole 13 amp sockets are still fitted in motorcaravans – even though double pole 13 amp switched sockets have been available for some time. The Concept Range sold by W4 Accessories is an example. Without

Mains hook-ups

A site hook-up is limited in its supply. Some supplies are as low as 5 amps; others as high as 16 amps. Some sites offer two levels of supply and charge accordingly. Ask the site warden about the amperage rating.

Using the figure given (amps), multiply this by 230 (volts) to establish the total wattage it can supply. For instance if a site offers a 10 amp supply, 10 x 230 = 2300 watts.

Now look closely at your appliances to see their wattage rating. Typically these are:

Light bulb	60W
Small colour TV	50 W
Fridge	125 W
Battery charger	100 W
Microwave cooker	1200 W
Domestic kettle	2,000 W

Now add up the wattages of the appliances you hope to have in use at any one time to assess whether you'll overload the site supply. If you do, you'll activate the hook-up pillar's trip switch and will have to ask the warden to re-instate the supply. Prepare for a frosty reception . . .

A hook-up cable should be connected to the motorcaravan before coupling up to the mains pillar.

A test device confirms if the supply polarity is correct or reversed.

question, it is worth changing the original single pole switched sockets for double pole versions. This is an inexpensive modification after which reversed polarity no longer poses a threat.

Portable generators

In a remote location a generator can be extremely useful. On a crowded site, however, the noise is undoubtedly intrusive.

A portable generator's output is also limited and whereas a model like the Honda EX650 is impressively quiet and conveniently compact, its output of 650 watts at 60Hz doesn't offer a great deal of scope. Moreover, voltage-sensitive appliances have to operate at 50Hz, at which setting the maximum output is even lower.

A further point relates to microwave oven operation – which a number of motorcaravanners hope to run from their generator. If you own a microwave rated at 600 watts, this figure relates to the oven's output as opposed to the input it requires. To establish which generators could run an appliance, the advice from specialist suppliers Phoenix Power & Equipment is to double the oven's

quoted wattage and then deduct 10%. Hence a microwave oven rated at 500 watts, would need a generator producing at least 900 watts. Regrettably, this is creeping into the small industrial size units which are considerably noisier and less compact than the 'leisure' models.

That aside, generators have a useful place and on some motorcaravans there's a metal-lined locker for transport – but it's not vented so you cannot operate the machine *in situ*. On larger motorcaravans a special compartment is made to accept permanently mounted machines. Models like the WTA (now being sold within the Electrolux range of products) or the Onan generators are often fitted to large motorhomes and starter controls are sometimes situated inside the vehicle. On an American RV, this kind of provision is commonplace.

Inverters

Another way to gain mains power is to draw current from the low voltage system and to convert it into a 230v supply with an inverter. Models like the Xcell from Driftgate 2000 are well respected;

Concept Range from W4 Accessories features double-pole switching.

The rear moulding on the Concept Range confirms the double-pole switching design.

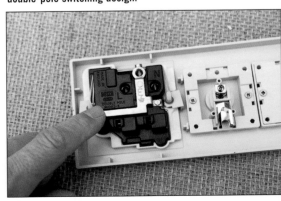

Electrical systems

Some motorcaravans include a lined locker for transporting a portable generator.

The starting and control of permanently installed generators is sometimes controlled by a remote panel.

so too are the 'fit and forget' Power Box products from P.E.L. Fitting a Power Box is illustrated in Chapter Eleven.

Other models like the PROwatt are also popular, and the Statpower inverter is made to connect into a cigarette lighter. No less unusual are miniature inverters made by Classic Leisure Lighting which are so small they can be hidden inside a lamp holder. They allow a lamp fitted with a 230v 10 watt long life 'warm' lamp to draw its power from a 12v source.

Where lighting is concerned, an inverter is excellent, but the supplying battery effectively limits the possibilities. For example, a 250 watt inverter – even if 100% efficient – is going to draw more than 20 amps from a battery when working to its limit. In consequence a 60Ah battery would be completely discharged in less than three hours. In reality, the battery discharge rate is even more rapid because no inverter can be 100% efficient; some power loss is unavoidable.

However, if you want to run a couple of 60 watt bulbs and nothing else, the limitations are less severe, especially if you follow the earlier advice and fit a 90Ah battery. That will produce good lighting for a number of hours.

The inverter-driven lamps from Classic Leisure Lighting draw current from the 12v system.

A miniaturised inverter can be mounted in a lamp holder.

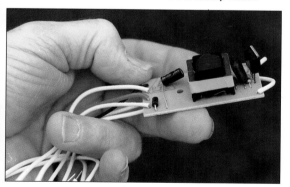

The Power Box inverter is a well-respected 'fit and forget' unit.

Gas supply systems and appliances

The most common fuel for heating and cooking in a motorcaravan is liquefied petroleum gas (LPG). This is produced in two different forms and an understanding of its characteristics, storage and supply ensures that the fuel is used effectively and safely.

Gas is not the only fuel used in a motorcaravan; mains electricity is sometimes used for heating a living area whilst 12v DC electricity usually operates the fan in a blown-air system.

Furthermore a central heating and hot water facility which uses diesel fuel, is discussed in Chapter Ten; but gas is the most common fuel and in this chapter, safety is a crucial consideration and receives constant mention throughout.

Characteristics of gas

The term Liquefied Petroleum Gas (LPG) is given to the fuel used in nearly all motorcaravans. This is usually supplied in steel cylinders, although some motorcaravanners have a bulk tank fitted underneath their vehicle. For owners embarking on long continental trips, a bulk, refillable tank has its merits because there is no standardisation in the types of cylinders sold in different countries.

LPG in its natural state is neither poisonous, nor does it have a smell; so a leak could occur unnoticed. For consumer safety and to ensure that leaks do not go unnoticed, a 'stenching agent' is added to the gas during processing to give it a distinctive odour.

In addition, LPG is heavier than air, so 'drop out' holes (sometimes called gas dispersal holes) are built into a motorcaravan to provide gas escape routes if a leak were to develop. It is for this reason that vents built into the floor and under gas appliances should never be covered up. Anyone buying a second-hand vehicle should carefully check that a previous owner has kept all ventilators unobstructed.

There are two types of LPG: butane and propane. Their characteristics are different, but as long as the correct type of regulator is fitted to the cylinder, motorcaravan appliances in Britain are manufactured to operate from either gas without need for adjustments. Differences between butane and propane are:

Butane:

– has a higher calorific value than propane which means it is a more efficient heat producer. Accordingly butane is the preferred choice when conditions are suitable.

– does not change from its liquefied state to a gas vapour when temperatures are lower than 0°C (32°F) at atmospheric pressure. The liquified gas freezes in the cylinder – so it is not the preferred gas of winter motorcaravanners.

– is heavier than propane, so although the smallest Calor Gas cylinders for the two products are the same size, the propane version holds 3.9kg (8.6lb), and an identical sized cylinder filled with butane holds 4.5kg (10lb) of liquefied gas.

Propane:

– changes from a liquefied state into a gas in temperatures as low as −40°C (−44°F) – so it is ideal as a winter fuel. Regrettably, suppliers on the Continent only seem to sell butane, though some processing companies add a small quantity of propane to butane cylinders in order to give improved cold weather performance.

– in its liquefied state it is lighter than butane. That's why, in two cylinders of identical size, there is less propane by weight than butane;

– has a vapour pressure between three and four times that of butane at 15°C and it's for this reason that different regulators are needed for the two gases; so if you change from one gas to another, you must change the regulator as well. Regulators are discussed later.

54

Before taking to the road, it is important to turn off the gas supply at source. There are isolation valves in modern motorcaravans to cut off the supply to different appliances within the system, but the best precaution is to turn off the supply *at the cylinder*. This should be part of every motorcaravanners' routine, prior to starting the engine.

Supply and storage

Portable LPG cylinders are sold in a number of sizes, some of which are more suited to a motorcaravanner's needs than others. A Calor cylinder is obtained by way of a hire agreement, where a fee is paid when using the products for the first time; therefore ownership of the cylinder remains with Calor Gas Ltd. If you cease being a Calor customer, the hire fee can be reclaimed, provided the original document can be produced. In contrast, the arrangement with Camping Gaz is different – you *do* purchase the first cylinder and merely exchange it when empty for another.

An advantage with Calor Gas is that this normally permits changes of gas type; so an empty 3.9kg propane cylinder can be exchanged for a 4.5kg butane one. Similarly a 4.5kg butane cylinder can usually be changed for a larger 7kg cylinder. Occasionally there are restrictions, depending on shortages.

Calor cylinder sizes

3.9kg (8.6 lb) propane
4.5kg (10 lb) butane
6kg (13.2lb) propane
7kg (15.4 lb) butane
13kg (28.7 lb) propane
15kg (33lb) butane
19kg (41.9lb) propane
Calor Gas butane cylinders are painted blue
Calor Gas propane cylinders are painted red.

Note: *The larger cylinders (13kg propane, 15kg butane and 19kg propane) are often used on permanent pitches but are normally too large for safe transport. Locker compartments are not designed to accommodate cylinders of these sizes.*

Camping Gaz cylinder sizes

0.45kg (1lb) butane
1.81kg (4lb) butane
2.72 kg (6lb) butane
Camping Gaz cylinders are painted blue.

Note: *Only the 2.72kg butane cylinder is a practical proposition for motorcaravanning. The two smaller cylinders might be kept for emergency back-up to operate a cooker burner but they are really intended for use in small tents.*

The design of a motorcaravan gas locker should incorporate an effective means of securing a cylinder and there are distinct disadvantages if there isn't room to accommodate a back-up supply cylinder. Some motorcaravans only have single cylinder lockers which is most unsatisfactory.

Various methods are used to anchor a gas cylinder; a collar and webbing straps are provided in this Swift motorcaravan.

Gas availability

Calor Gas is widely available in Britain, and is sold in several different sized cylinders. Both butane *and* propane are sold by Calor Gas but the company doesn't operate abroad.

Camping Gaz is another product available in Britain, but the largest cylinder (the 907) is only a modest size 2.72kg (6lb). Moreover, propane is not available in Camping Gaz cylinders.

Camping Gaz is available in over one hundred countries although prices vary. It is notably inexpensive in Spain because butane cylinders are used in many less affluent homes, so it receives a heavy subsidy from the Spanish Government; with regard to propane in Spain, this is normally only supplied for commercial vehicles. Camping Gaz is not available in Finland or Sweden and is seldom stocked in Norway.

Other products are available abroad and in Germany there are several examples, such as SKG 5kg propane cylinders. However, higher operating pressures are employed in Germany, so before using this product a different regulator is needed, together with an adaptor to suit a Calor propane regulator coupling.

A substantial 'drop-out' ventilator is essential at the lowest point of a gas locker.

The internal gas locker in a van conversion must be effectively sealed from the living quarters.

It is essential that the locker incorporates a substantial drop-out ventilator at the lowest point of the enclosure. Remarkably, some motorcaravans produced by notable manufacturers, have had drop-out ventilators which are higher than the floor of the enclosure. Since the gas is heavier than air, an escape would lead to dangerous gas accumulation below the level of the vents.

On a coachbuilt motorcaravan, it is relatively straightforward to manufacture a purpose-built storage locker with external access. In a van conversion the task is less easy and some manufacturers construct an internal locker, albeit with thorough sealing of the access door. This ensures cylinder storage is isolated entirely from the living quarters.

It is also important that a gas locker is not used to accommodate any electrical appliances – particularly a leisure battery. Leakage *can* occur at a cylinder valve and if a spark is generated when coupling to the terminals of a battery, an explosion could easily occur.

On returning home, many owners remove gas cylinders from the vehicle as a precautionary measure. This is fine, but storage of the cylinders at home presents new problems. Under no circumstances should cylinders be left in a cellar, for example, since leaking gas would have no means of escaping. *Gas Safety Regulations (Installation & Use)* state clearly that propane cylinders must not be stored inside any dwellings; nor should they be stored anywhere that lacks low level ventilation outlets. A shed or outhouse might prove suitable; but it is safer to adopt the practice of the suppliers whose cylinders are kept in a roofed storage cage situated well away from any source of flame.

Pressure regulation and supply control

A key component in a motorcaravan gas supply system is a regulator. This fulfils two functions:

1. It ensures the delivery of gas from a cylinder is at a stable and constant pressure in accordance with the needs of the appliances. It thus smooths out the tendency for a full cylinder to deliver gas at a higher rate than one which is nearing exhaustion.
2. It incorporates a union so that the flexible feed pipe to the supply system can be coupled up safely to the cylinder without fear of leakage.
One of the annoying features of LPG systems is the absence of a universal coupling. To connect to a propane cylinder the regulator is manufactured with a carefully machined and threaded insert (male) which creates a close register when

Gas engineering qualifications

For some time it has been stated that work on gas connections, flues and supply systems should only be undertaken by a competent gas engineer. More recently, however, this prescription has been deemed too vague and some advisers insist that only a CORGI registered engineer tackles this kind of work. Others assert that the requirement is even more stringent and state that a CORGI qualified person must have successfully completed a course which embraces training in LPG installations in leisure vehicles. This caveat is added because some CORGI registered engineers are only trained to deal with domestic household installations.
NOTE: *CORGI stands for Council for Registered Gas Installers. Registration is a requirement for those who install and maintain LPG installations as laid down in the Gas Safety (Installation & Use) Regulations 1994.*

Always transport a cylinder in its *upright* position. If a cylinder is laid on its side, the liquefied gas *might* prevent the pressure relief safety valve from functioning correctly. Gas can also escape from a faulty valve and when it's acknowledged that in the transfer from liquid to vapour there's approximately a *two hundred times increase in volume*, the potential hazard is clearly apparent.

A regulator is a key component in a motorcaravan's gas supply system.

To achieve leak-free coupling to a Calor 4.5kg butane cylinder, there's a flexible washer; this must be changed at frequent intervals.

tightened up within the receiving socket (female) of the cylinder. No washer is involved – merely a close metal-to-metal location. The coupling method is the same on all Calor Gas propane cylinders and you'll need to keep a spanner handy.

Regrettably butane couplings are less straightforward because there are several different types. For instance, on a 4.5kg Calor cylinder, there's a threaded female nut; this has to be positioned over the threaded male outlet and

tightened anti-clockwise. The reverse thread often surprises newcomers to motorcaravanning and a spanner is needed to form a tight joint. There is also a small washer held within the regulator coupling nut which must be changed periodically. Spares are available for a modest sum from any Calor specialist.

On both the Calor propane cylinders and the Calor 4.5kg butane cylinders, a robust turn wheel on the top opens or closes the gas supply valve.

Disconnecting a 541 regulator from a 7kg Calor Gas butane cylinder

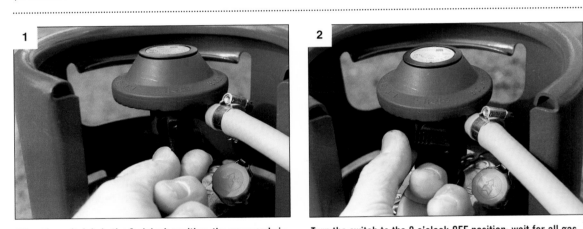

1

When the switch is in the 6 o'clock position, the gas supply is ON.

2

Turn the switch to the 9 o'clock OFF position; wait for all gas flames to go out.

3

With the switch in the OFF position, the disconnecting lever can be lifted and the regulator removed.

4

The orange safety cap must be replaced on the cylinder – even if it's empty.

Sealing washers and pressure regulation

• Remember to buy a supply of sealing washers if you use a Calor screw-on butane regulator. The washer in the black screw-on blanking cap that you get with a new cylinder must not be transferred for use in a regulator as it is not made of the correct composition.
• For the technically minded, a butane regulator is rated at 28m bar (11.2 inch water gauge); a propane regulator is rated at 37m bar (14.8 inch water gauge). So if a service engineer connects a glass 'U' tube holding water to a butane supply, the pressure is sufficient to force the water 11.2 inches up the tube; propane would force the water 14.8 inches up the tube. Nowadays most gas engineers measure this with a gauge.
• The practice adopted abroad often differs. In Germany, for example, current installations now operate at 30m bar; previously, older installations operated at a higher pressure of 50m bar. This has implications for anyone purchasing a second-hand motorcaravan abroad.
• A regulator is set at the time of manufacture and must *not* be dismantled. A diaphragm inside moves up or down to adjust the flow of gas and a lever mechanism monitors and regulates operation. There is *nothing* to service and the units are sealed at the time of manufacture; a regulator should be renewed periodically and certainly at three year intervals.
• A regulator has a tiny hole in the casing. If this becomes blocked, the diaphragm is unable to move inside. A problem sometimes occurs when a motorcaravanner stays on a site for a prolonged period during the winter and places the cylinder alongside the vehicle. If moisture gets into the 'breather hole' and freezes, the diaphragm can get stuck in the fully open position. Should you find that the flame on a cooker becomes far higher than normal, this 'over-gassing' situation is nearly always the result of regulator malfunction.

When motorcaravanners find it necessary to use Camping Gaz, it is normal to purchase an adaptor that screws into the top of the butane cylinder. This also incorporates a control wheel and enables the type of Calor butane regulator already described to be coupled into a Camping Gaz supply.

The larger butane cylinders from Calor Gas adopt a different coupling method. As the sequence photographs demonstrate, the regulator has to have a special clip-on coupling. The gas cock now forms part of the regulator itself whereas on the smaller 4.5kg product the turn wheel is part of the cylinder.

To summarise, if using different types of cylinder, three different regulators are needed – plus an adaptor if you want to connect up to a Camping Gaz cylinder: These are:

• A Calor screw-on propane regulator – with open-ended spanner.
• A Calor screw-on butane regulator to suit 4.5kg cylinders – with open-ended spanner.
• A Calor clip-on butane regulator to suit 7kg cylinders.
• Either an adaptor to enable a Camping Gaz 2.72kg cylinder to be coupled up with a Calor screw-on butane regulator, or a Camping Gaz regulator with on-off control.

Cylinder state

Assessing the amount of gas remaining in a cylinder can be difficult. There are several devices intended to give a clear indication of the fill, including weighing accessories.

If using Calor cylinders, one procedure is to establish their weight when empty by referring to the information on the aluminium collar below the valve. This is expressed in lbs/ozs – if you prefer to work in kilograms, pounds have to be divided by 2.2046. Then the cylinder should be weighed on bathroom scales to establish by how much its weight exceeds the stated empty weight.

Alternatively the cylinder pressure can be monitored using one of the gauges from Gaslow; these are available individually or incorporated in a Gaslow regulator. They also serve a further role as leak detectors, which is explained later.

To assess the condition of a cylinder using a Gaslow gauge, the system must be in operation with at least one appliance in use. Taking into account the load imposed by the appliance(s) a Gaslow gauge then indicates if the supply is in a good state, a mediocre condition, or approaching exhaustion. Earlier gauges used a needle which

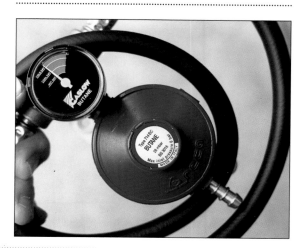

A Gaslow gauge can be used to assess the amount of gas in a cylinder and it also indicates if there is a leak in the system.

A competent and practically-experienced owner should find no difficulty in replacing the flexible hose on a gas supply system. However, fit *new* clips every time you replace the hose. As regards the rest of the supply system, this should always be entrusted to a gas engineer who has been trained in the installation of LPG systems.

The Truma Duomatic L kit automatically changes the supply from an empty gas cylinder to a full one.

A control panel with the Truma Duomatic L is mounted inside the motorcaravan to indicate the state of the gas cylinders.

pointed to 'traffic light' segments in the dial; the red section warned of a nearly empty cylinder whereas the green segment indicated that all was well. On the latest gauges it is the segment that moves, and to achieve even greater accuracy there are separate read-outs for use on 'cold days', 'cool days' and 'hot days'. This is a good system, but it only gives an indication of cylinder condition when appliances *are being used*.

Changeover systems

Running out of gas is always inconvenient. Even if there's a back-up cylinder, the business of disconnecting the regulator and coupling up to a new one is a nuisance, especially if it's raining. It is even more annoying if it happens when a meal is being cooked or in the middle of a cold night when the heating system is crucial for comfort. This is why a changeover system is so useful – especially one which is completely automatic.

The simplest and least expensive types, like the Gaslow manual changeover, merely involve turning off the failed cylinder and opening the valve on its replacement. Since both connections are permanently in place, the task takes seconds to complete.

Automatic types are even more convenient – though progress should be monitored periodically so that steps can be taken to remove and replace an emptied cylinder. In many systems the exhausted cylinder can be disconnected and taken to a dealers for exchange without upsetting the one that's operating; there's no risk of gas leaking when one cylinder is uncoupled.

As regards the Truma Duomatic L automatic changeover, there's a control panel for mounting in the living quarters which bears red and green LED indicators. This enables you to keep a close watch on the cylinders without having to go outside. There is also a defroster to ensure the Duomatic L doesn't freeze.

Pipework and installation

After the cylinder and regulator, the supply route starts with a length of flexible hose. The following points should be noted:

• The flexible hose is neither a plastic nor natural rubber; it is made from a special composition to comply with British Standard 3212.
• There should only be one flexible hose in the entire system – to couple up with the gas cylinder. Elsewhere, metal pipes must be used, copper being the most common material.
• Where the hose is pushed on to ribbed unions, it is important that hose clips are used.
• Flexible hose deteriorates very little when kept in stock at a suppliers. In use, however, it is affected by sunlight and atmospheric conditions. It must be inspected annually and replaced if there are any signs of cracking or general deterioration.
• The hose bears a date on the side to indicate when it left the factory; this may be a year or so *before* purchase, depending on stock turnover.
• It is important to note the *precise* date when new hose is installed since it should be changed

Flexible gas hose bears a date on the side to indicate when it was manufactured.

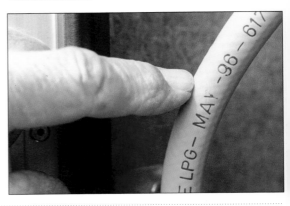

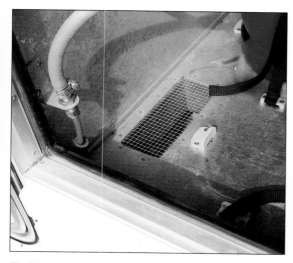

Flexible gas hose is connected to the rigid supply pipe in the gas locker.

Compression fittings feature three items – a cap nut, an olive and the component itself.

periodically. The *Calor Gas Dealer Directory (1995)* recommends this is done at five-year intervals or more frequently if there is evidence of deterioration; for instance, hose sometimes loses resilience and stretches at ribbed unions.

The inboard end of the flexible supply hose terminates with a bulkhead connector, after which the supply pipe is rigid.

On account of the risk of a serious accident, neither the rigid gas supply system nor the connections to gas appliances should be modified, repaired or coupled up by non-qualified DIY enthusiasts. In the *Calor Caravan Check Scheme* booklet (May 1995 Edition) it states, *'Gas installation is an expert's job and by law must only be undertaken by an experienced gas fitter.'* A CORGI registered engineer fulfils this requirement.

This view is firmly adopted here and technical descriptions about the supply system are provided for information only. Arguably the task of connecting up copper gas pipe using a proprietary pressure fitting is not difficult – particularly for anyone familiar with the similar pressure fittings used in

domestic plumbing; but the inexperienced person will not know how much to tighten a coupling to achieve a joint of leak-proof integrity. Over-tightening can deform the pipe and a leak is inevitable – as it is if the coupling is under-tightened; so the instruction is clear: leave this to a qualified LPG engineer.

Copper pipe for gas systems is made in the following sizes:

5mm (³⁄₁₆in) outside diameter (OD) = feed to a gas lamp; seldom seen today.
6mm (¼in) OD = feed to many types of appliance e.g. the fridge.
8mm/10mm (⅝in) OD = main trunk feed in a motor caravan; feed for space heating appliances.
NOTE: *Some fittings designed for metric pipe will not fit imperial pipes.*

Pressure couplings are made to suit the pipe diameters, with reducers permitting branches to adopt different sized pipes from the main trunkway. The accompanying diagram shows the key components such as the 'olive' and the 'cap nut'.

When connections are formed, the cap nut is fitted on the supply pipe first, followed by the olive. The pipe is then inserted into the coupling as far as the stop point and the cap nut tightened.

As a cap nut is tightened, the olive bears harder against the shoulder of the fitting and is squeezed inwards, gripping the gas pipe tightly.

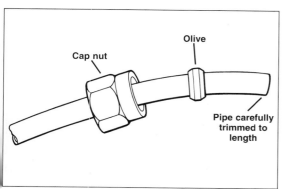

Cap nut
Olive
Pipe carefully trimmed to length

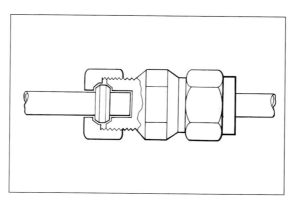

Bending copper gas pipe can be done by hand; but a pipe-bending tool is used for more precise work, especially when forming acute angles.

In a gas supply system, isolation valves are fitted so that individual appliances can be controlled separately.

When a compression coupling is formed, it is pointed out in *The Dealer Information Booklet*, published by Calor Gas, that jointing compounds should not be used. A jointing compound is to seal 'thread to thread' couplings.

Bending copper gas pipe is often done by hand; but for more precise work, especially when forming a tight bend, a pipe bending tool is used. This supports the walls of the pipe and prevents kinking. It follows the same principle of operation as a pipe bender used for domestic copper water pipes.

As regards the final coupling to appliances, this often employs a thread-to-thread union rather than a compression fitting. In this instance, a special LPG jointing paste is required to seal the threads and Calortite is the recommended choice.

In modern installations, it is also necessary for individual appliances to be controlled by a separate isolation valve. If an oven were to develop a fault on holiday, for example, the supply to this appliance could be completely shut down whilst leaving other appliances still useable.

Leak Detection

Whereas work on a gas supply system should not be undertaken by a DIY owner, exercising vigilance over the integrity of the system is different. A wise owner, for example, might want a leak detection device fitted and some types are available that you could fit yourself. In addition, if you want reassurance that couplings are sound, there is no reason why you shouldn't check them using a leak detection liquid.

The procedure is to have the system switched on at the cylinder and to keep all appliances off. Cigarettes and naked flames should be extinguished. Couplings are then smeared with either a proprietary product or a solution made

of diluted washing-up fluid. Once applied, check for bubbles – which indicates a leak. It is usual to apply the mixture with a small brush and to hold your fingers around the joint to prevent the fluid running away. If you find a leak, switch the system off at once and get the coupling tightened or replaced by a gas engineer.

A more convenient way to monitor a system is to fit a Gaslow gauge at the gas supply cylinder. These products were mentioned earlier because they have an additional function of indicating the pressure in a cylinder. The test procedure is as follows:
• Turn off *all* gas appliances.
• Turn *on* the gas supply cylinder; the gauge should show a green segment.
• Turn *off* the gas supply at the cylinder.
• Provided there is no leak, gas will be held in the supply pipes and the gauge will remain green for a prolonged period.
• Using a standard Gaslow product, if the gauge remains green for at least a minute, the system is sound.
• Note that over a longer period, the gauge will eventually return to the red sector.

An Alde leak detector can be installed in the supply line – bubbles in the sighting glass indicate the passage of gas.

Gas supply systems and appliances

The First Alert Gas Alarm emits a loud sound when the smell of gas is detected – it is an easy product to fit.

Another way to keep a long-term check is to have an Alde leak detector fitted into the supply line by a gas engineer. This incorporates a small glass sighting chamber filled with a glycol liquid. To conduct the test, switch the gas supply on and turn all appliances off. When a red test button on the top of the detector is depressed, a regular flow of bubbles in the sighting chamber gives away the fact that gas is escaping somewhere in the system.

Different again are leak detectors that give an audible warning when a sensor detects gas. This type of device *could* be fitted by a careful DIY owner. For instance, the First Alert electronic alarm warns the occupants of a leak, using a piercing 85dB siren. The unit has to be connected to a 12v DC supply and should be fixed to a secure base in an appropriate location. Recognising that LPG is *heavier* than air it needs fitting low down.

Cooking appliances

Cooking facilities in a motorcaravan comprise a hob as a standard item; larger vehicles often include an oven, too. A grill is normally included in British models as part of the hob design. In total the kitchen usually forms a prominent part of the living space, with accompanying work tops, sink, drainer and so on. It is only in respect of rubbish disposal that British manufacturers are poor in providing a facility for accepting kitchen waste.

Motorcaravans built abroad are often very different in design. Even luxury vehicles like the German Hymer coachbuilts have a diminutive kitchen area. It appears their users resort to cooking less frequently and prefer to 'eat out'. Very few models imported from the Continent feature a grill since toast is seldom on the menu. Importers of foreign products often have to fit

In this DIY project, units were fitted to a plastic laminated board first and installed later as a module inside the new kitchen.

Since 1994, gas appliance manufacturers fit a flame failure device on each hob burner.

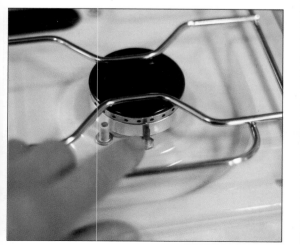

Manufacturers like SMEV often integrate a hob into a complete sink and drainer unit.

different appliances in order to make the kitchen more acceptable to the British public.

As regards appliance design, technical innovation has been much in evidence. For example, many cooker hobs fitted in the early 1990s were equipped with an electronic igniter on each burner, a facility many regard as essential. The procedure is to hold down the igniter button whereupon a succession of sparks is generated. The gas control is then depressed to deliver gas to the burner and ignition is instantaneous.

Since 1994, it has also been mandatory to have a flame failure device (sometimes called a 'flame supervision device') fitted to all gas burners. If the gas on a burner blows out, the device immediately cuts off its supply. You will see the small probe that projects into the flame of the burner; when this is hot, an electric current is generated. The current then flows to an electro-magnetic gas valve that stays open all the time the probe is hot. However, as soon as the flame is extinguished, current is no longer produced; the electro magnet in the gas valve fails and a small spring closes off the supply. The only point to note with this system is that the gas valve should be over-ridden when lighting the burner, in order to give the probe time to get hot. That's why a gas tap has to be held down for a few seconds when igniting a burner.

All modern appliances now have to bear the CE approval mark and this is an assurance that the product has passed requisite safety testing procedures. It is important to ensure that the appliance is suitable for the type of fuel, i.e. butane, propane or both, and for the supply pressure developed by the regulator. Appliances are CE marked for different countries of destination and those used in the UK will be marked clearly on the appliance label badge and on the packaging. Not unusually, items like a hob are integrated into a complete kitchen system incorporating a sink and drainer as well.

Owner improvement work

Constructing a kitchen or improving an existing layout is a task that many DIY owners tackle successfully. Appliances are supplied with clear installation instructions and safety elements are emphasised.

Anyone who is competent in carpentry can undoubtedly prepare the aperture to install an oven or hob unit, making certain that the structure is sufficient to bear the weight of the units and the buffeting that occurs when driving along bumpy roads.

Clearances are crucial elements, too, and an appliance's installation manual will draw attention to the spacing needed between adjacent combustible surfaces. The construction of shielding may also be necessary, though it is disturbing to note that even in professionally constructed motorcaravans, curtains are sometimes perilously close to a cooker. In some interior layouts, a cooker is situated immediately behind a cab seat, which also has implications when dealing with a spitting frying pan. Misgivings are also voiced about climbing out of an over-cab bed when there's a cooker directly below; so the

This mock-up of a Truma room-sealed space heater shows how the combustion air intake and exhaust flue are taken to the outside.

The heat exchanger in a room-sealed appliance usually has fins moulded on its casing to release heat efficiently.

The Carver Fanmaster can be fitted to the rear of many recent Carver heaters and DIY owners often carry this out themselves.

Once fitted to the rear of a Carver space heater, ducting is coupled up to the Fanmaster to distribute heat around the motorcaravan.

Carver's ducted air kits are available for owners who want to improve the distribution of warm air around the living area.

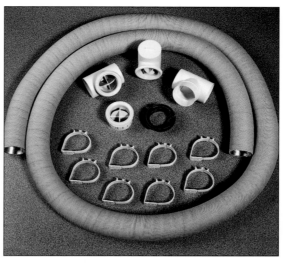

Carbon monoxide detectors

Devices that warn owners when carbon monoxide is present are now available for motorcaravans. For instance the SF330 carbon monoxide detector is a CE approved device measuring 120 x 82 x 37mm and weighing 200 grams. It's easy to wall-mount the product. Installation doesn't eliminate the need to have gas appliances checked regularly, but it gives an added element of safety. This product is available from DIY superstores.

location of kitchen units needs particular consideration if you are engaged in a DIY conversion.

With these cautionary notes, the final one concerns the provision of gas to the appliance. Whilst carpentry work is something that a competent owner/builder might tackle themselves, it is important to reaffirm the point made throughout this chapter about creating a gas supply and coupling up to appliances. *This part of the installation should be entrusted to a CORGI registered gas engineer qualified in LPG work in respect of motorcaravan systems.*

Space heating appliances

The open burner 'gas fire' is no longer used in motorcaravans for safety reasons. Apart from the risk of something falling on to the exposed flames, the system takes oxygen from the living space and waste is discharged into the living area as well. In extreme cases there might be a risk of carbon monoxide poisoning.

The appliances are now called 'space heaters' and these have to be 'room sealed'. This means the burners are housed in a compartment that is sealed from the living area. Combustion air is drawn directly into this sealed section from the outside and in a similar way, exhaust gases are returned back outside via a flue.

Heat generated in this combustion chamber then has to be directed into the living area. This is achieved by directing the hot air through a 'heat exchanger' which is purposely designed to

With all working parts enclosed, the Truma E2400 draws air from the living space, heats it, and redistributes it via a network of ducting.

Popular for many years, the Truma E series blown air heaters incorporate a balanced flue/air intake and can be fitted into very small spaces.

Propex heaters can be installed in small spaces although the gas cylinder location shown here seems most unsatisfactory. A cylinder should be housed in a locker sealed from the living quarters and with a drop-out ventilator.

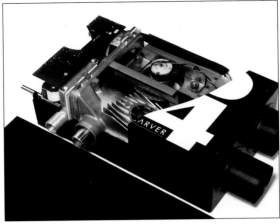

The Carver P4 Compact blown air heater is an efficient unit that is standard in many of the smaller post 1997 motorcaravans.

Roof-mounted flues must be kept clear of debris; even spiders' webs can upset the delicate balance of a space heater's operation.

release heat efficiently. Many heat exchangers are thus manufactured with moulded fins – rather like the fins on an air-cooled motorcycle engine.

In consequence it is the heat exchanger that warms the interior rather than the gas flames themselves. To assist in the distribution of heat, many appliances also have a fan, which directs warmed air along a network of ducts. Outlets in the system then ensure that heat is distributed throughout the interior. Closed rooms like a shower cubicle can then receive warm air which is piped from the space heater.

If you don't have a ducted warm air facility, a fan-driven distribution system can often be added at a later date. For instance the Carver Fanmaster can be installed on many of their heaters and

there's a pre-formed mounting point on the rear of the casing. Attaching the unit is straightforward although it needs a 12v DC supply from the low voltage system to operate the fan. The Fanmaster has a 1.5 amp 18 watt motor that should be fused at 5 amps.

In addition, the Fanmaster also incorporates a mains-operated electrical element that draws 8 amps at 2kW; so whilst its function is to distribute warmth from the space heater, it can also warm the air using independent integral electric elements. This can produce heat at manually switchable output levels from 0.1 to 2kW. Temperature is regulated using a wall-mounted controller. Note that gas and electrical heating are not operated at the same time.

The Truma Ultraheat adopts similar principles although with this appliance it is possible for both gas and 230v systems to be operating simultaneously. A further distinction is that the 230v element is bolted directly to the heat exchanger instead of being an integral part of the fan on the rear of the casing. As regards output this is:

1. 1kW from the electric element,
2. 2kW from the electric element,
3. 3.4kW from the gas burner,

For quick warm-up both gas and electric systems can be used; when the heater reaches 2kW the electric heating element is switched off automatically. This is a safety feature of the Ultraheat system.

Many practically skilled owners add a ducting system to their motorcaravans and, using proprietary components from specialists such as Carver and Truma, the task can be fairly straightforward. Hiding the ducting discreetly is the main challenge, although it is possible to obtain

Heating appliances

- There are no servicing tasks on gas heating appliances that an owner can carry out.
- Space and water heating appliances must be checked by a qualified gas engineer in accordance with manufacturer's instructions – an element that should come within the annual habitation service check.
- In addition to checking the appliance, the flue will also be given a safety and efficiency check.
- Ensure that you are given a written account of the servicing work that has been completed.
- The Carver Fanmaster incorporates a number of safety devices including a cut-out button that comes into operation in the case of overheating. This can occur, for example, if all the outlet ducts are closed off or obstructed. Owners can re-set this device themselves taking into account the following procedure: wait until the appliance has cooled down, open all the outlets, and disconnect the mains supply at your consumer unit. Now re-set the trip button which is situated on the side of the fan casing, remembering that in some motorcaravans, access to the trip button isn't easy.
- Many space heaters feature a piezo ignition system where you have to depress a button several times to create a spark at the burner. More recently, however, electronic ignition systems have gained in popularity. They're a standard fitting on compact units like the Carver P4 and the Truma E Range. In some instances it's possible to convert an older Piezo system to electronic ignition. A dealer can advise what upgrade kits are available.

specially reinforced sections to take routeways beneath the floor without too much loss of heat.

Large motorcaravans sometimes have 'wet systems' in which radiators are used. The 3000 Compact central heating system from Alde, for example, is installed in the latest motorcaravan from Buccaneer. This motorcaravan also incorporates the Alde 2968 engine heat exchanger which operates in conjunction with a Fiat engine's heating system.

In small motorcaravans, compact heaters are more suitable. These are completely enclosed (apart from the air intake, air distribution outlet and flue). An integral fan distributes the warm air and a great benefit of these products is that they can be mounted in discreet locations within lockers, small wardrobes and so on.

The examples from Truma are well-established products that operate with remarkable efficiency. Ignition is electronic and in spite of its compact size, the heat output from the Trumatic E2400 model is a noteworthy 2.4kW. Heat from the unit is transmitted through ducting and like all room-sealed heaters, it can be left operating all night. Output is thermostatically controlled to ensure that the level of warmth remains at a consistent level.

A similar product is the Propex unit, a British product taken over by Carver in 1994. This has now been re-designed completely and re-launched as the Carver P4 compact blown air unit. The P4 is a self-contained unit featuring a low profile side wall flue. With 1.2kW or 2.2kW output settings, the specification includes automatic ignition, thermostatic control, and operation on either butane or propane. It is fitted in post 1997 models but is also easy to fit to older motorcaravans.

Owner improvement work

A competent DIY owner could undoubtedly install many of the space heating appliances available as far as the carpentry work is concerned. Installation instructions are very detailed and some manufacturers include paper templates that are useful when apertures have to be formed.

The final gas connection work and testing needs to be done by a CORGI registered gas engineer. Similarly, on appliances in which a mains electricity supply is needed, this too should be entrusted to a qualified electrician.

Lastly, the connection of a flue is a critical safety matter that should also be carried out by a gas engineer. A small leak might lead to an escape of carbon monoxide and fatalities in motorcaravans are well-documented.

Servicing and safety check

Like cooking appliances, space heaters also need an annual safety check and service. This is not something the owner can tackle.

Several tasks will be carried out and one is to check the shape of the gas flames. A problem in motorcaravans is that there are periods when gas appliances might not be used for an extended spell. This is when dust and cobwebs can accumulate. It often comes as a surprise to learn that the humble spider often upsets gas appliances; filaments of a spider's web across a pilot light can distort the shape of the flame and prevent the main burner from igniting.

It's the same with the flue. Even a spider's web spun across a flue at the roof outlet can upset the exhaust efficiency enough to prevent a space heater switching from pilot to main burner. So general cleaning is one of the elements of servicing and the labour charge for this is modest.

Water heating appliances

Availability of hot water is a great asset and few motorcaravans are built without the inclusion of a water heater. There are three main types:

1. Storage water heaters (Carver Cascade, Rapide GE, Belling Malaga, Truma Storage).
2. Water heaters integrated with a space heater (Trumatic C range, Atwood Confort 3, Alde 3000 Compact).
3. Instantaneous water heaters (Morco, Rinnai).

Note: *The American manufacturer Atwood ceased marketing products in Europe in 1997. Spares, however, continue to be available in the UK.*

Storage heaters have the advantage of being inconspicuous, can easily be mounted in a bed box and operation uses a remote controlled panel. Their balanced flue is discreet, too, and more recent versions incorporate a mains heating element as a secondary heat source to the gas burner; this can be operated at the same time as the gas burner to speed up heating time. Notwithstanding the twin source of heat, the storage vessel still takes time to heat up from scratch and the quantity of available hot water is limited too. There's also the matter of weight. Few

The controls in this Swift Royale provide convenient remote operation of its Carver water heater.

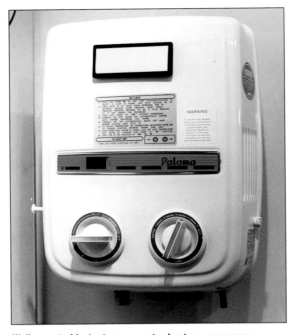

Wall-mounted instantaneous water heaters, once very popoular, distribute an excellent flow of hot water.

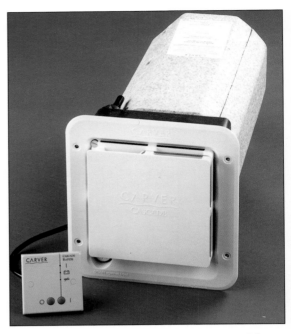

The Carver Rapide series of water heaters features a 9 litre (2 gallon) storage tank.

people drain down the water before taking to the road and water is significantly heavy. A Carver Cascade, for example, holds 9 litres (2 gallons) thereby taking up 9kg (20lb) of payload capacity.

Instantaneous water heaters don't have this weight disadvantage but have recently lost their popularity, on account of the fact that the gas burner is exposed. A constructed flue above the unit is now a requirement, and the appliance takes up valuable wall space. On the other hand

instantaneous appliances can produce hot water without any delay and continue to produce it all the time there's a cold water supply and gas to heat it. However, see *Safety* box.

There are also combined heaters. These are extremely efficient but are bulky units which tend to be used in larger vehicles. For instance the Alde 300 with its radiator system is fitted into Buccaneer's 1998 models. The Atwood Confort C was fitted to the Murvi Morello in 1996 and 1997 models. Currently the Trumatic C Combi heater is being fitted to Swift Kon-Tiki 1998/1999 models and

The Trumatic C Combi is a highly sophisticated unit whose operating functions are controlled electronically.

One alternative to a winter drain-down is to fill the water system with a potable anti-freeze.

all the operating functions of this sophisticated appliance are monitored electronically. The combined space and water heater is also fitted with a release valve which empties the water heater reservoir automatically when air temperature drops to 2°C. Provided the manual over-ride hasn't been selected, when winter frosts arrive unexpectedly early, this is a most useful feature for an owner who has overlooked the all-important system drain down.

Owner installation and upgrades

Instantaneous heaters and storage units like the Carver Cascade are often fitted by experienced DIY owners. The installation instructions are usually clear and Carver includes paper templates to indicate the cut-out needed in the side of the vehicle.

Nevertheless, this is an ambitious undertaking and the point about leaving the gas connection work to a qualified gas engineer is re-stated.

Upgrade kits are also available to improve earlier Carver Cascade models. For instance the Cascade 2 can be upgraded to achieve the faster drain-down of the Cascade 2 Plus.

In addition, the Cascade 2 Plus GE includes a 660 watt mains heating element. However, the latest Cascade Rapide now has an 830 watt heating element and if you buy a tank repair kit, this includes a replacement 830 watt element on the package.

Upgrades like this can be carried out by your dealer, although competent owners have also installed the components successfully.

Owner care

It is important that a water heater is included in annual inspection and service work at an approved dealership. As with other gas-operated appliances, servicing and repair work fall outside the scope of DIY endeavour. Draining-down work, however, is an exception.

Frost can seriously damage a water heater. For instance in the Carver Cascade units, the water storage casing can be forced away from the heating section when freezing water expands in the chamber. Inside an instantaneous water heater, extreme damage can be sustained within the labyrinth of narrow bore water pipes.

There are two ways to ensure this doesn't happen. One is to drain down the unit entirely and to leave it empty over the winter months. The other is to fill the entire system with potable anti-freeze, although Carver does not recommend this for their water heaters.

The latter strategy is favoured in the United States and a potable anti-freeze is now available in the UK under the Camco accessory range. This is imported by Alde UK. All you have to do is to pump the recommended quantity of this specially formulated product into the system and to leave it there until the weather improves.

The other option to drain down the system is

Early Carver water heaters took a long time to drain down completely; this model was still discharging small amounts of water after 25 minutes.

A recent innovation from Carver is a blocking device for sealing off an emptied water heater while the rest of the water system remains in use.

described in the manufacturers' literature. With a Carver Cascade unit the instructions are:

1. Open all taps over sinks and basins;
2. Remove the drain plug on the appliance;
3. Leave the water to drain out completely – this may take an hour or more;
4. Replace drain plug to keep out spiders and insects.

Early Carver heaters take an age to drain and it is wise to leave one of these units discharging water for a couple of hours if possible. More recent models release all the water at a much quicker rate.

Instantaneous water heaters can also take time to drain down, and although there is a release point on a Rinnai heater which merely needs loosening, it should ideally be removed completely. A receptacle left underneath will catch water over a prolonged period, so the drain plug won't need replacing for several days.

As a final update, Carver has recently introduced a closure device that isolates the water heater in winter but allows the rest of the water system to continue running; so if you've drained the heater but subsequently need the motorcaravan for a short trip, you can run the water system to make water available for brewing tea or heating a kettle without the water heater cylinder filling up automatically as it usually does. The insert necessary to achieve this has been available through dealers since early 1998.

Water supply and waste systems

The water system in smaller motorcaravans is usually quite different from the provision made in large models. In some small campervans, fresh water is drawn from a portable container, whereas in coachbuilts, water is stored in a large on-board tank.

Water systems in motorcaravans vary in a number of ways. The type of pump, the taps, the refilling arrangement, the filter system and the waste water facility, all differ from model to model.

The supply system

Small campervans are seldom built with on-board water tanks because they take up a significant amount of space. This is particularly true in respect of small van conversions and adapted multi-purpose vehicles. Instead, portable water containers are used – one for fresh water and one for waste.

Portable containers

Many owners of motorcaravans fitted with on-board tanks still find it necessary to pack a portable water container as well. This is because a number of sites are not equipped with a motorcaravan service point where a fresh water tank can be re-filled and a waste tank emptied. It comes as a surprise, for example, to find that a number of top quality holiday sites in France are not thus equipped. With this feature missing, the motorcaravanner often has to fetch water in a portable container just like the owners of smaller vehicles.

As a rule, motorcaravanners prefer plastic jerrican water containers, because their angular shape allows them to be readily stowed in a locker.

In a few motorcaravans, there is a purpose-built internal locker in the kitchen for accommodating a small capacity portable water container. This is the case with some Reimo conversions, but again, valuable space is then lost so the alternative is to position the water container on the ground outside the motorcaravan on arrival at the site. Needless to say, this means that an external water inlet coupling has to be fitted to the vehicle following the practice adopted by trailer caravanners.

Small campervans similarly need a portable container for waste water. Several types are available and most receptacles feature a side input point which is brought into use when the container is laid flat, thereby achieving clearance beneath the waste outlet. These waste containers have a normal emptying point on the top and both are equipped with screw caps.

On-board water tanks

Whilst a system involving portable containers has its merits, most motorcaravans are built with on-board tanks – one for fresh water, and the other for waste. Incidentally the word 'waste' in this context refers to water discharged from a sink or wash basin. Only the large American motorhomes have a special holding tank for sewage as well.

As regards tank location, there are two options: to either mount the tanks below the floor, or store them within an internal bed box. Some manufacturers, e.g. Auto-Sleepers, prefer the first option because this means that internal locker space isn't wasted by housing these large receptacles within the living area; but there is a disadvantage with this arrangement. In winter, the water in any pipes and tanks situated under the floor soon freezes and this has severe implications if you want to tour in cold conditions.

It is for this reason that many motorcaravans have the fresh water tanks mounted internally. This is certainly a better solution for the all-year-round owner.

However, all is not lost if your motorcaravan has an under-floor tank system. Special kits, manufactured by Carver, permit an alternative winter arrangement. This allows fresh water to be fed into the system from a portable water container that is temporarily connected up indoors. Typically this is positioned in a shower tray and a water

Portable water containers are used if there is insufficient space to mount an on-board tank.

On many larger motorcaravans, the freshwater tank is mounted in a bed box.

Water containers

• If using an external fresh water container, fit a bung or inlet cover so that insects, vermin and slugs don't make an unwanted entry. The Whale Watermaster submersible pump incorporates a plastic cap to achieve protection.
• When a bung is fitted, make sure it has a small breather hole. If this is missing and the pump is efficient, the container will collapse when water is removed.
• When stowing water containers, accessory specialists like Gardner of Wakefield manufacture purpose-made nylon carrying bags which are ideal for this purpose. They offer protection if you hastily leave a site in rain and have to stow the muddy container alongside other items in a locker.

coupling has to be built into a side wall of the cubicle. Obviously the adaptation involves some alterations being made to the pipe runs, but many DIY owners carry this out successfully.

Another way to overcome freezing water in an underfloor tank is to fit an immersion heater. These are supplied by Caravan Accessories Kenilworth (CAK).

With regard to monitoring water levels in tanks, it is customary to include a gauge that is mounted in the living area. In Swift motorcaravans there is an indicator for the waste tank too, but this is unusual. Because food particles can upset the level monitoring mechanism, the majority of manufacturers do not connect a waste water gauge; so you get into the habit of emptying the waste tank whenever you drive to a service point to take on fresh water.

On the subject of emptying waste tanks, it is important that the water is emptied into an approved gully, manhole or purpose-built soakaway. Emptying on to a grass verge is unacceptable. On some continental sites, the owners haven't developed motorcaravan service points and direct you to a storm water drain. This is not a satisfactory arrangement and would not be tolerated at UK holiday venues.

With regard to developments, Assembled Supplies (Electrical) Ltd (ASL) exhibited a new level indication system at the Caravan and Outdoor Leisure Show at Earls Court, in November 1997. This is referred to as a 'non-intrusive' level indication system because there is nothing installed inside the tank. Instead there are metal plates mounted on opposite sides of the exterior of the receptacle. The tank thus acts as a capacitor

which forms part of an electronic circuit. As water level changes, so does the value of the capacitor and variations are then indicated on a meter.

Another feature of the ASL initiative is the inclusion of a switching device in the electronic circuit which switches off the pump automatically whenever the supply tank becomes empty. This is very useful because pumps may sustain serious damage if allowed to run in a dry state for an extended period.

Installing tanks

An experienced DIY enthusiast is unlikely to find the installation of a water supply tank difficult. A standard shape rectangular tank is available from Fiamma, but for less conventional shapes, specialists like Amber Plastics or CAK supply tanks in a wide range of shapes and capacities.

Some enterprising self-build enthusiasts with plumbing knowledge have even adapted a length of unplasticised polyvinylchloride (PVCu) domestic soil and vent pipe and fitted it with saddle couplings to provide inlet and outlet points. Screw-on end caps seal the pipe and provide inspection ports for cleaning. In this case all the necessary components

CAK water specialists hold stock of over 180 less conventionally shaped tanks.

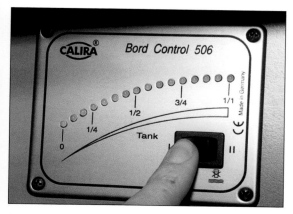

The LED water level gauge fitted in Murvi motorcaravans is from the German manufacturer, Calira.

Tank access

Before buying a motorcaravan, look at the emptying arrangement. The hose and release cock are easier to reach on some models than others; and check the way the hose is clipped back into place, because some systems are decidedly poor.

Note the arrangements for filling the tanks, because if you cannot drive within close vicinity of a tap, you will need to purchase a long hose. Alternatively a tank may be refilled in stages using a portable water container, if this is the case, a funnel might be needed to direct water into the filler tube.

Some models, e.g. recent Swift Kon-Tiki motorcaravans, provide a 12v socket alongside the filling point to accept a Whale tank refill submersible pump, so although you need to carry the water container from the tap to the vehicle, you don't have to engage in strenuous lifting. The submersible pump does the filling work as the accompanying photographs show.

would be purchased from a plumbing or builders' merchant. For a small 'campervan' needing a low capacity supply, this idea is a sound one.

On the subject of access ports, when comparing products check there's a large screw cap for cleaning the inside of the tank. This might not need to be done often but it is always surprising what accumulates over several seasons.

To complete an installation a number of components will be needed and a specialist like CAK can supply everything required. Outlet unions, couplings, pipe, stop cocks and so on are all listed in their catalogue.

Water level gauges are also included in the Plug-In-Systems range of low voltage gauges and under the Zig brand name as well. The light-emitting diode indicator fitted in Murvi motorcaravans is supplied by Calira in Germany.

Taking the Plug-In-Systems product as an example, the fitting leaflet shows clearly what is involved. Probes from the sender unit come in several lengths to suit different tank depths and these can be cut to meet your requirements.

As a final warning, before tackling a tank installation project, always spend time reflecting on the merits of different locations. Needless to say, water is heavy: 1 litre weighs 1kg (2.2lbs) or if you prefer imperial measures, 1 gallon weighs 10lbs; so a large container might upset the ride characteristics of the vehicle if it is inappropriately located. Whilst it makes sense to tour with a tank containing only enough water for a roadside picnic, many motorcaravanners fill their tanks brimful prior to leaving a site.

Direct supply and waste provision

In America, many camping grounds enable campers to create a direct link between a 'recreational vehicle' (RV) and the site's drainage and supply facilities. On pitches offering this opportunity, fresh water, waste water and sewage service points are coupled up to the vehicle's

holding tanks using purpose-designed connectors. Elements like a TV aerial link and a telephone line are not unusual either.

Whilst this development hasn't been in great evidence in Britain, the Superpitch has now been available for several years. There are over fifty sites which have pitches specially equipped with Superpitch service points and there's little doubt that this number will increase. As a rule, few British motorcaravans are fitted with the appropriate connectors and, to enjoy the benefits, a vehicle's water and waste systems have to be modified using Superpitch components.

On a similar note, some dealers like Brownhills Motorcaravan & Leisure Centre also sell the necessary couplings for RVs and will install the system in their workshop. Whilst this is specific to these vehicles, the Greenford and Thetford coupling systems used on North American RVs can also be coupled into the UK Superpitch using

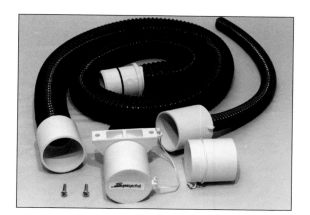

A motorcaravan waste and fresh water system needs special couplings to take advantage of a Superpitch facility.

73

pipe; once everything is fitted, the tap is left permanently on. Needless to say, these conversion kits both feature a pressure reducer so that water delivered direct from the rising main doesn't damage the motorcaravan's plumbing system. If UK sites have some way to go before matching their North American counterparts, there's a clear indication that changes are taking place.

Pipework

Whilst motorcaravan appliances and service systems are generally of a very high order, the plumbing system is often disappointing. Plumbing for both fresh water and waste water systems can be surprisingly rudimentary.

Waste water systems

Looking at the waste first, many manufacturers use ribbed convoluted pipe and this can usually be found under a kitchen sink or washbasin. In some cases, pipe that is ridged on the outside is lined with a smooth surfaced tubing on the inside; but this is unusual. The problem is that ridges in the pipe easily trap food particles like rice, peas, and other remnants. In time, this deteriorates and because there is no deep seal water trap under a motorcaravan sink like we have at home, smells easily seep into the living quarters.

It is also disappointing that on a number of motorcaravans, water empties from a sink or washbasin at a decidedly slow rate. Even on some top-of-the-range models, this element is disappointing. In many cases an improved system isn't difficult to fit and many handy owners have completely replaced the original waste pipes. Regrettably, manufacturers seem reluctant to adopt the kind of improvements carried out by a number of practically minded owners.

Improvement work on a waste water system

In a motorcaravan, a waste water system can be made up quite easily using the domestic PVCu waste pipe sold at builders' and plumbing

adaptors. Superpitch designates these adaptor couplings as Kits 9 and 10 respectively.

A coupling arrangement for all services remains relatively unusual in Britain; the idea of connecting up permanently to a water tap is much more common. A number of sites have special pitches in which the visitor has the benefit of a private stand pipe and a private drainage point. In response to this, Carver sells the 'Waterline' which connects up to a Carver Compact inlet. Equally, Whale markets the 'Aqua Source' which either connects directly into a Whale Watermaster socket or, with an adaptor, into a Carver Compact inlet.

Water entering one of these wall-mounted inlets then has to be routed directly into the pipework, by-passing an inboard tank. The tank has to be isolated from the system temporarily by fitting a stop cock.

The Carver and Whale products feature 'food quality' hose which is coupled directly to the stand

For coupling permanently to a stand pipe the Whale Aquasource includes different tap adaptors.

At the motorcaravan, the Aquasource has to couple into a Watermaster inlet socket.

merchants, as well as many DIY Superstores. This is the type of 'plastic' waste pipe many of us have under our sinks and washbasins at home.

When connecting up the pipe, all joints are formed using a proprietary 'adhesive weld' sold for the purpose. With a brush mounted on the screw cap, it's easy to apply; but preparation is important. The collar of each coupling and the end of the pipe should be perfectly clean. If you rub the surface with a light grade of abrasive paper, the dulling effect helps the surfaces to 'key-in' successfully.

During construction, the position of the pipes should be checked with a spirit level to ensure that whenever the vehicle is parked level, there's a distinct fall throughout the system. The job demands patience rather than a high level of skill, but the reward is that water will discharge through the pipes at notable speed.

In some motorcaravans, making modifications to the entire system isn't possible without embarking on serious alterations. Pipes are often hidden and there is also the problem that the outlet on sinks and basins is too small for coupling up to domestic waste pipe. However, in one improvement project it was found possible to construct a routeway in domestic PVCu pipe and then to insert the smaller bore convoluted pipe into the new system directly below the sink and basin outlets. Foam (sold in aerosol cans at builders' merchants) was then injected into the junction to fill the gap where the thinner ribbed pipe rested within the larger diameter domestic pipe. This prevented smells escaping from the system.

When making this union the dissimilar pipes were coupled directly below the sink and in a vertical plane. The tail of the original ribbed pipe was draped 100mm (4in) inside the larger domestic pipe to ensure there was sufficient overlap to prevent a leak. As stated earlier, the discharge rate of waste water was most impressive.

Fresh water systems

Like waste systems, many fresh water supply systems are also disappointing. There remain a number of manufacturers who continue to fit flexible hose and clip systems in their motorcaravans. In fact some of the most reputable manufacturers adopt this primitive arrangement claiming that it seldom gives problems, but many users would challenge this statement.

The trouble with flexible hose is that over a prolonged period, kinks often develop; for example, on older models it is not unusual to find that the water flow rate is disappointingly slow. Typically the pump gets blamed, but a closer investigation usually reveals there's a constriction in one of the feed pipes. As a general rule, this appears where the hose turns a sharp bend or bears against a sharp edge. Once a section of flexible hose develops a kink, it is seldom possible to return the distorted piece back to its former shape.

There is also the problem of leaking joints. In a motorcaravan, a remarkable number of hose clips

are needed to couple up branch pipes and to connect into appliances. Worm driven clips are not fault-free and any hint of weakness is aggravated by the movements sustained when driving on bumpy roads. It's no surprise that a joint will occasionally fail, and when a failed joint is hidden behind a panel or in a restricted area, effecting a repair can be quite involved. In a motorcaravan the case for installing semi-rigid pipe with push-fit couplings instead of a hose and clip arrangement is a very strong one.

Semi-rigid plumbing with push-fit couplings is far from new. In fact as long as thirty years ago, beer was pumped in many club houses and bars through similar food-quality semi-rigid plastic hose. Nowadays the system is commonplace, yet curiously there are only a few manufacturers like Swift and Herald, who use a push-fit plumbing system on their coachbuilts. On some of the more recent models, semi-rigid pipework is combined with sections formed using the hose and clip system.

If circumstances necessitate adopting a strategy where both types of pipe are fitted in the same motorcaravan, there's no problem because adaptors for coupling-up both pipes are available. Similarly there are unions which accept semi-rigid pipe in one end and where a threaded coupling nut is fitted on the other. This type of union enables you to connect semi-rigid pipe up to a diaphragm pump manufactured with threaded couplings.

A particularly innovative item in the range of semi-rigid pipework components is a short length of plastic channelling that has a moulded 90° bend. This is used where a length of semi-rigid pipe has to be led around a sharp corner. Without this component, the pipe would kink irreparably. To avoid this, the section is pressed into the angled channelling so that its sidewalls are supported. In consequence, the bend in the pipe is sustained at a consistent curvature and a kink cannot develop.

This channelling is one example of the many couplings and components in Whale's semi-rigid plumbing range. In addition there is also a pipe cutting tool to ensure that a cut section of the

Over a prolonged period, kinks can develop in flexible hose; the flow of water is then seriously restricted.

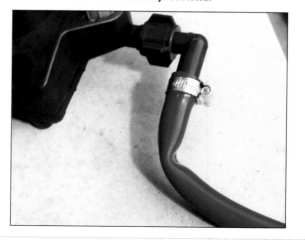

Laying-up tip

When leaving a motorcaravan for a prolonged period, remember to put plugs in the sink and basin outlets. This prevents smells from the waste water system creeping into the living space. Buy a spare plug for the shower tray as well.

75

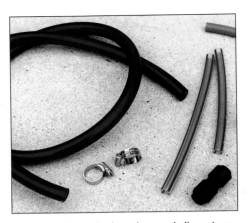

The choice of supply pipe – hose and clip system on the left; semi-rigid pipe with push-fit couplings on the right.

By using different couplings, this Shurflo pump is connected up to both flexible hose (left) and semi-rigid pipe (right).

The black channelling is made to support semi-rigid pipe so that it doesn't kink when turning a 90° bend.

12mm or 15mm (outside diameter) pipe is cleanly and squarely formed. This is important when coupling into a fitting.

More recently, Carver has joined Whale's initiative and has launched a similar push-fit system. It remains to be seen how long it is before these systems become a standard feature in motorcaravans.

System requirements in both types of fresh water system

Irrespective of the pipe system and connectors installed, there are several components that may also be needed.

Non-return valve

Once pipes are primed, it would be a disadvantage if the water drained back to the tank or water supply vessel every time a tap was turned off. Where a diaphragm pump is installed (as described opposite under *Water pumps*), its mechanism doesn't permit water to drain through its chambers when the motor isn't operating, so a non-return valve isn't normally needed.

However, small motorcaravans that are often fitted with a submersible pump are different. When the pump stops operating, water in the pipes will drain down, passing through the pump's casing, and effectively emptying the entire supply system. This means there's a delay in the water-flow when the tap is turned on the next time. To prevent this, a non-return valve can be fitted into the pipe as near to the water source as possible. This ensures that residual water is held in the pipes. This is beneficial – but it has obvious implications if a vehicle is going to be laid up for winter.

Drain-down tap

The above points show the advantages of holding water in the supply pipes when a motorcaravan is in use. In winter, however, manufacturers state that a drain-down of the entire system is essential to prevent frost damage. This is wise advice although whether this precautionary measure is always necessary depends on where you live.

Winter temperatures in Scotland undoubtedly fall far lower than they do in Penzance, so if you live in an area with low winter temperatures, the need to drain all residual water from the system is obvious.

Some owners never drain down their entire system in winter, and the pump, pipes or water filters manage to avoid damage from frost. Flexibility in the plastic components will cope with expansion if there's only a light frost; however, water heaters are different and *must* be drained down (as discussed in Chapter Five), irrespective of where you live in Britain.

Taking note of the risks, it is regrettable that motorcaravan manufacturers recommend a complete drain down – including removal of residual water from the pipes – yet seldom fit drain-taps in their systems! Accordingly, one of the hose or pipe connections has to be disconnected in order to drain the pipework, which is a poor arrangement. Fortunately, fitting a

Hose and clip plumbing

- **When replacing a failed joint, don't be tempted to re-use the old worm-drive clip – buy a replacement. Worm-drive clips are often known as 'Jubilee clips'.**
- **Buy good quality clips even if they cost a little more. There are poor quality imitations on the market whose ridged drive is all-too-easily deformed once a tightening pressure is applied.**
- **Prior to fitting a new clip, apply a small drop of oil on the worm wheel and also on the ridges of the tightening strip.**
- **Make sure the end of the hose is trimmed neatly and squarely.**
- **To ensure the hose is flexible, immerse the end in very hot water for several seconds. If you work quickly so that the plastic doesn't cool, you'll find the Jubilee clip will pull more tightly into the warmed hose.**
- **Some clips may have a sharp edge that could split the hose if over-tightened – so tighten with care.**
- **Most clips don't over-compress, but if you're connecting up to a plastic tube, like the coupling point on a tap unit, be careful not to tighten it to the point of cracking the product.**

Push-fit semi-rigid plumbing

• Forming a joint is extremely easy with a push-fit system. Make sure the pipe is cut cleanly, then merely insert the section into the coupling and push it fully home. A water-tight connection is immediately achieved.

• Inside each coupling there is a small collar known as a 'collet'. This can be removed if you want to see what it looks like – but it is normally left in place, and it shouldn't be taken out when forming a joint.

• The collet grips the outside of the pipe, so if you try to pull the joint apart, the collet is driven against the surface of the pipe with increasing force and disconnection by muscle-power is virtually impossible.

• Notwithstanding the grip achieved by the interaction of these key components, a connection *can* be disconnected by holding the exposed part of the collet firmly against the coupling itself. While pushing the collet towards the coupling, the pipe will disconnect when pulled in the opposite direction.

• To ensure a coupling isn't accidentally disconnected by pressure on the exposed part of the collet, the Whale system includes cover caps which should be merely pushed over the finished joint. The cap shields the collet, thereby preventing unintended disconnection.

drain tap isn't a difficult job for a practically-minded owner, even though it ought to have been installed when the motorcaravan was manufactured. The tap has to be located:

a) where it's easy to catch the drain-off water
b) at a low point in the system
c) at a point 'upstream' of a non-return valve or a diaphragm pump since these components prevent water passing through.

Surge damper

Where a diaphragm pump is fitted, it is sometimes found that the motor operates with irregular pulses. This is usually solved by fitting a small chamber within the pipe feed known as a 'surge damper'. Several motorcaravan manufacturers now fit one of these as standard – but don't let the shape confuse you – this is not an in-line water filter which sometimes has similar dimensions.

Note: *The surge damper must be mounted vertically with its connection at the bottom.*

Water taste filter

The filters discussed in the following section on pumps are only designed to remove grit and water-borne solids. Taste filters are different and their charcoal content improves the palatability of water. This type of filter is mentioned under *Filter Systems.*

Water pumps

Motorcaravan water pumps fall into two categories: models that need priming and models that don't.

Some products are unable to start the pumping action until water is introduced into the casing of the unit, thus expelling the air; this is what is meant by 'priming'. Typically a pump that needs priming is made with a small impeller or 'paddle wheel' that spins around, pushing water through the casing and along the pipes. This is known as a centrifugal pump.

In contrast, a self-priming pump usually

A tap fitted into the water system enables an owner to drain all residual water from pipe runs.

A surge damper fitted into the system smooths the flow of water.

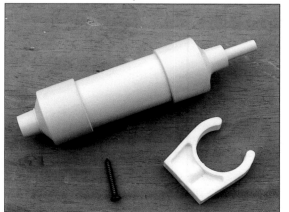

77

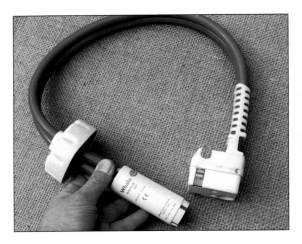

The Whale Watermaster submersible pump is a robust one.

The Evenflow pump is an example of a modern diaphragm pump.

Straightforward installation and easy filter cleaning is a feature of the Clearstream 700 diaphragm pump.

incorporates pistons that move up and down within sealed chambers; this type of pump will start to draw water along an empty pipe even when the chambers are empty. To most people the perception is that the pump is able to 'suck' water up from a water container rather than merely pushing it along the pipe. A physicist might politely point out that it's not a matter of 'suction' but of vacuum creation and pressure. The subtle difference is not important to our understanding here. More important is to state that the self-priming devices fitted in motorcaravans are called diaphragm pumps.

Examples of the two types are:

Non-priming pumps – Whale GP74 (seldom seen today), submersible pumps (made by a number of manufacturers)

Self-priming pumps – Fiamma models, Shurflo models, Whale Evenflow Pumps, Whale Clearstream Pumps.

For the purpose of this section, the focus will be on submersible pumps and their more expensive counterparts, diaphragm pumps. However, irrespective of the type used there has to be a switching arrangement.

Pump switching

Before an electric pump can deliver water, the tap has to be opened and the 12v electric motor switched into operation. One of three switching methods can be used:

1. Manual switch

Any 12v switch could be mounted in a kitchen to operate the pump once a tap has been turned. Foot operated push switches are available as well as conventional finger-operated rocker switches. None of these are fitted normally although they could be installed as a temporary cure if a fault develops elsewhere.

2. Microswitch

These tiny units are mounted in the body of a tap so that the motor is switched into action as soon as

the tap top is turned. Damp is their enemy and if water or condensation settles on their casing, electricity can track across the tiny gap between the switch contacts. When this happens, the microswitch needs changing – a topic covered later under *Taps and shower systems*.

3. Pressure-sensitive switch

This type of switch can be mounted:

a) in-line – i.e. within the feed pipe itself
b) integrally within the body of a diaphragm pump
c) as part of the water inlet socket of a submersible pump system – as in the Whale Watermaster product.

A pressure-sensitive switch recognises that when a tap is turned, an 'opening' appears in an otherwise sealed system. The switch mechanism is then activated thereby bringing the pump motor into action. Unfortunately if there's a small leak in any of the pipe connections then this can cause the motor to start as well. So it's not unusual to hear a pump clicking in and out very briefly because of a drop of pressure in the system. This is especially disturbing in the night so motorcaravans fitted with pressure-sensitive switching include a separate over-ride switch on the 12v control panel. Indeed it becomes a habit to switch off the pump last thing in the evening – or even during the day if false switching occurs often.

Over-frequent false switching can be resolved by altering the sensitivity of a pressure switch and most units feature an adjuster screw to 'fine tune' the system, but if there's a leak at one of the connectors this should be repaired promptly to prevent water ingress.

Further information on switching systems is mentioned in the subsequent sections on diaphragm pumps and taps.

Submersible pumps

Whilst the submersible pump is an example of a non-priming pump, the device normally achieves a state of prime as soon as it's dropped into a water container. Water fills the casing, air is expelled, and as soon as the motor is set into motion, water is pushed along the system with notable force.

Submersible pumps are normally only fitted for the water supply system on smaller motorcaravans – though the Whale Superfill 80 is often used on large coachbuilts to lift water from a container so that it's easier to fill an onboard tank. They can equally be used in this way to fill the flushing reservoir of a cassette toilet. In both cases, a 12v connector will need to be fitted to the outside wall of the vehicle at an appropriate location.

On a small motorcaravan using an external plastic water container, an input has to be fitted to the wall of the vehicle. This has two functions: it couples the supply pipe into the motorcaravan system; and it connects the two feed wires that will operate the submersible's motor. These wires are usually hidden within a section of the plastic tubing.

Advantages
• A well-designed submersible pump achieves a good flow rate.
• Good quality models are robustly built.
• A submersible pump is much cheaper than a diaphragm pump.
• Noise level is low during operation.
• Recent Whale submersible pumps incorporate an anti-air lock hole in the top of the casing.

Disadvantages
• When the mechanism fails, a submersible pump cannot be repaired.
• If the casing cracks, water will penetrate the motor compartment and cause a short in the 12v system. If this occurs, a fuse in the pump circuit will 'blow', thereby ensuring that damage isn't caused elsewhere.

In view of the 'throw-away' nature of the less expensive submersible pumps, owners whose water system relies on one of these units know the wisdom of always carrying a spare.

Airlocks in submersibles

If a submersible pump doesn't deliver water after it has been dropped into a water container, there are probably air bubbles caught in the casing.

To expel air bubbles, disconnect the feed pipe from the motorcaravan. Keep the pump under the water and swing the feed pipe so that the unit bumps several times against the side of the water container. This dislodges air bubbles, some of which are sometimes seen rising in the water. Alternatively air is dispelled through the upper end of the hose.

To reduce the likelihood of air bubbles getting caught in a pump casing, more recent products feature an air release hole in the top of the casing. The Whale 881 is an example.

Diaphragm pumps

These well-engineered products are widely fitted. Their mechanism is elaborate and there is nothing an owner should attempt to repair inside. If something goes wrong the importers or manufacturers offer an overhaul and repair service. Despite this, there are a number of tasks an owner should carry out – such as cleaning the filter.

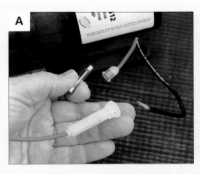

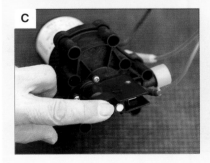

• If a diaphragm pump fails, first check the in-line fuse. One is often fitted alongside the unit (A).
• If water delivery is intermittent, the sealing 'O' rings inside the mechanism sometimes fail and air gets into the system. Eventually the water flow will fail completely.
• Excess noise is sometimes caused because the mounting screws are so tight that the rubber feet underneath the unit are compressed. The base on which it is mounted then acts as a sounding board and amplifies the sound. Loosen the screws, or if necessary, replace the rubber feet (B).
• If the pressure-sensitive switch needs adjustment on a Whale Evenflow model, the adjusting screw can be found hidden under a blob of white silicone sealant (C).
• On other models the adjustment may be more conspicuous. On the Whale Clearstream 600 it is accessed by removing a protective blue cap (D).

The mechanism of a diaphragm pump can be badly damaged by grit and the filter fitted with the product must be kept clean. Cleaning procedures are covered under *Filter systems*.

Advantages
• Output and flow rates are usually exceptionally good.
• Well engineered products.
• Powerful ability to lift water – the Whale Clearstream 700, for example lifts water up to 1m (39in).
• Kind to batteries.

Disadvantages
• When the mechanism fails, the pump usually has to be sent away for repair.
• The product is expensive.
• Some models are inclined to be noisy.

Pump installation

The submersible
Anyone involved in a DIY project might consider fitting this type of pump. The only major task is cutting a hole in the side of the vehicle to mount the input coupling. If you purchase a Whale Watermaster model, a cutting template is provided. Forming a hole and applying a sealant has been discussed in Chapter Three.

A notable feature of the Watermaster product is that a pressure-sensitive switch is built into the input socket. There is also an adjusting wheel to alter its degree of sensitivity, but you are not obliged to use the pressure-sensitive switch arrangement and can fit taps with microswitches if you prefer. There are three terminals on the rear to enable you to exercise your preference, and the fitting instructions show how to make the appropriate connections.

An adjuster on the Watermaster coupling alters the setting of the pressure-sensitive switch.

The diaphragm
The instructions for fitting a diaphragm pump are clearly presented. The job involves mounting the unit, connecting a 12v supply, and coupling up the water pipe. Different connectors are available – for example the Whale Clearstream 700 can be supplied with couplings to link with semi-rigid pipework or couplings to connect to 13mm (½in) flexible hose.

One point is particularly important to follow – the grade of 12v cable used. For instance the Whale Evenflow pump requires 2.5mm² cable (cross sectional area) which achieves a continuous current rating of 21.5 amps. Cable selection was discussed in Chapter Four, and the manufacturer's specification must be followed to ensure efficient operation of the pump.

Clearstream pump installation

The Clearstream pump is held in place by four fixing screws; these shouldn't be over-tightened.

An arrow moulded in the casing indicates the direction of the water flow.

Coupling up the pump to a motorcaravan's 12v supply should be done with 2.5mm² cable.

Cleaning grit filters

A screwdriver is needed to gain access to the water filter on a Clearstream 700; the cap is held tightly in place.

When the cap is lifted clear, the mesh filter is revealed.

The grit filter on a Carver submersible can be removed for cleaning.

Cleaning an Evenflow in-line grit filter

The in-line filter on an Evenflow pump has to be disconnected from the pipework.

Once a retaining clip has been removed, the two sections of the filter can be separated.

The gauze filter can be lifted clear of its housing for cleaning.

Fitting a Carver taste filter

Carver Crystal cartridge water filters improve the taste quality of water.

To support the filter, an attachment clip can be fixed to a suitable surface.

After connecting up to the supply hose, the filter is secured in the retaining clip.

Filter systems

In the section on diaphragm pumps, the point about keeping grit out of the mechanism was emphasised; hence the filter must be fitted on the suction side of the pump to prevent grit entering. The sequence photographs on page 81 show how to remove the filters from two different pumps. The Evenflow filter can also be quickly cleaned by removing it and running water through it in the reverse direction under a running tap.

Water 'taste' involves an entirely different type of filter. Admittedly these products remove solid particles as well, but their main function is to improve water palatability. Don't confuse these with water purifiers used by adventurers embarking on cross-continental expeditions – water purification systems are elaborate and may need an electrical power source to kill water-borne bacteria.

Taste filters are usually fitted in-line as close as possible to the drinking water tap, and examples are available both from Carver and Whale. Fitting this type of filter is an easy job for a practically-minded owner as shown in the photographs on the previous page. The only problem is remembering to replace the unit at frequent intervals. An average user could reasonably expect a filter to last a season; but some motorcaravanners leave them in place for several years. Quite apart from failing to achieve its objective, an old taste filter might act as a health hazard.

Taps and shower systems

The design of taps and shower heads has changed significantly over the last decade. To the disenchantment of many owners, some taps have proved extremely unreliable and one of the country's leading motorcaravan manufacturers has received more customer complaints about these components than anything else. In many instances the faulty items are imported products whose unit price had been their main attraction.

One reaction to the problem was to fit domestic-style mixer taps which undoubtedly look appropriate in a large motorcaravan. The only problem has been that the rate of flow from a 12v pump sometimes looks rather feeble after the more familiar output from domestic taps over the sink at home.

As regards a tap's requirements, it has to open or close the waterway at the turn of the top. With the low level of pressure in a motorcaravan system compared to a mains supply, there shouldn't be a problem with this.

In some taps, the turn of the top has to operate a micro-switch as well. As explained earlier, not all models are fitted with a pressure-sensitive switch. But if your motorcaravan has microswitches,

Changing the microswitches on Whale taps

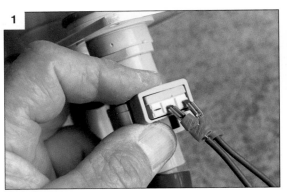

Feeling in the dark under your sink, locate a plastic collar clip.

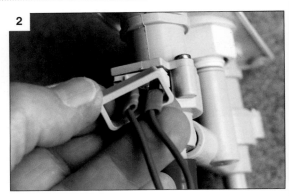

Ease the clip off the switch mounting point.

Gently pull the microswitch from its two locating pins.

Move the switch to a more convenient position; replace with a new one and reverse the operation.

Domestic taps have been fitted into several motorcaravans such as the Swift Royale.

always have a spare in case damp gets into the existing unit.

On some imported taps, if the microswitch fails, it is impossible to reach it to fit a replacement and the whole tap has to be thrown away. On Whale taps the more recent models present little difficulty as the photographs opposite and below demonstrate. The main problem is reaching the

underside of the tap – it helps to be a contortionist when changing microswitches behind a kitchen sink. Provided the unit can be reached, the following points explain how to change the microswitches on Whale Elegance and Whale Modular products:

• Ensure the tap top is completely turned off;
• Switch off the 12v supply;
• Reach under the sink and remove the rectangular plastic collar that keeps the switch in place;
• If it slips from your grasp, don't worry; the collar will remain on the two wires that are connected to the switch;
• Detach the switch from its two tiny locating pins;
• Since you haven't detached the cables from the terminals on the switch you can bring the whole assembly into view;
• Disconnect the terminals, introduce the replacement switch and re-couple the cables.
• Continue in reverse to reinstate the assembly.

Overall the job isn't too difficult, but the latest tap from Whale is even easier to work on. The new Elite mixer taps are available in two versions – both *with* and *without* microswitches. However, if you need to change a switch, you don't need to contort yourself in the kitchen cupboard underneath the faulty tap. Everything is done above the sink – with the whole operation in view. It's a great improvement as the photographs below show.

Changing the microswitches on Elite mixer taps

1 Working from above, prise out the hot/cold plug to reveal the tap lever attachment screw.

2 Remove the tap lever, then lift off the switch activating plate, noting its position carefully.

3 Prise up the microswitch from its cradled location with a small screwdriver.

4 Pull the switch clear to disconnect the terminals; then replace with a new microswitch.

83

Refrigerators

In a motorcaravan, a refrigerator is one of the most important contributors to comfortable living. However, successful operation is only achieved if the appliance is correctly installed, maintained and regularly serviced.

Periodically, a fridge has to be disconnected and removed completely so that it can be cleaned and adjusted if necessary. After a winter lay-up in particular, fridge operation should be thoroughly checked in preparation for the summer season. Fortunately, routine maintenance work can be carried out by any practically minded motorcaravan owner, and installation of a new model is not too difficult either.

Operation

Cooling is achieved in a refrigerator when chemicals are circulated around a network of pipes. As the chemicals circulate they change state and this has the effect of drawing heat from the compartment in which foodstuffs are stored.

In the refrigerators used in our homes, chemicals are circulated by a compressor and you will often hear the motor spring into life when a thermostat recognises the need for further cooling. This system works well but is seldom employed in the enclosed living space of a motorcaravan because the noise from a compressor can be intrusive. To achieve silent operation, chemicals in the appliance are thus circulated by the application of heat.

Appliances of this type are referred to as *absorption refrigerators* and the heat needed to circulate the refrigerants comes from one of three sources:

• a 12v DC heating element
• a 230v AC heating element
• a gas burner.

All three operating modes achieve efficient performance, although the best one to choose depends on circumstances. For instance, when stopping on a pitch where mains electricity is provided, it is logical to use a 230v hook-up. Alternatively, on a site where there is no electricity, you would switch over to gas operation.

It is also possible to operate a fridge from gas while the vehicle is in motion, but this is potentially very dangerous. Moreover, it is illegal to enter a filling station with a gas appliance in operation – an explosion could have terrible consequences. Equally it is not permitted to board ferries and Le Shuttle with a gas appliance in operation. So when taking to the road, always switch the operation over to the 12v supply.

Motorcaravanners often believe that 12v operation is not going to be very efficient; but as long as the vehicle's alternator achieves a good output and provided the electrical supply system from the engine has been correctly wired, cooling is extremely efficient. The only disadvantage when operating on the 12v option, is that the level of cooling cannot be controlled – the fridge will work 'flat out' all the time the engine is running. Check the food in the fridge doesn't freeze solid as this can occur when driving for extended periods, especially if the weather is cold.

Procedures for making changes to the operating mode of a fridge are explained in owner's handbooks and when you use a motorcaravan frequently, the task of switching over becomes a simple routine; however, if you haven't used your motorcaravan for a long time, it is not unusual to forget the steps you have to follow. This is why the Electrolux AES refrigerators, first introduced into the UK in 1995, are so attractive.

Automatic Energy Selection

Automatic Energy Selection (AES) employs electronic switching which make all the decisions for you in accordance with a programmed priority system. For instance, if the fridge can sense the availability of a 230v supply, the unit will automatically start to operate on mains in preference to gas or a 12v supply; however, on a site with no mains hook-ups, the appliance will operate on gas – as long as the cylinder is switched on.

Once you take to the road, always turn off the gas supply at the cylinder for safety reasons.

On a conventional refrigerator you then have to operate a selection switch on the panel to

Whereas some American RV fridges are designed to run on gas when on the move, it is strongly recommended to turn off a gas supply at the cylinder before taking to the road. On Electrolux refrigerators made prior to 1992, the burner flame is not extinguished just by turning the temperature control to its lowest setting. Any model with a red ignition push button on the fascia is one of the earlier appliances. Only more recent Electrolux fridges incorporate a gas shut-off valve in the temperature control knob.

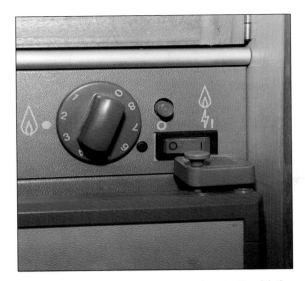

Earlier models with a red ignition button do *not* extinguish the gas flame merely by turning the gas control knob to its lowest setting.

Fridge capacity is good, but avoid packing food so tightly that air cannot circulate within the storage compartment.

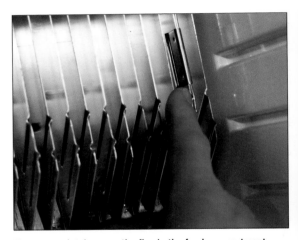

Never completely cover the fins in the food compartment; they create cooling and provide a mounting for the thermostat temperature sensor (indicated).

Packing tip

Leave some of the cooling fins at the rear of the food compartment exposed as they are the means by which the operating system at the rear of the casing draws heat from the food compartment. Be careful not to dislodge the thermostat which is clipped to the fins, as this will result in incorrect readings, resulting in the refrigerator becoming overcool.

prompt 12v operation – though it will only commence when the engine is running. On an AES model, the changeover is effected automatically and as soon as the engine is running, the 12v system is brought into use. Even if you accidentally leave the gas cylinder switched on, an AES refrigerator still takes the 12v supply in preference to gas.

During the development work on the AES principle, it was noted that in the event of a motorcaravanner forgetting to turn off a gas cylinder, the fridge would subsequently return to gas operation whenever the vehicle was parked. Clearly this would be unacceptable when stopping at a filling station. To overcome the problem, the manufacturer programmed a twenty minute delay into the automatic selector; but note that this time lapse *only* takes effect in the transition from 12v to gas operation. The switchover delay effectively resolves the filling station problem – presuming a vehicle can be re-fuelled and driven away within twenty minutes, but of course, the issue doesn't arise if you always remember to turn off the gas cylinders prior to driving the vehicle.

Getting the best from a refrigerator

Several courses of action will ensure you get the best results from a motorcaravan fridge:

Prior to departure

Before leaving home, it helps to pre-cool the food storage compartment. Do this by adding several items, such as cans of drink, then operate the appliance for around three hours. If you can hook up to a mains supply you will save gas, but you will need an adaptor in order to connect the industrial-style hook-up plug into a household 13 amp socket. You should also fit a portable RCD device in the socket to offer

protection to anyone working near the trailing lead. These items can be purchased in DIY stores.

The following points should be observed:

• Only transfer perishable items like milk, butter and bacon, when the temperature has dropped.
• Avoid packing food so tightly that air cannot circulate around the storage area.
• Never completely cover the silver cooling fins inside the food storage area. For example, cooling efficiency is often impaired when an owner pushes a shrink-wrapped pack of beer cans hard up against these fins at the rear of the food compartment.
• Before taking to the road, *always remember to secure the door catch.*

On-site

Several elements can hinder refrigerator efficiency. These include:

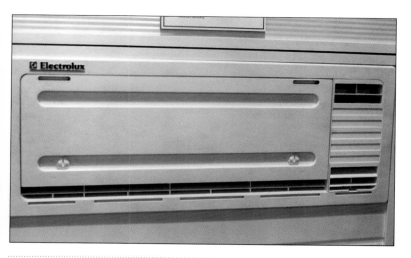

Winter covers from Electrolux should be fitted when outside temperatures fall below 10°C (50°F).

Ignition problems
If initial attempts to ignite the burner are unsuccessful, this may be because there is air in the gas line. However, repeated attempts usually purge the air quite quickly. Should there be continuing difficulty, it is probably time to have the appliance serviced. As part of the service work, the ignition electrode will be cleaned and realigned, see *Servicing a Refrigerator*, page 92.

Ventilators obscured
Ensure that the ventilators on the outside are not obscured, for instance, cooling efficiency is often impaired on motorcaravans if the external door covers the vents when fully open, especially in hot conditions. A similar disadvantage occurs if the refrigerator vents fall within a fully enclosed awning.

Voltage loss
On crowded sites, particularly abroad where electrical standards might not be as strict, power from a 230v hook up is often reduced. It can fall as low as 190v and cooling is seriously affected as a result. Under these circumstances, switch back to gas operation as you will often find this overcomes the problem.

Cooling loss
Open the fridge door as briefly as possible. Regrettably, some recent motorcaravans have a false door front that completely hides the fascia controls. While the door may match other kitchen furniture, it means the refrigerator has to be opened to alter the cooling control or energy selection switches. Subsequently, loss of cooled air is unavoidable.

Overcooling
When motorcaravanning in the winter, outside temperatures may bring the reverse problem – overcooling. It is not unusual to find that milk, cucumbers, and yoghurt are frozen solid. In reality, this is only likely on models fitted with a gas valve such as the RM212, RM4206, RM4230 and RM4200. It doesn't occur on models fitted

with a gas thermostat like the RM2260, RM4237 or the RM4271.

Winter covers
If your refrigerator over-cools in cold weather, Electrolux manufactures 'winter covers' which clip on to the ventilators, thereby restricting the flow of air across the rear of the appliance. It is recommended to have these fitted whenever the outside temperatures fall below 10°C (50°F).

Ventilators from other manufacturers may not accept winter covers, so a makeshift answer in cold conditions is to partially cover some of the fins with cooking foil, although this is neither glamorous nor entirely effective.

Note: *Winter covers are not draught excluders. If wind blows into your motorcaravan through the outside vents, the refrigerator has been incorrectly installed, see* Ventilation, *page 89.*

On returning home
On completion of every trip, remove foodstuffs and leave the door partially open – fridges usually incorporate a catch that holds the door slightly ajar so that air can circulate around the inside.

At the end of the season, clean the inside of the refrigerator with a weak solution of bicarbonate of soda. Electrolux recommends a teaspoonful is added to half a litre of warm water. Other cleaners should not be used – some types have led to cracks developing in the cabinet lining material.

If you lay-up the motorcaravan, consider having the refrigerator serviced by a motorcaravan service engineer prior to the start of the new season.

Installation

Although the following information provides guidance for DIY motorcaravan converters, it also provides a point of reference for anyone buying a motorcaravan or for existing owners who have found the efficiency of their fridge disappointing.

Stain removal

To remove stubborn stains from the interior of your fridge, use a very fine wire wool pad, lubricated with water to reduce its abrasive effect. If applied gently, this will remove marks without damaging the plastic lining material.

87

Choosing a location

A refrigerator is a heavy appliance, especially when full, so its position in the living quarters may have an effect on the suspension, especially if it is situated at the extreme rear of a vehicle. Similarly, whilst a chest-height installation affords convenience on site, it would inevitably contribute to body roll when cornering. Finally, if the chosen position results in its ventilators being obstructed when the entrance door is fully opened, the efficiency of the unit may be significantly impaired.

Levelling

Since the movement of chemicals is hindered if a fridge is not level, the installer should first park the motorcaravan on level ground. Thereafter, a spirit level is used when installing the refrigerator so that its level position coincides with that of the vehicle.

On an Electrolux refrigerator, the reference point for verifying a level plane is the shelf in the small freezer compartment. Of course, a very short spirit level is needed to take a reading here. The exception is the RM123 which has a sloping shelf; on this model the spirit level should be placed on the base of the food storage cabinet.

Note: *i) All Electrolux refrigerators manufactured before 1986 had to be completely level to operate. A tilt in excess of 2–3° could impair operation. Since this date, all higher specification models are described as 'tilt tolerant'. Some models will*

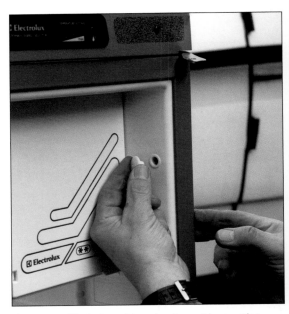

More recent Electrolux refrigerators have side mounting points – plastic caps hide the heads of the screws.

operate at an angle of 3° (eg RM122 and RM4206); others operate at 6° (eg RM4217, RM4237, and RM4271).

ii) On the road, a fridge will seldom be level, particularly when driving along a carriageway with pronounced camber. However, as long as a level position is achieved periodically – which is the case on normal roads – chemical circulation will take place and cooling will occur.

Structural fixing

When on the road, the living quarters in a motorcaravan receive a considerable shake-up, especially on bumpy country lanes. To resist this, a refrigerator needs to be carefully secured. It is prudent, for example, to fit small wooden blocks on the floor at the rear of the unit. Normally, blocks are not needed at the sides because support is afforded by the adjacent kitchen units to which the appliance is anchored.

Side anchorage used to be achieved by driving screws through furniture on either side and directly into the metal casing of the appliance. As long as they penetrated no further than 12mm (½in), the interior plastic lining wouldn't be damaged; however, models like the RM2260 and RM2262 were manufactured with a projecting flange around the front; this incorporates fixing points.

In addition, Electrolux refrigerators made since 1994 incorporate holes in the sides of the food compartment. This means that long screws can be driven from the *inside* outwards, thereby achieving anchorage from adjacent structures – usually kitchen cupboards. The heads of the screws are then concealed by a white plastic cap that matches the inner lining of the food compartment. Whichever method of fixing is adopted, three objectives must be achieved:

Correct installation is important and the need to fit a metal shield deflector at the rear is emphasised by the manufacturer.

Installation method

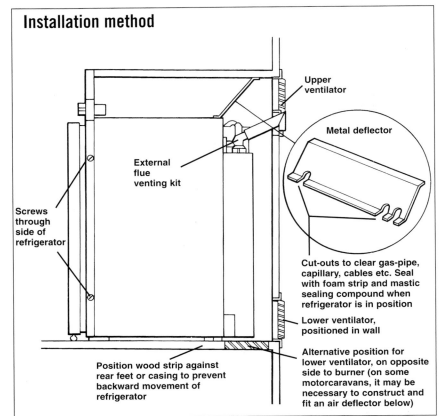

Upper ventilator

Metal deflector

External flue venting kit

Screws through side of refrigerator

Cut-outs to clear gas-pipe, capillary, cables etc. Seal with foam strip and mastic sealing compound when refrigerator is in position

Lower ventilator, positioned in wall

Alternative position for lower ventilator, on opposite side to burner (on some motorcaravans, it may be necessary to construct and fit an air deflector below)

Position wood strip against rear feet or casing to prevent backward movement of refrigerator

- The fridge should be in a level position when the vehicle is parked on level ground.
- It must not shake loose when driving on rough roads.
- The appliance should be easy to remove for servicing.

Ventilation

In both the heat of summer and the cold winds of winter, a motorcaravanner will experience problems if the manufacturer has disregarded the ventilation requirements specified by Electrolux.

Sealed ventilation path

For efficient and successful operation, it is critical that the operating system mounted on the rear of the casing is kept cool. When this is achieved, an Electrolux absorption refrigerator will operate efficiently in air temperatures as high as 38°C (100°F). However, when a motorcaravan is parked in a non-shaded spot on a hot, sunny day, temperatures inside the vehicle can rise to considerably higher levels. It is for this reason that the rear of the casing must be completely sealed off from the interior of a motorcaravan and a sealed ventilation path formed over the cooling components.

In addition, a deflector needs to be fitted on top of the casing. This directs warmed air that has passed over the cooling unit towards the upper ventilator that is mounted on the wall of the vehicle.

To help installers create a sealed ventilation path, Electrolux manufactures an aluminium shield, complete with deflector, that should be mounted to the rear of the casing. This is referred to as the IK1 Kit. Alternatively, a custom-made shielding arrangement can be formed using sheet aluminium

In this self-built motorcaravan, a deflector shield is made up from aluminium sheet.

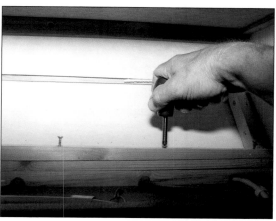

Once positioned correctly, the deflector is screwed down to wooden strips mounted on the fridge, and pipe apertures are filled with sealant.

remnants – a strategy which most motorcaravan manufacturers prefer.

In van conversions, where the curved profile of a side wall has a complex shape, a custom-made shield is often more appropriate. The IK1 Kit is better suited to coachbuilt motorcaravans where the sides are made from flat foam-bonded panels. Whichever approach is followed, the need to shield and isolate the rear of the refrigerator from the living quarters is a crucial installation element.

It is most regrettable, therefore, to find that some motorcaravan manufacturers disregard this requirement – in spite of the instructions and diagrams given in the refrigerator installation manual. Two problems arise if the ventilation pathway at the rear of the appliance is not kept entirely separate from the living space. First, the refrigerator will not operate to its maximum potential in hot temperatures, and second, in cold weather, draughts blowing through the wall vents will penetrate directly into the interior of the motorcaravan.

If you suspect an incorrect installation, feel the work top or draining board directly above the refrigerator. If it gets hot, then it is certain that warmed air from the rear of the cooling unit is not being correctly deflected to the outside via the upper ventilator.

Prior to installing a fridge, sections from an IK1 kit are positioned and checked; a sealed ventilation path at the rear is an essential feature.

89

Some motorcaravanners fit a fridge fan to the upper ventilator to enhance air flow in hot weather.

Rain is discharged effectively from an Electrolux ventilator and water penetration is highly unlikely.

Ventilation components

If an installation is correct, warmed air will rise across the rear of the appliance. There should be no need to fit an electric fan to accelerate air movement. Notwithstanding this advice, motorcaravanners whose holiday venues are in hot regions often add a small 12v-operated fan within the sealed section at the back. A refrigerator fan is marketed by Peter Miller Leisure products and this is easy to attach to the upper ventilator.

The size of ventilators is also critical for good performance. On models with less than 2cu. ft. storage capacity, the ventilators should provide at least 240cm^2 of free air space; models offering more than 2cu. ft. storage require ventilators achieving at least 300 cm^2 free air space. Note that this is reduced if an insect gauze is added on the inside of the grille.

The A1609 and A1620 ventilators made by Electrolux achieve these requirements although they are comparatively expensive. It is for this reason that a few manufacturers fit other types – though some versions lack the leak-proof design of Electrolux units and driving rain can penetrate. Equally, some of the less expensive ventilators are not made to accept winter covers, although this problem also occurs with earlier types of Electrolux ventilator too.

Owners of older motorcaravans often decide to upgrade their refrigerator ventilators to the A1620 versions since these accept winter covers and integrate the flue outlet neatly within the design. This changeover necessitates increasing the dimension of the aperture and you should check there are no obstructions before tackling this upgrading work.

The position of ventilators relative to the appliance is another issue. The top vent should be located so that its upper edge is at least 55mm above the casing of the refrigerator. The upper

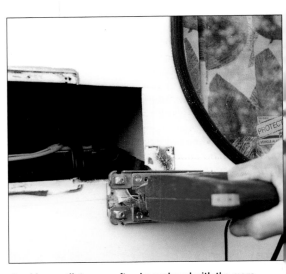

An older ventilator can often be replaced with the more recent Electrolux A1609 unit, but the aperture may need increasing in size.

vent should be located so that the lower edge is in alignment with the top of the appliance. On the other hand, the lower vent can either be positioned in the side wall or in the floor. If the latter option is preferred it should be situated as far from the burner as possible so that draughts do not extinguish the flame. It may also need a deflector plate fixed under the floor so that dirt isn't driven into the vents when driving the vehicle.

The refrigerator flue

The provision of a flue is necessary in order to disperse the products of combustion created when the appliance is operated on gas. Note that

Refrigeration

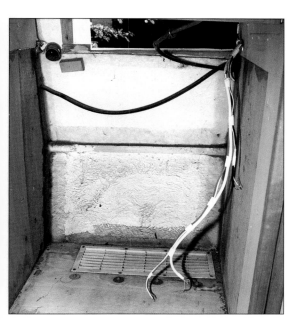

A floor mounting for the lower ventilator is an acceptable alternative to fitting the unit in a side wall.

this is an entirely separate element from ventilation. The fact that the flue outlet is accommodated in the latest ventilators is purely for tidiness. On older installations the outlets were kept separate.

The assembly of the flue pipe supplied with an Electrolux fridge is straightforward and its installation is clearly described in the fitting instructions. These should be carefully followed and the tubing supplied should not be extended in length since this could lead to an imbalance in the gas/air mixture.

Mains connection

The 230v mains connection is easy to carry out. An Electrolux refrigerator is supplied with a three-core flexible cable which needs coupling into the motorcaravan's mains supply. Typically there is a separate spur for the fridge and this is protected by its own miniature circuit breaker on the mains consumer unit. This is described further in Chapter Four. The current rating for the mains connection should be no greater than 5 amps.

Low voltage connection

A problem with 12v operation is the fact that voltage drop can be experienced if the connecting cables are too long and of insufficient diameter. Requirements are shown in the illustration below.

The source is taken from the vehicle's alternator which is an ignition-controlled supply (the current only flows when the engine is running). However, a second, permanent supply is needed too, because many fridges now have an electronic ignition system (which is undoubtedly more convenient than piezo crystal spark ignition), so a separate feed is drawn from the leisure battery as shown in the diagram.

Key elements in the supply are:

• A 15 amp fuse situated close to the positive terminal on the vehicle battery.
• A relay – this is an electric switch which operates as soon as the engine is running. Current can then flow from the vehicle battery to the refrigerator, recognising that the alternator will be charging the battery to compensate for the considerable drain. This will be at least 8 amps; the rate of consumption is 96 watts. Suitable relays are available from both Lucas and Hella and as soon

The 12v connection to an Electrolux refrigerator must follow the manufacturer's specifications, to avoid a voltage drop.

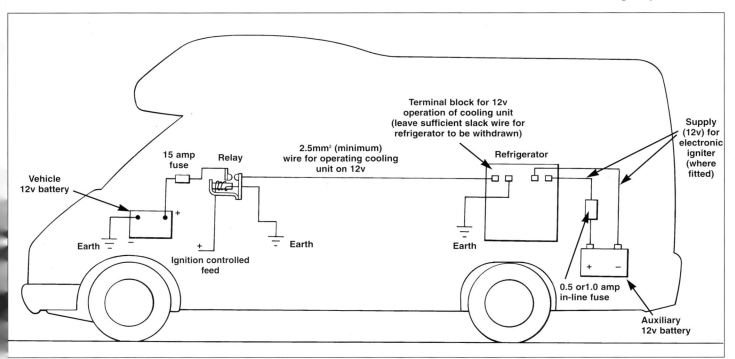

Connection to a 12v supply uses a connection block that is fastened behind the fascia control panel.

as the engine is switched off, the relay will automatically arrest the flow of current to the refrigerator. Consequently, the vehicle battery is protected and the owner then needs to switch the refrigerator over to gas or to hook up to a mains supply.

• To ensure minimum loss of current, Electrolux recommends the connecting cable to be at least 2.5mm^2 (21.75 amps continuous current rating). Cable of this type is supplied as standard if you purchase a Hella fridge relay kit but it is also available from any automotive specialist dealing with car electrical products.

• Whilst the connection could go directly to the refrigerator, it is usually routed via a 12v distribution control box. Typically these have a separate switch for the refrigerator supply and there will be another fuse in the box — usually of 10 amp rating.

• From the control box, the positive and negative feeds are coupled to a terminal block on top of the refrigerator casing, just behind the control fascia.

• A 12v feed to the electronic igniter for the gas burner (where this form of ignition is fitted) will be a separate source taken from the leisure battery rather than from the battery that serves the vehicle's engine.

Gas operation

Requirements for the gas supply include:

• An independent gas cock in the supply to the fridge – this is usually situated adjacent to the casing, in a kitchen cupboard.

• Copper feed pipes of 6mm (¼in) outside diameter (OD) – you must not make the final connection to the appliance with flexible gas hose.

• A flue arrangement – this is *entirely different* from the ventilation system as described earlier. On the outside of the vehicle, the flue cover plate used to be entirely separate from the ventilator grilles. In 1994, however, Electrolux introduced the A1620 grilles that combined both the flue outlet and the upper ventilation outlet into a single plastic moulded unit.

• An ignition system – in the 1960s and early 1970s, the gas burner had to be lit with a match. However, push-button igniters that use a piezo crystal to generate a spark have long since replaced this system. In the mid-1980s, electronic ignition was introduced and this is now much more common. In order to create a light at the burner, the spark gap has to be set to 3mm and the components should be free of soot.

• Gas escape provision must be included when a unit is installed – it is not sufficient to rely on the lower ventilator grilel to provide an escape route for leaking gas since it might be fitted with a winter cover. Accordingly a purpose-formed 'drop-out' hole of 40mm (1⅝in) is needed, thus providing a direct outlet to the exterior.

• The union for coupling into the supply system is situated on top of the appliance, just behind the control fascia. Whereas an experienced DIY owner might be able to secure a fridge in its location, the final connection to a gas supply should not be tackled. This should be entrusted to a competent gas engineer who will form the joint using an approved threaded coupling. In a thread-to-thread union, a jointing compound like Calor-tite will be used.

There will also be a generous length of excess copper pipe on the top of the appliance so that it can easily be drawn forward from its housing when planning removal for servicing.

Servicing

As with any appliance, particularly a gas-operated unit, periodic servicing is very important. This not only ensures that the fridge operates efficiently; it is a safety element, too.

Despite this, some motorcaravanners who *never* have their fridge serviced may find that the appliance continues to perform well, season after season, but there is nothing more annoying to find that it finally fails on holiday, especially in hot weather.

Recognising the different levels of use, Electrolux recommends that servicing should be an annual task, although the point has been conceded that in certain instances a biennial service might be adequate. Either way, servicing itself is fairly straightforward. Rather less straightforward is the task of disconnecting the appliance from its housing and transferring it to a work bench. This is because some motorcaravan manufacturers fit the appliance in the early stages of construction, and then build furniture around it, making retrieval and reinstatement annoyingly difficult.

Since much of the work involved in servicing demands competence and experience working with gas appliances, it is not a task that a DIY enthusiast should tackle. On the other hand, a labour charge could be reduced if the owner were able to remove the fridge from its housing. Reinstatement could also be considered, although re-making the gas connection should be carried out by a gas service engineer.

To illustrate the work that your dealer should carry out when you ask for a refrigerator service, the accompanying illustrations highlight the key tasks.

The work breaks down into the following sections:
• With the fridge on a bench, the service engineer will remove the flue outlet pipes that are connected to the top of the burner tube. This tube is effectively

Servicing a refrigerator

The flue outlet on the top of the burner tube is disconnected first.

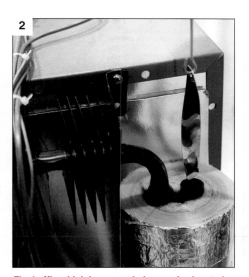

The baffle which is suspended on a wire has to be removed from the burner tube for cleaning.

In use, the baffle suspension wire rests on the burner tube, thereby assuring the critical position of the baffle is achieved.

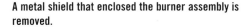

A metal shield that enclosed the burner assembly is removed.

The burner is disconnected from its mounting.

Gas ignition

Gas only flows to the burner when the tip of the thermocouple has warmed up and the operating valve has opened. During the warming-up period, you have to open the valve manually by holding in the gas control knob for a few seconds.

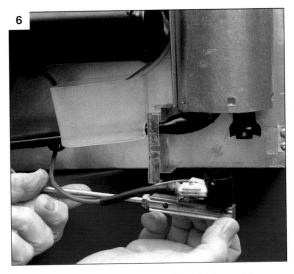

The burner assembly is pulled away from the base of the burner tube to stay clear of falling soot.

Using a special wire brush, deposits are removed from the burner tube.

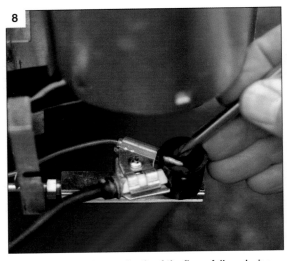

The screwdriver points to the tip of the flame failure device which will need cleaning.

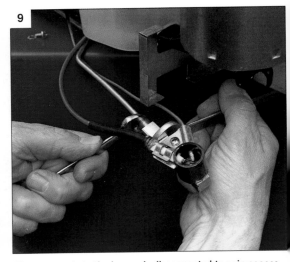

The gas supply to the burner is disconnected to gain access to the jet.

a chimney clad in an insulating material. Wrapped within its insulation are the heating elements for 12v and 230v operation.

• A baffle is lifted out of the burner tube. This is a twisted piece of metal sheet suspended on a wire and its position within the tube is critically determined by the length of this wire. One servicing task is to clean off any carbon deposits from the baffle.

• At the base of the burner tube, a metal wind shield that encloses the burner is removed.

• The burner assembly is now disconnected and pulled gently away from the base of the burner tube. Using a special wire brush supplied by Electrolux, the engineer will now clean all carbon deposit from the tube.

• The burner assembly will be cleaned, too, including the tip of the flame failure probe which is called a 'thermocouple'.

• The burner is now unbolted in order to gain

access to the tiny gas jet. This will be replaced; under no circumstances should the original jet be cleaned as the size of the aperture is critical. Even brushing it with a finger tip can upset the delivery of gas. There are many jet types to suit different models.

• After reassembly, the tip of the ignition probe is repositioned, if necessary, to achieve the 3mm clearance needed for a spark gap.

• The thermocouple looks like a thin copper tube. The lower tip is heated by the flame; the upper end is connected to the gas control unit just behind the fascia. When the tip is heated, a tiny current flows along the thermocouple and this holds open a spring-operated gas valve using an electro magnet, but sometimes the attachment nut loosens, and gas fails to reach the burner because the thermocouple is not opening the gas valve. During a service the tightness of this nut is checked.

• After a general inspection of the appliance, a

94

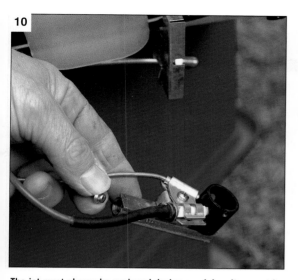 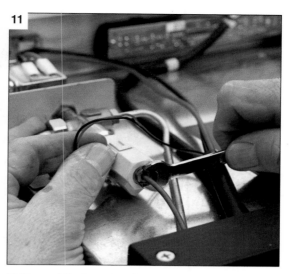

The jet must always be replaced during servicing; it cannot be cleaned.

Tightness of the thermocouple connection behind the fascia is checked.

bench test will be carried out to confirm the refrigerator is fully operational. It will then be re-installed in the motorcaravan and all couplings to gas and electrical supplies will be reinstated.

Other types of refrigerator

At present, Electrolux refrigerators are used in nearly all motorcaravans. However, in 1996 one manufacturer fitted a semi-portable compressor refrigerator into a multi-purpose vehicle conversion. This was imported from Australia.

On very small motorcaravans, there is also merit in having a compact portable refrigerator. For example the Camping Gaz CTL 350 is a neatly designed product that operates from gas, mains or a low voltage supply.

Also, a portable refrigerator, such as an Electrolux RC1600, situated in an awning can prove useful as an additional purchase.

Electrolux motorcaravan refrigerators: helpful hints

1. Defrosting should be carried out regularly.

2. The refrigerator door should be left open when it is not to be used for some time.

3. Liquid or items with a strong odour should be well packaged.

4. Ensure the ventilation openings are unobstructed.

5. The door is secured by means of the travel catch when the caravan is on the move.

6. Ensure only one mode of operation is used to run the refrigerator at any one time.

7. If the refrigerator fails to work on gas, check that:
    a) The gas cylinder is not empty;
    b) The gas valves are open.

8. If the refrigerator fails to work on 12v check that:
    a) The 12v supply is connected to the refrigerator;
    b) The fuse on the 12v supply is intact;
    c) The 12v switch is on.

9. If the refrigerator fails to work on 230v check that:
    a) The 230v supply is connected to the refrigerator;
    b) The fuse is intact if a 13 amp plug is fitted;
    c) The 230v switch is on.

10. It is recommended that a service engineer checks the refrigerator once a year. There is a nation-wide network of Electrolux service specialists.

(Reproduced courtesy of Electrolux Ltd)

Furniture and furnishings

Some motorcaravans are fitted with deep carpets, velvet curtains and florid fabrics, but this 'carpet-slipper' comfort does not suit everyone. An immaculate interior is hardly suitable for owners who enjoy outdoor pursuits – muddy boots and wet rainwear soon leave their mark.

Recognising that some owners enjoy passive leisure activities, motorcaravans are often designed with plush interiors. Other models however, are more appropriately designed for users with interests like fishing, mountain biking, walking and water sports. For instance, the use of plastic laminates on furniture items produces surfaces that are easy to clean. Similarly, the use of a vinyl floor covering with optional carpet pieces is far more sensible for the active owner, so appearances and practicality are important. The following guidance is intended to help existing owners, readers planning to purchase a second-hand model, and DIY converters who are fitting out their own motorcaravan.

Interior cleaning

Regular 'housework' pays dividends. Portable vacuum cleaners and hand-held products are useful appliances; some are cordless re-chargeable models whereas others are made to plug into a cigar lighter. The latter type is fine for cab cleaning but unless the plug system is modified, the length of flex limits use further afield.

In addition to vacuum cleaning, it is also advisable to carry out more thorough cleaning work every now and again. Removing seats and seat backs to a bench outside and cleaning them with a proprietary cleaner is well worth the effort. In fact it is often surprising to see how dirty a cleaning cloth becomes when wiping away the cleaning fluid.

Domestic cleaning shampoos are often suitable for motorcaravan furnishings and shampoos from specialists like Stain Devils are popular. You will also see on instruction labels that some carpet cleaners also clean upholstery surfaces as well. Have a look, too, at vehicle upholstery cleaners. Products like Auto Glym Car Interior Shampoo are

suitable for cleaning most motorcaravan fabrics, especially velour covers. The three-part process is as follows:
• Spray the Auto Glym cleaner directly on to the fabric
• Stipple the fabric gently with a soft brush to agitate the fibres
• Wipe the material with a clean cloth. Be prepared for a surprise – the cloth will be surprisingly dirty!

If you can work outside, cleaning fumes are able to escape and dampness will not lead to condensation forming in the vehicle; so when planning a general clean like this, try to delay the job until the weather is warm – but don't delay cleaning work if it involves removing stains.

Dealing with stains

Everyone has the occasional accident, but if there's a regular risk of stain damage – perhaps from dogs or young children – it may be wise to have some loose fitting protective covers made for selected seats. These are usually machine-washable as the label will confirm. The subject of covers, however, is dealt with in greater detail later.

It's also useful to keep a small container of general-purpose stain remover as a permanent item in your motorcaravan, but bear in mind that a 'do-everything' cleaner is seldom as successful as a cleaner made specifically to deal with a particular blemish.

Equally it is useful to note that a number of kitchen products can be used for stain removal. In fact a useful cleaning kit can be made up using the following:

• Absorbent white cloth
• Spray mister bottle
• Blunt, round bladed knife
• Nail brush

Models with ornate, carpeted and florid interiors are fine for passive leisure – but less suitable for outdoor sports enthusiasts.

The Swift Kon-Tiki removable carpet sections laid on a vinyl floor offer full versatility of use.

The eminently practical furniture and furnishings in a Murvi motorcaravan are ideal for active leisure enthusiasts.

- Salt
- Lemon juice
- White methylated spirits
- White vinegar
- Household ammonia
- Biological washing powder
- Glycerine
- Borax.

Some of the more common stains can be removed using these household products:

Chewing gum

Freeze using ice cubes packed in a polythene bag, tap away the brittle gum with a knife handle.

Alternatively use Scotch 3M Clean Art – this comes from stationery specialists and is formulated to remove deposits left on book covers by gummed-back price tickets. Similarly it can be used to dissolve chewing gum.

Grass stains

Remove using a mixture of two parts white methylated spirits with one part water. Spray with water mist then dry.

Coffee stains

Soften using glycerine and leave for 25 minutes. Sponge away with clean water.

Tea stains

Treatment for coffee often works for tea as well. Alternatively sponge the area with a mixture of 1.5ml of Borax added to ½ litre of cool water.

Blood

Sponge with salt water solution followed by a mild ammonia and water mix. Blot at every stage, finish with clean water, avoid heat while drying.

Vomit

Sponge area with water to which drops of ammonia have been added. Then apply washing powder and water mixed into a dense paste, leaving it for 30 minutes. Brush this away before finishing with fresh water.

Wine

Remove colour using white vinegar and water. Alternatively make a mix of lemon juice and salt, then apply a washing powder paste as described for 'vomit'.

Some car interior shampoos will clean motorcaravan upholstery as well.

Sauces and ketchup

Soften with glycerine and remove excess. Sponge with 50–50 mix of white vinegar and water. Biological washing powder mixed to a paste may help to shift the final dye marks, but remember that some sauce stains are very resistant.

Worktop stains

Lemon juice is often successful in removing a discolouration.

Refrigerator staining

See Chapter Seven for dealing with stains inside the food compartment.

Replacing cushion foam and covers

Sitting and reclining comfort is especially important. However, being seated during a journey is quite different from sitting when parked on a site. Equally we all have different preferences when it comes to cushion resilience.

Foam failure

In some motorcaravans, seat foam often loses its resilience surprisingly early in the life of a vehicle. Usually it's because a cheap product was specified

Dealing with stains

• Treat a stain as soon as possible; the longer it's left, the harder it can be to remove.
• When applying a treatment, use a clean, white, cotton cloth – an old sheet is ideal. This is because the dye on a coloured or patterned rag can sometimes seep into the fabric you're cleaning.
• Always remove stains first, before submitting a fabric to the dry-cleaners.
• Identify the cause of a mark before applying a cleaner. An incorrect product can sometimes set a mark permanently.
• Before applying a treatment, always try it first on an inconspicuous corner of the fabric to make sure there is no unexpected reaction.
• Where there's a surface deposit, scrape away any remnants with a blunt-bladed table knife before applying a cleaning chemical to prevent a stain from spreading.
• Be gentle – fibres can be damaged with rough, scrubbing actions.
• If removing a mark from a velour seat cover, work in the direction of the pile to avoid damage.
• Be sparing with liquids, blotting periodically to avoid deep penetration into the foam below the cover.
• Remove all traces of cleaning fluids afterwards – some compounds leave a mark of their own.
• A final application of water is best done using a mist spray – the spray bottles sold in garden centres are ideal.

and the foam soon starts to 'bottom out'. This means you abruptly hit the under-base when sitting down firmly. Fortunately, many cures are available from motorcaravan upholstery specialists. These include:

Top-up foam

Since the original foam has compressed slightly, there's often room within the cover to add a thin layer (typically 25mm/1in) of high resilience foam. Although the cover has to be opened to insert the top-up layer and then re-stitched, this is soon done with factory machinery and the cost is usually quite reasonable.

Foam replacement

Replacing the foam with a high resilience product is the best answer – several specialists provide this service. Contact suppliers for samples so that you can check the compressibility of different materials.

Creating a multiple-layered foam

Specialists like Caralux can usually bond two or three layers together to produce a composite foam; for example, a more resilient foam is usually

99

preferred as the lower layer, with a softer product bonded on the top. Specialists like the Caravan Seat Cover Centre are also able to create a 'his 'n hers' mattress when a double bed is made using bonded foams of different characteristics.

Producing shaped cushions isn't difficult for a professional upholsterer either. Making a 'knee roll' (the raised front portion of a bench seat that gives support behind the knee) is a simple task. The specialist prepares the foam section using a guillotine and bonds the piece in place using spray-on adhesive.

If you decide to have a new foam core, the finished job is even smarter if a final 'fibre wrap' is added. This is a white fibrous synthetic material often used as padding in quilted anoraks and the effect is to round off the angular corners of block foam.

Most owners would prefer to have the re-fill operation completed professionally; however, mail order services are available for owners wishing to pick open a cover and later re-stitch it up again. If you order foam by mail order, it is usually wise to make some clear drawings of cushion shapes and to provide paper templates as well.

Spring interiors

These have been used for several seasons in more expensive motorcaravans; they can also be specified if you're having re-upholstery work done.

For the mattress on a bed, a spring interior type is the preferred choice of many owners. However, on a bench seat used while you're travelling, a spring interior mattress will often produce a bouncy ride. Equally there are instances where the forward edge of this type of seat is inclined to collapse, thus reducing leg support. Good support on a travel seat, together with safety belt security, is especially important.

So the case for preferring this type of core fill isn't completely straightforward. It partly depends

on whether it's for a bed base or a seat used when travelling.

Cover fabrics

A cost-effective way to improve the appearance of seating is to fit loose covers. These are sometimes made of a stretch fabric and a zipped version is undoubtedly better than one that uses tie tapes. Some loose covers are machine washable.

A problem with these products, however, is that they sometimes slip around the cushion. An answer is to have upholstery buttons made up; these are pulled through both the fabric and its foam core using an industrial needle. Careful use with an opened metal coat hanger and some insulation tape achieves the same result. Tags on the back secure each button but if you want to remove the cover for laundering, the securing tape has to be cut.

Without doubt, loose covers with zips are useful as a temporary measure, for instance, when young children are at their 'sticky finger' stage, though a more permanent improvement involves fitting new made-to-measure covers.

Provided you pre-arrange your visit, several motorcaravan upholstery specialists will make and fit covers while you wait at their factory. With a large motorcaravan this is likely to be a full day's work and the service is comparatively costly – but the results can be stunning.

Prior to booking an appointment you should first send for fabric samples; the range of materials on offer is quite remarkable. Not only do patterns differ, but there are tweeds, velours and print cottons to contend with.

In addition there are options in respect of edging trims. These include:

Taped edges – usually a budget alternative, often used on a cushion base where the backing fabric is stitched to the main material.

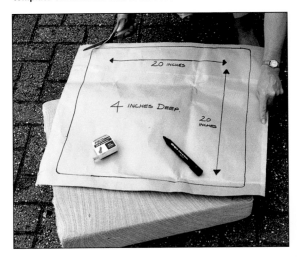

Replacement foam can be bought by mail order, but a template ensures the size is correct.

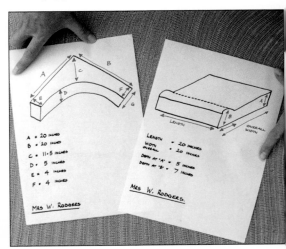

Diagrams showing unusual shaped foam are helpful when ordering by post.

Spring interior cushions can be ordered but may give a bouncy ride on a travel seat.

Piping – either made in matching material or in a contrasting colour.
Ruche – decorative, woven tape that gives a smart appearance.
Cord – used in a number of recent models, often with spiralling striped colours in the lay of the cord.
Cut ruche – a fluffy edging that suits more ornate interiors.

These trims are usually applied by a machine that stitches the main fabric to the edging trim and encapsulates the foam in a single operation. On the other hand you may prefer the covers to be made with a zip, which makes dry cleaning at a later date a feasible proposition.

Without doubt, some indefatigable owners tackle this kind of refurbishment themselves; but if they don't own an industrial sewing machine the results aren't always successful. On the other hand, running-up a stretch cover is easier, and some motorcaravanners make these themselves with pleasing results.

Cab seating

Improvement work is often needed in the cab area as well. Once again this is a job for a fabric trimmer although pre-made seats can be

Cut ruche is an ornate edging finish on motorcaravan cushions.

Cab seating is available in a variety of designs from Speedograph Richfield.

purchased as replacement items. A swivel base can also be purchased that enables a cab seat to be rotated and used within the living space.

So the choice is whether to have existing seats re-trimmed – or replaced. Some owners like to upgrade for high back 'captains' seats' and these are available with adjustable arms, rake adjustment and lumbar support features.

Specialists in this field, like Speedograph Richfield, will even create a custom-made seat using the same fabrics that have been used in the living area. If a customer can supply these, the resulting re-fit can have an attractive match that is reflected throughout the vehicle's interior.

Furniture construction and repair

Considerable skill is shown by the cabinet manufacturers who fit-out motorcaravans. Three criteria need to be met:

1. Structures have to be strong enough to withstand the rigours imposed by bumpy roads and uneven surfaces.
2. The entire structure has to be light.
3. The finished product should look attractive.
There's no doubt that many amateur converters with joinery experience are successful in producing smart, strong furniture, but the shortcomings are usually in respect of weight. Even an owner who merely wants to add a small shelf typically adds unnecessary weight.

The point to appreciate is that both materials and construction methods are very specific for the

Safety

In modern motorcaravans, covers have to possess a resistance to cigarette or match ignition and new models carry a label verifying their integrity. Sometimes, however, the resistance is lost after dry cleaning and the manufacturer should be consulted about this. To reinstate fire-resistance qualities, fabrics can often be re-treated.

101

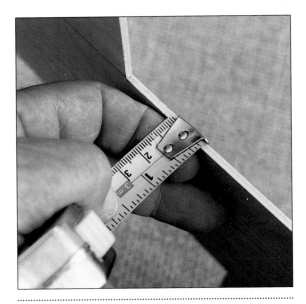

The print-faced decorative ply used in motorcaravans is only 3mm thick.

be made in English Ash, for example, but the main body of the piece is no more than thin ply. Alternatively a door is often hollow and built using two pieces of faced 3mm ply held apart by spacer blocks. Hardwood lipping around the edges then adds the final touch and makes the unit look heavy and strong. It's only when an unhinged door is lifted that the reality suddenly becomes apparent.

Once this unique feature is recognised, the skilled woodworker can undoubtedly match the techniques used by manufacturers. Using a steel edge and a sharp woodworking knife, it is easy to cut 3mm ply with several passes of the blade. A clean edge is instantly achieved.

Normally the fixings used by the home constructor would be specially treated woodscrews together with an appropriate adhesive – instead of staples which are often used by a converter for speed of construction. However, if you buy an electric staple gun, you will find the abrupt impact often causes less damage when assembling a structure than repeated blows with a hammer.

Another point to remember is that many manufacturers periodically sell surplus stocks of hollow doors that can be used or modified. The photographs on the facing page show how a hollow door was reduced in size and an insert slipped into the core to act as a spacer. A wood adhesive like Evo-Stik Resin W is applied prior to introducing the spacer piece to create a good bond. A 'G' cramp holds the assembly temporarily in place for 24 hours, using some scrap timber to protect the surface of the workpiece from direct pressure and to extend the zone of compression.

The exposed edge is finally covered with small lippings cut on a circular saw bench. Veneer strip is an acceptable alternative but because it's so thin it is less bump-resistant. The lipping is held in place with an impact adhesive but additional strength is achieved using veneer pins. Panel pins

job, so the decorative veneered chipboard used in our homes is far too heavy for use in a motorcaravan. Conventional plywood is much the same.

The decorative faced plywood used by motorcaravan manufacturers is only 3mm thick and is unusually light. This product, unfortunately, is seldom available from DIY stores and usually has to be purchased direct from a motorcaravan manufacturer. Alternatively it can be supplied to order from a board specialist. The 'wood effect' is generally achieved using a mock grain veneer printed on paper and stuck to the surface of a light grade of plywood. The result looks very convincing, but on no account should it be rubbed down with abrasive paper, as the paper veneer will simply rub off.

To achieve a smart finish, hardwood trim is often used as a surround moulding. This is the only concession in the weight-watching battle. Hence the frame of a roof level locker door might

Hardwood surrounds give lightweight doors a smart appearance.

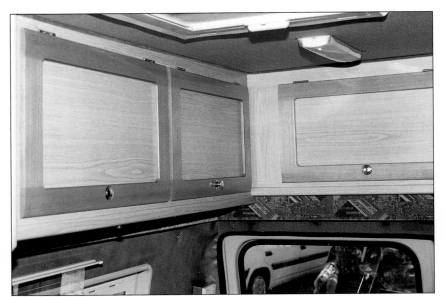

A Rabone Chesterman cutting guide is helpful when preparing 3mm ply with a woodworking knife.

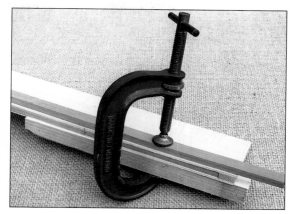

When a hollow door is reduced in size, a spacer has to be glued into the void.

A 'G' cramp will hold the assembly firmly in place while the woodworking adhesive sets.

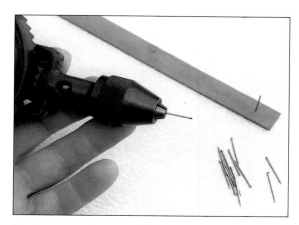

A strip has been prepared to cover the edge of the modified door.

Slender veneer pins are used in a hand-drill to prepare pilot holes in the edging strip.

are too thick and the narrower veneer pin is less visible. However, you will need to drill pilot holes to prevent the lipping from splitting. Some woodworkers nip off the pointed head which helps to overcome this problem, but it's better to drill a pilot hole.

If you don't possess slender twist drill bits, use one of the pins themselves. Cut off the head with pliers so that the pin seats well in a hand-drill chuck, then offer up the pointed end and keep the drill turning quite fast. It gets hot as it penetrates the lipping, but it does the job well.

Another recommendation if you want to strengthen a small shelf made from 3mm ply, is to cut some 8mm (or thicker) hardwood lipping and prepare a groove in it on a saw bench. Alternatively use a combination plane. As the accompanying photograph shows, this is glued and slid on to the edge of the ply to add surprising strength to an otherwise flexy and lightweight sheet.

Similar weight-saving strategies include the use of hardwood battens to provide a rigid bed base. This strategy is often used by manufacturers and it helps to reduce the normal tendency for condensation to form under bed mattresses. Finally, as regards furniture catches,

hinges and handles, specialists like Woodfit supply a whole range of items. In addition, stays, ventilators and plastic turnbuttons used in the caravan trade can be purchased by mail order from CAK of Warwick.

A grooved lipping piece is used to give strength to the edges of a 3mm plywood shelf.

Chassis, suspension, towing and tyres

The chassis, suspension and tyres on a motorcaravan affect both driving characteristics and the comfort of passengers. In addition, the undergear determines whether it is possible to tow a trailer, yet not surprisingly, it's the interior which determines many people's choice of a motorcaravan.

There is nothing particularly attractive about equipment below the floorboards. Nonetheless, owners who have no idea about the type of chassis or the suspension on their motorcaravan are overlooking a critical contributor to comfort when they're on the road.

Equally there are many purchasers who order a motorcaravan without checking if their chosen vehicle could be used for towing. Should they decide at a later date to tow a small trailer for holiday gear, or leisure equipment like a dinghy, a jet ski or a motorcycle, there's often an unpleasant surprise in store. A large number of motorcaravans cannot be fitted with a towbar, so although the title of this chapter may sound rather 'technical', several points need to be looked at more closely – starting with the chassis.

Chassis variations

It was pointed out in Chapter Two that a panel van doesn't have a chassis in the traditional sense. Like a car, its structure has strong box sections that are integral with the construction of the steel floor panels. In consequence, the earlier part of this chapter is not applicable to motorcaravans based on 'van conversions'. Later sections, however, which look at suspension and towing matters are undoubtedly important.

It is when a motorcaravan is constructed on a bare chassis that several design features should be checked at the time of choosing a model. Work usually starts with what is known as a 'chassis cab' and a Peugeot Boxer example is illustrated in Chapter Two. In contrast the A-class builder commences operations from an even more radical beginning since there is no cab shell either.

Whichever approach is being followed, the motorcaravan can be built on different chassis 'foundations'. Each is fundamentally dissimilar and

it is helpful to understand the features associated with the three variations used by the manufacturers.

The original commercial chassis

A number of motorcaravans are built on a chassis principally designed for commercial applications. Commercial users are the key source of revenue so few base vehicle manufacturers pay recognition to the particular needs of motorcaravan builders. Ford is one of the exceptions, as mentioned later.

Using a standard commercial chassis as the base for a motorcaravan has both advantages and disadvantages.

Advantages
- The structure is rigid.
- The chassis has been developed in conjunction with the vehicle as a whole.

Disadvantages
- A robust commercial chassis is heavy – a factor which affects payload potential.
- Whereas chassis members are thoroughly painted, a galvanised finish might afford better protection.
- There are few projections outside the main longitudinal members to provide support for a motorcaravan floor panel.
- The structure is quite high above the ground, necessitating prominent steps on the finished motorcaravan.
- The higher the finished vehicle, the greater the likelihood of body roll when cornering.

In addition to these points are the disadvantages of retaining the original suspension system; however, the subject of suspension design is mentioned later.

Notwithstanding these features, a number of motorcaravan manufacturers build on the standard commercial base. Special reinforcement is therefore

104

needed in the composite floor panel and together with the construction of the exterior walls, the builder has to take into account the limited support on either side of the main chassis members.

Ford-modified chassis design

Better support is achievable for motorcaravans built on the Ford Transit base. Acknowledging the motorcaravan builder's needs, Ford has created a number of modifications on the rear-wheel-drive Transit. The development was first announced at the Earls Court Caravan and Leisure Show in Autumn, 1994.

The modified chassis cab product was immediately used by Herald Motorcaravans whose base unit is always exclusively Ford. A short time later, Auto-Sleepers also used the modified chassis on the company's Ford-based coachbuilt models.

Designers at Ford's special vehicle engineering division lowered the height of the main longitudinal chassis members by 75mm (3in). This reduction is made on both the medium and long wheelbase versions. In addition, the main members incorporate a facility to attach outriggers and side assemblies that provide support for the wider floor needed on a motorcaravan.

To assist the motorcaravan manufacturer further,

Installation of an AL-KO Kober AMC conversion to a Fiat Ducato chassis cab

1

With the vehicle supported and a guiding jig in place, the original chassis is sawn away from the cab.

2

The original chassis is severed; some of its parts will be reclaimed and re-mounted.

3

The junction point to the rear of the cab is cleaned and prepared for welding.

4

Using a jig to achieve accuracy, connecting flanges are welded to the stub chassis behind the cab.

5

Several components from the original chassis will be re-used including the wheels and the brake assemblies.

6

The AL-KO Kober chassis is constructed of hot dip galvanised sections that are bolted together.

106

the rear closing member of the chassis is removable, thereby allowing the builder to extend the construction rearwards. With extension units bolted to the main chassis, this ensures the rear section of the living quarters is fully supported. However, since a rearward extension means that the standard exhaust system isn't long enough, an altered design takes the pipe to one side.

Other differences in this motorcaravan 'package' include a special Transit cab with a much higher level of comfort than would be provided in a commercial vehicle. Additions include higher quality seats, velour trim, electric windows, and additional noise reduction materials. Furthermore, the Ford rear suspension is different, too, and an anti-roll bar is fitted.

The AL-KO Kober AMC conversion

Another chassis designed specifically for motorcaravan construction is manufactured by AL-KO Kober and this can be fitted as a replacement unit on certain front-wheel-drive vehicles. The operation involves a radical alteration to the chassis cab unit supplied by the vehicle manufacturer. However, the conversion is approved by both Fiat and Peugeot whose vehicles are widely used by motorcaravan manufacturers. These modifications have proved successful for a large number of vehicles, including motorcaravans and over twenty thousand conversions have been completed since 1985.

The alteration itself involves the installation of a completely new purpose-built chassis together with an axle that is fitted with a different suspension system. However, the brake drums, bearing assemblies and wheels are retained from the original chassis cab.

The photographs below show a brief synopsis of the conversion process. A number of minor features are not illustrated, such as rearranging the road light system, altering brake hydraulics and so on, but the main constructional tasks are shown.

Motorcaravans built on this system derive a number of important benefits from the end product and an appraisal would include these points:

Advantages

• Computer-designed chassis members contribute to a very light construction without compromising rigidity.
• Installation of hot dip zinc galvanised sections ensure notable longevity.
• Where requested by the motorcaravan manufacturer, AL-KO Kober will fit a chassis that is 225mm (9in) lower than the base vehicle chassis.
• A lower floor height is a particular advantage in a motorcaravan conversion – both in respect of outside lockers as well as the living quarters.
• Access to the living quarters will be easier and a lower centre of gravity is now more easily achievable, giving reduced body roll on corners.

7

The cab flanges, coated with protective wax, are coupled to the new chassis; eight bolts are inserted.

8

A new extended hand brake mechanism is fitted to the AL-KO Kober chassis.

9

Using a rolling road, the brakes are checked and adjusted with concrete blocks simulating a typical load.

10

The replacement chassis is not only lower; there is better support for the floor panel.

Motorcaravans built on an AL-KO Kober chassis and rear axle conversion will have a plate mounted in the engine compartment giving details about:

Gross Vehicle Weight (maximum total vehicle weight).

Gross Train Weight (maximum total weight of vehicle with towed trailer).

Maximum weight Axle 1 (permitted axle loading, front).

Maximum weight Axle 2 (permitted axle loading, axle no 2).

Maximum weight Axle 3 (permitted axle loading, axle 3 – in the case of twin rear axle models).

Further details of the AL-KO Kober conversion are given in the AL-KO AMC Handbook which is included with the documentation of a new motorcaravan. If mislaid, copies are available from AL-KO Kober using the address given in the Appendix.

AL-KO KOBER CHASSIS CONVERSION WEIGHTS (KGS.)	
G.V.W.	3400
G.T.W.	4800
AXLE 1	1650
AXLE 2	1900
AXLE 3	

A red compressible spring assister on this Swift Royale improves the performance of the leaf springs.

• Single or tandem axle units can be fitted irrespective of the original back axle configuration.
• Increased load potential can be accommodated if requested by the motorcaravan manufacturer.
• Since the chassis sections are bolted together, replacement of a damaged unit may be possible without major re-construction work.
• AL-KO Kober-designed towing brackets and motorcycle racks are available for attachment to the chassis if required.
• The least expensive short wheelbase chassis cab model can be converted to a long wheel base unit, with the minimum wastage of original materials.

Note: *Further advantages in respect of the suspension system are detailed later.*

Disadvantages

• Additional items must not be welded to the AL-KO Kober chassis – this would invalidate the guarantee.

Note: *Great reliance is placed on the bolts, flanges and fabrication that connect the new chassis to the donor cab. This is not a method of conversion that could be tackled by the zealous self-builder.*

Clearly there is much to be gained by this constructional approach and it is used for ambulance conversions, buses and removal vans, as well as motorcaravans. Manufacturers currently using the AL-KO Kober chassis include Autocruise, Auto-Trail, Buccaneer, Compass, Elddis, Lunar, Machzone and Swift. However, this may only be on selected models.

The choice of chassis clearly has structural implications, but the suspension system is also an important part of the structure, being a main contributor to comfort.

Suspension systems

Ride comfort in a motorcaravan – particularly in the living quarters – is governed largely by the suspension. This can be a problem where a commercial vehicle is used as the base.

Leaf spring suspension

Often described as 'cart springs', the typical leaf spring arrangement used on most commercial

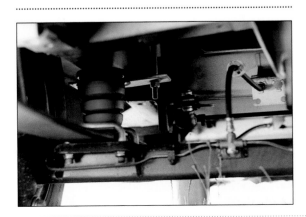

vehicles is fine for bags of cement or crates of lemonade. But the ride tends to be harsh and for a discerning motorcaravanner this form of suspension is seldom satisfactory without some degree of modification. The problem is especially evident on the uneven surfaces of country lanes or roads in France accompanied by a sign declaring *chaussée deformé*.

Problems also occur on twisting roads or roundabouts, where there is the disconcerting feeling of body roll, especially on taller vehicles where a high centre of gravity accentuates the problem. Poor loading, especially the carriage of heavy items in a roof box makes things worse. A similar feeling is experienced when a high-sided vehicle overtakes a motorcaravan on a fast road.

With this in mind, the designers of the Ford Transit add a rear anti-roll bar on the company's base units. Further improvements are made by the manufacturer with the installation of stiffer front shock absorbers on the front as well.

With regard to the Mercedes Sprinter and Vito commercial vehicles, these are both fitted with leaf springs but motorcaravan manufacturers usually add additional support to improve the ride characteristics.

Making improvements by the addition of support systems like air suspension units is also something that the owner can have done and this is described later.

Coil springs

Whilst frequently fitted on the rear suspension of cars, coil springs have not been prominent on commercial vehicles. However, the most recent Volkswagen Transporter is different. It features an independent suspension system at the rear using mini coil springs and a semi trailing arm configuration. The refined ride has been favourably reported in many independent motorcaravan tests.

As regards the springs, these are short coils mounted at a slight angle in order not to create intrusion into the habitation area. Rear coil springs on a car for example, typically take up space in the boot – hence the Volkswagen 'mini coil springs'. Moreover, the semi trailing arm is not unlike a wishbone arrangement and the benefit bestowed on the vehicle with the independent springing undoubtedly provides a comfortable configuration.

Manufacturers currently using the Volkswagen Transporter include Compass for the coachbuilt Calypso, Bilbo's with the high-top Nektar, Auto-Sleepers with the high-top Trident, and many more.

If a conversion is based on a car, the coil spring system is again likely to be employed. For instance the self-build Starcraft described in Chapter Eleven uses the original set-up from a Ford Cortina although uprated coil springs are fitted at the rear as a replacement for the original items.

Torsion bar

Different yet again is a system which uses a torsion bar. In this arrangement, a swinging arm suspension unit provides the mounting point for a wheel hub at one end and a long, fixed bar at the other. As the vehicle rides the bumps, the bar is subjected to a twisting action which it naturally resists. This is what is meant by a torsion bar and the system has been employed in many popular vehicles – the Renault 5 is a good example.

An engineer might point out that what appears a curious action to the lay person is no different from the similar twisting action that a coil spring has to endure. The only difference is that the torsion bar is rather like a coil spring that has been unwound to form a long rod.

When setting up a car, a torsion bar can be tightened by inducing a twist to alter the vehicle ride height and driving characteristics. In practice, a torsion bar system works well – although the bar takes up space. On a Renault 5, for example, the front torsion bars are 1.22m (4ft) long and run behind the sills of the car.

If this appears a rather clumsy arrangement, it is no problem in respect of the rear suspension employed in an AL-KO Kober AMC chassis. In this application, the torsion bars are mounted *within* the axle tube. The bars couple to the swinging arms that provide mounting for the wheel hubs, and replacement telescopic shock absorbers are fitted during the conversion to suit the system.

The AL-KO Kober torsion suspension undoubtedly provides improved road handling, and weight options of 3200, 3400, 3500 and 3850kg can be specified. In other words the payload can be increased to suit the motorcaravan designer's specifications – ultimately providing a motorcaravanner with more, or less, scope when loading up.

In motorcaravan tests, the improved ride achieved using an AL-KO Kober torsion bar system in place of the original leaf springs is frequently acknowledged. At the time of writing, development work is in progress with the aim of launching a complete replacement package intended for existing motorcaravans. If the product is launched it will permit owners of front-wheel-drive motorcaravans built on an original commercial suspension to have the leaf springs and axle completely replaced by a torsion bar system. If this conversion becomes possible, it would certainly be well received by many owners.

Shock absorbers

When considering a suspension system, many people presume – quite wrongly – that fitting higher specification shock absorbers will stiffen the springs and increase ride height. This reveals a misconception about the function and design of products commonly referred to as 'shockers'.

Driven without shock absorbers, a vehicle

A new shock absorber is fitted when the AL-KO Kober torsion spring axle is installed.

bounces along in wild leaps – as any Banger Racing enthusiast will have seen when a shocker has failed on the race track. Irrespective of whether it is a telescopic shock absorber filled with gas or one containing oil, the component's job is to dampen down the movements as a vehicle rides the bumps. Shock absorbers simply do what their name implies and a standard 'shocker' is not a spring device. Incidentally, gas shockers are often considered better than oil-filled versions but can be quite costly.

That said, it is true there are some special types of shock absorber that are manufactured with an additional coil spring mounted around the telescopic casing. Products like Monroe Load Levellers include a coil spring addition and were used on the Starcraft described in Chapter Eleven. Alternatively, the Monroe Ride Levellers are shock absorbers with an additional air inflation facility for height adjustment. Inflation can either be achieved with a foot pump at a suitably located Schrader valve, or by fitting the Monroe mini air compressor. Note: a Schrader valve is the type used on vehicle tyres.

Several specialist suppliers deal with suspension components like these and a prominent supplier to caravanners and motorcaravanners is Ashley Banks.

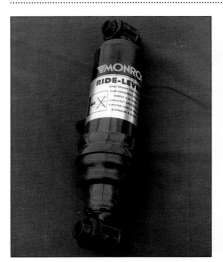

Monroe Ride-Levellers are shock absorbers that include an inflation facility to help the existing springs.

Heavy duty auxiliary springs for Talbot Express, Bedford Rascal and several other vehicles are available in the M.A.D. range.

Coil spring adaptation units are available from several specialists.

Leaf springs can equally be boosted up using an additional coil spring.

Spring assistance

Many motorcaravans can have their suspension strengthened by the addition of auxiliary springs. Products from the Dutch specialist M.A.D. are supplied by Ashley Banks and kits are available for twelve or more different chassis used by motorcaravan manufacturers. These include popular examples like the Fiat Ducato, Ford Transit, Talbot Express and many others.

Spring assister kits are also manufactured by Grayston Engineering Ltd and some are claimed to lift the tail of a motorcaravan by up to 100mm (4in). They are available for most popular base vehicles and can be ordered direct.

When considering different methods of 'firming-up' a leaf spring system, there are three alternatives:

• Fit a large bump stop that features a concertina construction.
• Fit an auxiliary coil spring.
• Fit an air-inflatable unit.

These additions usually locate in the central section of the leaf spring, directly above the axle mounting. Examples are shown in the accompanying photographs and air inflation types deserve special mention.

Air assistance

As regards pneumatic units, the Firestone air spring is employed in conversion kits from Driverite and Airide. The Airide system, for example, is supplied by Symonspeed and units can be fitted to Ford-, Talbot- and Mercedes-based motorcaravans. The inflation of Firestone air springs is done via a Schrader valve that is fitted in a suitable location. Typically the inflation point is mounted in the cab and the valve and its accompanying gauge enables you to use a car tyre pump or an air line to inflate the pneumatic springs and to monitor pressure.

On some base vehicles, the two air spring units are pre-fitted to a specially treated steel beam that is mounted across the chassis. In other instances, the air springs are fitted independently using 'U' clamps. Welding work is not involved.

The benefits of an air spring system include these points:

• Air pressure can be adjusted to suit the particular application and the loading,
• Any sagging at the rear of the motorcaravan can be remedied,
• Stability on motorways is improved,
• Body roll on corners is greatly reduced.

The system can be installed professionally although many DIY installers complete the work successfully themselves. Safe access is critical and it is not a pleasant outdoor job in winter weather. However, it is not as technically demanding as many owners imagine.

Towing

In many instances a motorcaravan is powerful enough to tow a sizeable trailer with a reasonable load. Its commercial origin usually means the engine has good pulling power, especially at low revs.

Touring caravanners work on the basis that to achieve the ideal match, the total weight of the trailer will not exceed 85% of the weight of the towing vehicle. This ensures that the 'tail doesn't wag the dog', and apart from micro motorcaravans, most models are likely to meet this recommended weight ratio, presuming the trailer towed is not carrying a cabin cruiser, another motor vehicle, or a similar heavy load.

Another matter to keep in mind is the 'gross train weight'. This figure, normally given in the base vehicle handbook, relates to the total weight of both

A pneumatic rubber spring assister can be fitted to help the operation of a leaf spring.

Chassis, suspension, towing and tyres

the towing vehicle and the trailer. Problems occur if you want to tow something heavy like a car, and a clear knowledge of the weights of both the motorcaravan and the fully laden trailer should be borne in mind.

Issues concerning the towbar (or 'tow bracket') are also important to take into account. As regards the new legal requirement that only an EC Type Approved towbar can be fitted, this only applies to light passenger vehicles – as explained in the Appendix. For the time time being, Directive 94/20/EC is *not* applicable to Commercial Vehicles. On the other hand, it seems unlikely that motorcaravan base vehicles will *always* remain exempt.

Rather more serious is the matter of *fitting* a towbar. For instance a major manufacturer like Witter lists brackets designed for many popular base vehicles including the Peugeot Boxer, Fiat Scudo and Mercedes Sprinter. However, these brackets are merely designed for an unmodified base vehicle. If in the process of the motorcaravan build-up there are additions introduced that extend beyond the original bumper, there is a chance the bracket will no longer be suitable. Equally there may be under-floor water tanks which obscure the critical points for its attachment, so before purchasing a bracket, it is essential to discuss the matter with the manufacturer of the motorcaravan.

It is much the same in respect of AL-KO Kober towing systems. The brackets are designed to bolt directly on to the AMC chassis, but if in the process of adding a motorcaravan body, key attachment points are obscured by panels, difficulties may arise.

Of course, there are always bespoke bracket designers, such as Watling Engineers, who are mentioned in Chapter Eleven concerning the Starcraft build-up. With older motorcaravans, purpose-made brackets could possibly be fabricated.

In some instances, a custom-made tow bracket can be specially designed by specialists like Watling Engineers.

As regards new models, the issue of the new *Type Approval Regulations* may create insurmountable difficulties. Time will tell.

Finally there is the issue of towing a small car for use on site. This practice is popular in the United States and it is also growing in Europe. Legal issues arise if the vehicle is merely pulled on an A-frame since it effectively becomes an unbraked trailer.

When carrying a car on a trailer, the position is clear and vehicle trailers are fitted with an over-run braking system as standard. However, trailing a car independently without a trailer, and by using what is known as an 'A frame' instead, doesn't avoid the requirement.

To achieve compliance, there are now coupling systems which bring the towed vehicle's own brakes into play. This meets the braking requirements, but there's still the need to ensure that the total weight of the car and the motorcaravan doing the towing, doesn't exceed the listed gross train weight.

Further advice on towing with an A-frame is available from Car-A-Tow, suppliers of the Easy Stow towing frame. As stated earlier, the matter of towing behind a motorcaravan is far from straightforward.

Tyres

Just as driving characteristics are dictated by chassis design and the suspension system, tyres play an important part, too.

Tyre pressures – which should be checked regularly – will be given in the base vehicle's handbook. However, recommendations for commercial loads may not always be appropriate for a motorcaravan, so a manufacturer is the first point of contact for confirmation about tyre pressures. Owners' clubs are often helpful as well.

Current practice is not to rotate tyres to equal out wear, although it's usually acceptable to switch a front tyre to the rear and vice versa *on the same side*. This ensures the tyre will rotate in the same direction throughout its life.

When laying-up a vehicle for an extended period, tyre side walls soon sustain damage. Periodically move the vehicle a short distance to ensure a different section of the side wall is distended during the lay-up. To lessen the likelihood of wall damage during storage, some manufacturers recommend that tyre pressures are increased by 0.3bar (5lb/sq inch) for the lay-up period. Bear in mind that vehicles used irregularly usually need new tyres on account of sidewall damage rather than the fact that the tread has worn.

Procedures for changing a wheel, jacking positions, and the tightening order for wheel fixings is specific to each vehicle. Consult your vehicle and motorcaravan handbooks.

Irregular tyre wear indicates there's a suspension or steering fault. Getting a specialist to readjust tracking on the front steering assembly often solves the problem on the front wheels.

Remember the legal requirements about tyres. Seek advice at a specialist if you are in any doubt.

By law, the maximum gross weight of an *unbraked* trailer must not exceed 750kg (10cwt). Where a trailer and its load exceeds this weight, it has to be fitted with brakes. Typically the braking requirement is achieved by an over-run arrangement. This means that if the trailer starts to run into the back of its towing vehicle, the coupling head, i.e. the 'hitch' head, will be depressed and a piston arrangement then activates a mechanical braking system on the trailer.

10
Contents

Motorcaravan accessories

There is a wide range of accessories available to motorcaravanners. Fire extinguishers, security products, cycle racks, awnings and many more are covered in this chapter – but the most important accessories are those concerned with safety and security.

Whereas many of the products in this chapter are optional additions, the provision of fire extinguishing equipment should be considered as crucial.

Fire precautions

The modern motorcaravan is built with safety in mind and new models are often supplied with a fire extinguisher, a smoke detector and a fire blanket. Older vehicles, however, may not be equipped with these items and it is strongly recommended to make the appropriate purchases.

Fires can develop in a number of areas and the chief task is to get all occupants out of the vehicle. Whether a fire can be extinguished depends on the situation, but having the right equipment can 'buy sufficient time' to make sure everyone is out of danger.

When purchasing safety equipment it should be recognised that there are different *types* of fire, depending on the materials involved. These are classified as follows:

Class A: Solid materials, especially those of organic origin (e.g. paper, wood, fabrics).
Class B: Liquids (e.g. oil, petrol, alcohol, fat).
Class C: Flammable gases (e.g. butane, propane, hydrogen).
Class D: Unusual substances including metals (e.g. aluminium, lithium).
Class E: Electrical products (e.g. burning mains cable).

Fire extinguishers

Recognising these differences, the approach for dealing with a fire will vary. Sometimes a bucket of water is sufficient to extinguish flames, but on a fat fire the effect can be devastating. Water is also entirely inappropriate where electrical components are alight; even a jet of foam directed at a mains supply cable can lead to electrocution. Manufacturers respond by producing a range of products which comply with European Norm 3 (BS 5423 prior to 1st January, 1997).

Previously the liquid, powder or gas in an extinguisher was identified by the colour of the container. Older products still exist and the colour designation was: red for water, cream for foam, black for carbon dioxide, blue for dry powder, and green for halon (which has since been withdrawn). But this has changed and new extinguishers are either red, or silver and red. A colour indicator verifies classification and a code confirms its intended use.

When considering different products for use in a motorcaravan, it has to be recognised that some are not appropriate for confined spaces. Accordingly a dry powder extinguisher is recommended as the best 'all-round' type because it will deal with wood, fabric, burning liquids and gases; in addition it can be used on an electrical fire.

A problem with older types of dry powder extinguisher was the fact that the contents could compact – so the casing would periodically need inverting and given a good shake. This has largely been overcome and the latest formulation is less likely to suffer from 'caking up'.

Buying and using tips include:

• Consider where the extinguisher is going to be located.
• Keep a constant reminder of the date on the casing – extinguishers have a 'shelf life'.
• Check the pressure gauge, where fitted. These are useful features.
• Be familiar with the way the extinguisher is withdrawn from its rack.
• Ensure you know how the trigger is released and activated.

112

There are many types of fire extinguisher — but only some are suitable for use in a motorcaravan.

An extinguisher should be easy to reach but not mounted too close to a stove.

A fire blanket is an essential item for dealing with fat or pan fires.

Needless to say, fire safety is a large subject and advice on procedures and precautions can be obtained from the caravan clubs. For further information, a fire prevention officer could also be consulted, and it is wise, when stopping at a Caravan and Camping Park, to familiarise yourself with the equipment provided. Fire is not a subject to be taken lightly.

Safety regulations

To comply with the Safety Regulations 1988, upholstery fillings in *trailer* caravans built since that date have 'combustion modified' foam in all cushions, mattresses and seat backs. Motorcaravans are not covered by these regulations as they are classified as motor vehicles, falling within different legislation, but fumes emitted from burning upholstery foams can cause severe respiratory problems, so it is wise to have the foam upgraded.

In a trailer caravan, all upholstery covers have to possess a resistance to cigarette or match ignition too, and new models carry a label verifying their integrity. A motorcaravan can be treated similarly; this resistance, however, will be lost after dry cleaning – re-treatment by a specialist is then needed.

Fire blankets

The method for dealing with a chip or frying pan fire is to smother it with a fire-retardant cloth to cut off the oxygen. In some instances you can achieve the same result using a metal tray.

Nevertheless, a 'fire blanket' is a worthy purchase. Products used to be covered by British Standard 6675, but this is now changed to EN 1869.

Smoke detectors

In theory these are useful warning devices but in the enclosed confines of a motorcaravan, they are easily activated – for instance when an elaborate breakfast is being prepared. The fact that many owners remove the battery is testimony to the problem but in reality the owner should check if this action would invalidate the insurance or warranty of the vehicle. The practicality of having one of these devices is partly dependent on the size of motorcaravan and the location of the unit.

Security products

Electronic alarms and tracking devices help protect a motorcaravan against theft and break-in. So too, do clamps and other locking devices.

Storage and parking protection

When comparing security systems, it is important to recognise the difference between alarming a vehicle parked in town, and one that is parked for an extended period in an unattended storage compound.

Whereas an electronic alarm may be fine for short-term parking, reliance on this type of device during a long term lay-up may be unwise. Operation is dependent on the battery being in sound condition and in an isolated venue, activated alarms sometimes pass unnoticed.

When considering wheel clamps, it should also be recognised that light products intended for use on a site are very different from the heavy duty models needed in an unattended storage compound.

Test Schemes

With so many security products on sale it can be quite difficult to ascertain the level of protection they offer. However, this problem has been partly overcome by the institution of independent test houses. For instance in Britain, the 'Sold Secure' initiative provides manufacturers with an opportunity to have a device checked by independent testers.

To pass the stringent 'Sold Secure' test, a product has to 'survive a concerted series of attacks for a minimum of five minutes.' On mechanical locks, the test employs techniques used by thieves together with 'picking tests' carried out by expert locksmiths. Levers, demolition tools and heavy equipment are employed. If five minutes seems short, this is more time than many thieves are willing to spend attacking a product. Different procedures are used for testing electronic alarms, although the tests are no less searching.

Sold Secure

A free copy of the document that lists all successful products passing the 'Sold Secure' tests can be requested by contacting the scheme's administration centre at Northumberland Police Headquarters. The address of Sold Secure is given in the Appendix.

The address of Sold Secure is given in the Appendix.

Woodwork tip

If a fire extinguisher or fire blanket is to be fitted to an item of furniture built from thin plywood, a piece of 9mm (⅜in) ply should be affixed on the reverse side of the mounting point. Alternatively on a wall lined with plywood the material is too thin, so add 9mm ply on its face. This reinforcing ply can be fixed using an impact adhesive like Evo-Stik and sufficient short screws to distribute the load liberally. When the extinguisher framework is then installed, the fixings benefit from a total thickness of 12mm (½in) of solid material.

One type of security device disables the pedals on a motorcaravan.

This sturdy PGR wheel clamp has passed the 'Sold Secure' testing procedures.

The Centinel Security post can secure a motorcaravan parked in a drive.

Without doubt the institution of destruction testing is a most helpful initiative. Even better is the fact that members of the public can find out which products pass the testing procedures.

Levelling devices

To achieve a level parking position, wheels may need elevating and motorcaravanners often carry short lengths of wood to achieve this.

The alternative is to buy purpose-made blocks and chocks. Portable plastic ramps from Fiamma are popular and a double width version is available to suit motorcaravans with twin wheels.

A more expensive model from Fiamma is the Level System ALU. This includes a chock to keep the wheel firmly on its slope. Serrated surfaces reduce slipping and Fiamma's ALU product is undoubtedly more suitable when motorcaravanning in wet or wintry weather.

Another product called the Flexator from AirMuscle Ltd employs an air lifting arrangement. Initially the motorcaravan is driven onto a Flexator which is then inflated with a foot pump – though pocket-sized, battery-driven compressors are also

Sectional link trackways help to control sinking on a muddy pitch.

available under the Jo-Jo range. A neat feature of the Flexator is the loop of rope attached to the unit. Experienced motorcaravanners will know that on muddy ground, a driven wheel sometimes ejects a lifting block with dangerous force. If this happens with a Flexator, the motorcaravan immediately drops to the ground, enclosing the rope and arresting the ejection of the device.

Elevating devices are undoubtedly part of the motorcaravanner's equipment. However, on muddy ground it should be recognised that sinkage can also induce a list on the vehicle. To avoid this, manufacturers like W4 Accessories market drive-on sectional link trackways. These are available from most dealers.

Awnings and roller blinds

When based on a site for several days, an awning offers more living space and also stakes a claim to a pitch when a motorcaravan is away from the site. Roll-out blinds cannot do this of course, though they are much speedier to set up.

Free-standing awnings designed for motorcaravanners have a zip-up 'fourth side' to provide total closure when the vehicle pulls away to leave the site. In consequence these structures are not unlike a frame tent – although a fitted valance enables the awning to be linked to the motorcaravan. The effectiveness of this valance to create a weatherproof junction varies because the body profile differs significantly from vehicle to vehicle.

A further problem for the awning designer is the variation in vehicle heights. Some awnings e.g. Apache, are therefore made in high and low versions. Height is something a buyer should check, together with the motorcaravan door which must clear the canvas when opened.

A further point is that van conversion awnings sometimes only fit one of the entrance points. The Eurovent Autovilla and the Marechal Autocamp are exceptions because they can either be erected

Ramps from Fiamma are a popular levelling accessory.

The Flexator is a device that uses inflation to achieve the right height.

alongside the sliding side door or at the double rear doors.

Coupling should be checked when choosing an awning. The coupling problems of a free-standing awning do not occur with roll-out blinds since these are permanently fixed to the vehicle. However, a blind cassette is often difficult to attach to a curved surface and whilst a range of brackets are available from specialists like Electrolux (Trimline Blind), Fiamma and Omnistor, flat-sided coachbuilt motorcaravans present the easiest mounting situation.

If a blind is preferred, remember that some models will accept side panels to provide a complete enclosure. Needless to say, these have to be detached prior to moving from a pitch.

Bear in mind, too, that a blind cassette should never project dangerously from the side of the motorcaravan. This projection problem is neatly solved by the designer of the 1998 Auto-Trail Arapaho motorcaravan because the entire cassette is mounted within a deep recess made in the side wall.

When comparing awnings, bear in mind the merits of different materials:

Poles

Steel tubing

Strength is the point in its favour; weight is its disadvantage. A good quality anodised finish is used on higher quality awnings whereas less expensive products soon start to rust if the coating material gets damaged.

Aluminium

This type of pole is light and resistant to corrosion, but aluminium tubing lacks the rigidity of steel poles.

A good valance between an awning and a motorcaravan is the key to achieving a weatherproof junction.

Glass fibre

This tubing is strong, light, and subject to neither rust nor oxidisation problems. Its disadvantage is its flexibility and a winter motorcaravanner watches vigilantly when it snows. The weight of snow can flex the poles and might even cause the structure to collapse.

Fabrics

Cotton

Though usually less expensive than a synthetic fabric, cotton has the advantage of 'breathability'. In consequence it doesn't suffer from the condensation problems associated with impervious synthetics. However, cotton is less tolerant of ill treatment. If packed damp and left for several

Awning marks

Try to avoid erecting an awning under trees, as some species are notorious for releasing sap. The roof of the awning can soon be covered with the sticky substance. If you have a problem removing sap, or similar unusual marks, special awning cleaners are available. An example is Camco Awning Cleaner which is specially formulated to remove sap, mould, mildew, and grime.

The Apache motorcaravan awning is available in two heights to suit different vehicles.

117

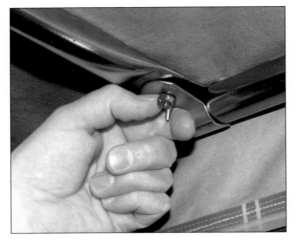

Sturdy anodised steel poles are a feature of the awning designed by Murvi Motorcaravans.

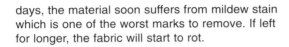

Many awnings have a protective plastic panel around the lower section of the side walls.

days, the material soon suffers from mildew stain which is one of the worst marks to remove. If left for longer, the fabric will start to rot.

Synthetic

There are many types of synthetic materials and some are as soft as cotton but more resistant to wear. Good synthetic fabrics are expensive and many types are not 'breathable' – so venting is essential to disperse condensation. Damp surfaces soon form on the inner surface of a non-breathable material, especially if the awning is used as an *al fresco* kitchen or as a drying area for wet clothes.

Mixed materials

In some products, the roof is a weather-resistant coated polyester, the main part of the wall is cotton and the lower section – approximately 30cm (12in) – is PVC. The PVC copes with splash-up damage in downpours and spray damage from canine leg-lifters!

Some roller blind awnings can have side sections attached to create a complete enclosure, as well as storm guys.

Adaptor plates are needed to enable a roller blind to be fitted to curved side panels.

Design Details

Awning accessories include:

• a pocket panel for storing holiday items,
• an inner tent which offers additional sleeping space,
• storm guys.

The benefit of having a ground sheet needs consideration, too. Traditional plastic sheets damage a grass pitch so there are special meshed carpets which are breathable. These can often be cut from a roll to meet specific requirements.

See for yourself

To evaluate an awning it is necessary to see it erected. Some dealers have permanent under-cover displays and Wellands at Crowborough near Peterborough has a particularly good 'see before you buy' service. Awning World at Chorley and Camping International at Gillingham are two other major suppliers with an indoor display facility.

Repairs and spares

Several specialist repairers advertise their services in motorcaravan magazines. There are also spare

Breathable matting for awnings is available cut to size.

Awning components are supplied by Blue Diamond Accessories.

Replacement poles are often sold at outdoor exhibitions.

parts specialists, whose goods are often displayed at open air rallies. The extensive range of items from Blue Diamond Products is a good example. Awnings are expensive but damaged items can often be replaced.

Roof racks

Awkward, but light items such as folding camp chairs can sometimes be conveniently transported on a roof rack. However, it is unwise to stow heavy equipment on a high-roofed vehicle since it can seriously upset its cornering capabilities. Low, fixed roof motorcaravans are

As long as they are light, bulky items can be stored on a roof rack.

the least affected by a roof rack load.

Unfortunately it has been fashionable recently to fit a semblance of a rack on many vehicles. These are cosmetic appendages rather than serviceable carriers. In many instances, tying points are missing and the roof cladding is exposed instead of being protected by load-bearing support rails running across the roof.

One approach is to have a rack tailor-made specifically for your motorcaravan. Some specialists design and build bespoke roof racks and reference is made to one such service in Chapter Eleven in the Starcraft case history.

Cycle and motorcycle racks

Heavily laden roof racks are not the only creators of instability on the road. A decision to carry a heavy load on the rear of a motorcaravan can also affect its road performance. It might also mean that the rear axle loading limit is exceeded – a fact that some owners seem to overlook when loading up items such as a heavy motorcycle. Additionally the method of attaching the rack to the vehicle needs careful consideration, too.

Many owners do want to take cycles or a motorscooter, so it is regrettable that so few manufacturers purposely construct a motorcycle carrying facility as an integral part of the chassis. Some Laika coachbuilt models feature a motorcycle rack and number plate/lighting board that can be slid out whenever needed. This is an

Roof racks and structure

When considering fitting a roof rack on a motorcaravan, remember that the structure of the vehicle must be sufficient to withstand three elements:
• The weight of the rack.
• The weight of the load the rack is carrying.
• The weight of a person standing on the rack when securing the load.
It should also provide suitable fixing points for securing the structure.

Slide out racks on some Laika motorcaravans are designed as part of the chassis.

A loaded cycle rack can impose a considerable strain on its mounting points.

excellent – though unusual – design feature. On most motorcaravans, racks are later additions, some of which are structurally safer than others.

Among the better examples are AL-KO Kober motorcycle racks. These are purpose-designed for installing on motorcaravans built on the AL-KO AMC chassis – a product discussed in Chapter Nine. The structure couples up with the AL-KO chassis itself and full integrity is thus achieved. The arrangement is very sound but unfortunately the product is quite expensive – not to mention the fact that many motorcaravans are built on a different chassis.

Although independent racks are available too, there are still a number of motorcaravans that need a purpose-made carrier. The product needs to be strong, light and fit for its purpose, so the idea of 'knocking-up' a DIY design is not a recommended option. It is better to seek the help of a specialist like the Hornchurch Motorcaravan Centre whose staff have made bespoke racks for many years. The designers are well aware of structural requirements in respect of the rack, together with the all-important attachment points on which the safe carriage of the load depends. Reference is

made to their work in Chapter Eleven with regard to the Starcraft motorcaravan.

Perhaps most problems occur with 'universal' racks, especially those intended to transport two or more cycles. Achieving secure fixings is the key requirement – on a bumpy road, the movement of cycles on a rack imposes considerable strain on the mountings.

Acknowledging this, Auto-Sleepers purposely bonds 12mm plywood strengthening sections into their GRP coachbuilt models, thereby providing a

When mounted on the doors of a van conversion, a rack sometimes imposes considerable stress on the steel panels.

Reinforcing panels are laminated in the bodywork on current coachbuilts from Auto-Sleepers to provide good fixing points.

120

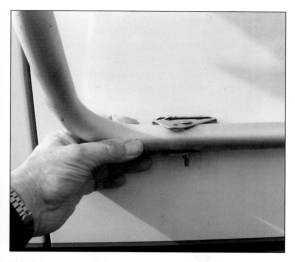

This fixing created unsatisfactory panel flexion when the cycle rack was fully laden.

Roof boxes can accommodate bulky items, but some types are not streamlined in shape.

sound mounting for racks like the Fiamma products. To guide an installer, Auto-Sleepers dealers have information sheets which show the precise location of these strengthening pads. Ply sections border the rear window and further reinforcing is bonded lower down on the rear panel as well.

However, it is on van conversions where problems are more acute. It is not normal for the metal panels on the rear doors to be given any reinforcement to absorb the stress imposed by a loaded rack and some fixings are notably weak. The metal door skin can flex badly when a rack is laden and the installation of a 'universal' rack is best entrusted to a skilled body specialist.

Notwithstanding these problems, difficulties are easily solved on a motorcaravan fitted with a bolt-on towball. Several bike racks are manufactured with a flange for installing behind the towball. The model from Witter is especially robust and includes an optional cranked bracket to ensure the supporting upright clears an obstruction e.g. a spare wheel. Bicycles can be carried on Witter's product when a trailer is coupled-up, as long as the noseweight limit is not exceeded. This product is shown in the opening illustration of this chapter.

Storage boxes

External storage containers are a popular way of increasing stowage space. Products from Omnistor and Fiamma are stocked by most dealers and several smaller suppliers are involved as well.

On American motorhomes these seldom place unreasonable loading on the base vehicle, but on smaller motorcaravans the owner should always be mindful of the vehicle's payload capacity. It is also important to emphasise that heavy loads should never be carried on the roof as the stability of a vehicle can be severely compromised when cornering.

In some cases the shape of roof boxes ignores

issues like fuel economy and the matter of aerodynamics seems to have been omitted from the designer's brief. Some motorcaravanners react by fitting the more streamlined designs intended for cars. This makes very good sense and the strategy is especially appropriate when planning to fit a roof box on a van conversion.

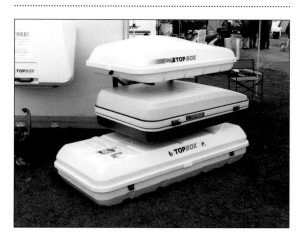

Streamlined roof boxes designed for cars are especially suitable for van conversion motorcaravans.

Rear storage boxes are a good alternative because they keep the weight lower down.

Whatever type of box is fitted, it is essential that its fixing points are sound. Equally, the motorcaravan manufacturer should be consulted for confirmation of what weights can be carried on the roof. This also raises the issue of access; to load some boxes it is necessary to climb on to the roof itself. If this is unacceptable, some storage boxes have forward-hinged and side-hinged lids which may provide alternative access – perhaps from a fixed ladder.

Without doubt, the business of fitting and gaining access to a roof box can be a problem and installing a rear-mounted storage box might be a better strategy. Rather surprisingly, storage boxes fitted on the back of motorcaravans are less popular in this country than abroad. However, their low position commends them both in terms of access as well as their influence on the vehicle's driving performance. Models bearing the Bak-Paka name are one example and these are often displayed at motorcaravan outdoor exhibitions; manufacturer details are given in the address list.

TV equipment

A concession to home comfort is to take a TV set on holiday. Sometimes a portable set can achieve a good picture using its own aerial, but the metal structure of most motorcaravans usually necessitates fitting an aerial outside.

Three items are needed in the set-up:

- Aerial
- Coupling
- Signal controller.

Aerial

Whilst its appearance is not particularly attractive, a directional aerial provides the best reception. Once on site, this has to be erected and then correctly orientated. With its labyrinth of metal elements, this type of aerial could not be mounted permanently on the roof of a road-going vehicle.

Accordingly an omni-directional aerial is preferred by motorcaravanners, even if signal gain is less effective. Most current products have the elements discreetly enclosed within a plastic casing and many motorcaravans have the

resulting 'flying saucer' designs permanently affixed to the roof. An adjustable mounting plate enables these products to be mounted on either a level or a mildly sloping roof. Alternatively, removable versions are available with temporary attachment achieved by suction pads.

Coupling

Whereas the coaxial cable from an aerial is usually routed through a prepared, weather-proof hole in the roof, some motorcaravanners prefer fitting a removable aerial. In this instance, the problem is finding a way to couple up the coaxial cable outside with the system installed on the inside.

Draping a coaxial lead through a window is not a tidy arrangement and the designers of Murvi motorcaravans sensibly resolved this by looking at components used in the marine industry – especially for cabin cruisers. The weather-proof coupling used on the Murvi Morello, for example, is a component supplied by Index Marine.

Signal controllers

Recognising that the quality of picture depends on the proximity to a television transmission station, most manufacturers of motorcaravan aerials also

The omni-directional aerial can usually be adjusted for mounting on a sloping surface.

A special control box can either amplify or reduce the strength of a TV signal.

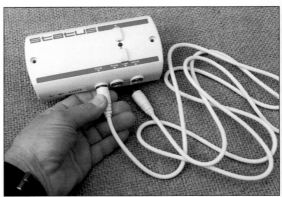

Directional aerials achieve better reception but have to be removed before driving away from the pitch.

The cable coupling fitted by Murvi is a weather-resistant model used in the marine industry.

All the necessary components for enjoying satellite TV can be purchased for use in a motorcaravan.

Reception advice

The subject of TV reception, aerials and transmission stations is complex. So, too, is the subject of mobile satellite equipment. However, the manufacturers of equipment are very helpful and sometimes they publish user-guides. In particular, a free booklet from Maxview entitled *TV on the move* is especially helpful. This is available direct from the company.

include signal control boxes. Using a battery-powered amplifier, a weak signal can thus be improved. Conversely you can be too near to a station – as occurs at the Caravan Club Site in South London which is situated directly below the TV transmission mast at Crystal Palace. In this instance the signal is too strong and most control boxes include an attenuation control that will reduce its strength.

Satellite TV

Larger motorcaravans can also be fitted with satellite dishes and several specialists supply tilting dishes, decoders and mounting poles. Typically the pole is mounted inside the motorcaravan with an interior control for adjusting the angle elevation of the dish. Some models even include a folding-down facility so the dish can be left installed on the roof but parked horizontally prior to taking to the road.

As a rule, these products are better suited to coachbuilt motorcaravans where the installation is easier and they are often fitted on American motorhomes where finding a mounting point on the roof seldom presents a problem. Further guidance on satellite TV in motorcaravans can be obtained from specialists like Grade UK, Maxview, Peter Miller Leisure and R. T. Marshall.

Blinds and flyscreens

More expensive motorcaravans are fitted with cassette sun blinds and flyscreens as a standard item. The silvered blind helps control interior temperatures on sunny days and most owners use the unit at night instead of pulling curtains since instant screening is achieved quickly and effectively.

Flyscreens are essential items for anyone spending the summer in places like the Lake District or the Western Highlands of Scotland. When midges start to swarm they can immediately turn pleasant moments into a disagreeable disaster. Even in hot conditions abroad a screen is useful since it allows you to sleep with curtains drawn, windows open and a protective mesh to keep insects at bay.

To be successful, flyscreen protection is needed on windows, roof lights and the entrance door. All-round cover is assured by housing the edges of the blind within the grooves of a cassette frame. Partial protection is pointless.

On large coachbuilts, A-class models and American motorhomes there is also a double door arrangement. A subsidiary inner frame fabricated in aluminium channel contains a mesh and this can be clipped to open in unison with the door or operated as a separate unit.

As regards window provision, blinds manufactured by Remis and Seitz are fitted in many of the more costly motorcaravans as standard items. However, they can also be fitted at a later date and products by Remis are especially appropriate for the DIY installer.

Products vary, of course, and at the 'budget end' of the market the cassette units have sun blinds and flyscreens which operate independently. More expensive units permit similar independence but by mounting one roller within the top rail and the second in the bottom part of the cassette, the manufacturer provides an opportunity to permit scrolling. This is where the blind from above and the mesh from below are clipped together, thus creating a double-sliding unit. It means you can have part mesh, part blind, according to the needs of a particular situation.

Another innovation is the introduction of double concertina blinds which absorb UV radiation more efficiently and where an aluminium laminated polyester surface provides a high level of insulation.

Scrolling on this Remis cassette includes an insulated concertina blind.

123

Fitting a Remis door screen

The lowest section of the frame is fitted first.

Aluminium sections are supplied separately and have to be assembled.

A peg on the moving cassette has to be located in a groove.

A nylon fringe on the main upright ensures an effective seal is achieved.

By mounting the roller in the closing rail, little space is needed around the door opening.

Once fitted, the Remis flyscreen gives excellent protection at the main entrance.

Blind retraction springs

If left in the lowered position for many months, a blind roller's retracting spring is kept permanently under tension. This has the effect of weakening it. Although the reason for leaving blinds lowered is to prevent sunlight from fading interior fabrics, it is helpful if blinds are raised for several days during an extended lay-up period. This relaxes the recoil spring.

If the spring gets tired and fails to lift a blind or a screen, it is usually possible to tighten the recoil mechanism. Look for tension adjustment points on either side of the frame and be prepared to remove the cassette from the wall to gain better access to them. Procedures for carrying out re-tensioning are often described in Owners' Manuals.

Bear in mind that insulation here means excessive heat can be kept out in summer and interior heat is more effectively retained in the winter.

Fitting guidance

To fit a cassette window unit, it is necessary to have sufficient free space around the opening in order to mount the frame. The surface should also be flat and window catches must not project into the motorcaravan in a way that would foul the action of the blind.

Sometimes this last problem can be overcome by mounting a prepared sub-frame of wood around the window aperture. Fitting the cassette to the raised base instead of the wall gives greater clearance when a blind is pulled down. It then clears any projecting window catches without difficulty.

Usually the four sections of a cassette have to be assembled to form a frame and you need to check carefully to ensure the construction is square. Any inaccuracy here will hinder the operation of the blind.

Like the window units, a Remis door screen is also easy to fit – provided there's a 15mm (⅝in) clearance on either side of the opening on which to mount the frame's main uprights. Compared to other door screens this is a very small dimension; and it is achieved because the cassette holding the rolled blind is moved across the opening when the screen is pulled. On other products the cassette is fixed permanently to a side frame, thereby requiring greater mounting space.

Other requirements relate to the door dimension – Remis frames are 1.8m high to suit a standard coachbuilt door and where the opening is 650mm wide. When installing the unit, a trackway is screwed to the floor. This houses the lower part of the screen and a frilled fringe ensures midges cannot creep around the sides of the mesh.

Overall the Seitz and Remis products are well constructed and as long as there is clearance around windows and doors, they are fairly easy to fit.

Air conditioning

Whilst a motorised fan can be helpful on a sunny day, an air-conditioning system brings particular benefits to the traveller in hot regions.

There are two types of air conditioners:

• Water evaporative units
• Refrigeration units.

Water evaporative units

To appreciate the principle behind a water evaporative system, it helps to try a simple experiment. On a hot day take a clean handkerchief, soak it in cold water, put a single layer of damp fabric over your mouth and breathe deeply. It is immediately apparent that the air being inhaled is cooled and this phenomenon continues until the handkerchief is dry.

Water evaporative systems like the roof-mounted Trav L Cool, distributed in the United Kingdom by CAK, adopt this principle, albeit in a much more sophisticated manner. Their advantage is their light weight imposing a load on the roof of only 8kg (around 17.5lb).

Whereas a water evaporative system may not lower temperatures as remarkably as a refrigeration device, Trav L Cool products are well respected. They are fitted as standard, for example, on some Hymer motorcaravans. As part of the installation, water supply tubing has to be connected to the

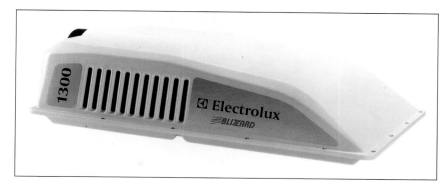

unit's filter from a compact water reservoir – normally discreetly fitted in a locker or wardrobe base.

A double-acting slow-running diaphragm pump circulates the cold water, some of which evaporates in the air cooling process. In temperatures around 30°C, water consumption is half a litre an hour and the 20 litre water reservoir keeps the Trav-L-Cool operating for around forty hours between top-ups.

Advantages of the product include:

• the unit can be mounted over a standard-sized roof ventilator aperture,
• a special cover vent on the outer casing acts as a warm air extractor while the motorcaravan is on the road,
• the product operates from a 12v supply.

Refrigeration units

Electrolux air conditioners are well-known and recently the range has been extended to embrace Blizzard models as well. Not surprisingly, a refrigerating unit is heavier than a water evaporative product and the smallest Blizzard 1300 model has a listed weight of 28kg (61.6lb). In consequence, the construction of a motorcaravan roof is a critical feature to check before installing this type of air conditioner.

The benefit of a refrigeration system is that it not only dramatically lowers temperature inside a motorcaravan but it reduces humidity, too. As regards installation, the interior height of the living area is hardly reduced because the interior control panel lies flat to the ceiling. Equally on the 1000 and 1300 models, this part of the product measures 340mm x 340mm – permitting it to occupy space usually taken by a normal roof vent.

Unlike the water evaporative product, the Blizzard units need a 230v 50Hz power supply and some motorcaravanners carry a generator, to overcome the limitation otherwise imposed when not stopping on a site with mains hook-ups.

Without doubt, Blizzard performance figures are impressive. All models can retain a temperature differential between the inside and outside air of 20°C (68°F).

For the present, models from Electrolux are the best-known in Britain. However, Carver has recently announced the forthcoming launch of the

Climatic – a 230v mains-powered system initially designed for internal installation. The unit could be installed in a cabinet or locker, and its variable blower can distribute cooled air via an existing blown air ducting system.

The appliance's light weight (19kg) is a feature of particular interest, coupled with the fact that the product can be installed either vertically or horizontally to provide scope when space is at a premium. More information on the Climatic is awaited with eager anticipation.

Oil-fired heating

Whereas air-conditioning is an asset in the heat of summer, winter motorcaravanners need the reverse – a good space heating system. Without doubt, there are many efficient gas appliances but recent development work has shown there is an alternative form of heating. Its fuel is either petrol or oil, depending on the engine in the base vehicle.

The Eberspächer heating system has been used for a number of years in the marine industry but

The Hydronic heater from Eberspracher involves a simple connection system.

Oil-fired heating hydronic 12V system

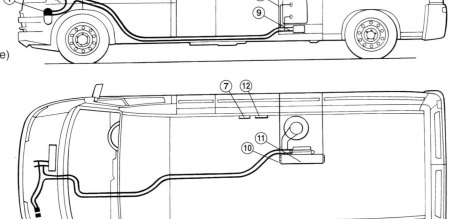

SCOPE OF SUPPLY

1. Hydronic 12v heater
2. 20mm internal diameter (I/D water hose)
3. 20 x 20 x 20mm T piece
4. 20mm I/D water hose
5. Fan matrix thermostat
6. 2 gallon calorifier
7. 1 bar. pressure relief valve
8. 15mm I/D water hose
9. 2kw Fan matrix unit
10. Open and closable outlet
11. Air diverter
12. Optional timer

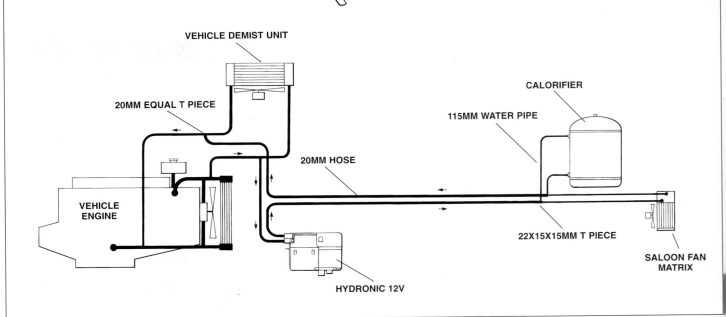

after recent work, a version is now available for motorcaravan applications. Murvi announced the product in 1997 as an optional extra on their award winning Morello. Around this time Island Plastics also started fitting one of these units in the Romahome Duo.

As an alternative to a gas system, this is a competitive product on account of its frugal consumption. A number of systems have been professionally installed and DIY fitters have also found the work is within the scope of an experienced practitioner. In upgrading work, it has also been noted that when it comes to warm air distribution, ducting previously installed for a gas warm air system can be re-commissioned.

Early reports have affirmed the economy of the system – a consumption of half a litre of fuel per hour or less when operating on full boost power is not unusual.

Most users fit a D4W Hydronic unit which uses diesel fuel but the B3W Hydronic version is also available for petrol engined vehicles. Either way, the remarkably small heater is fitted in the engine

compartment and its 230 x 160 x 86mm (9 x 6½ x 3½in) outside dimensions mean that it takes up little space.

The accompanying diagram shows a typical installation layout which offers the following advantages:

• Fuel for the unit is taken directly from the vehicle's fuel tank,
• A fan unit is fitted in the living compartment for warm air distribution,
• Three heat levels are available – 4.0kw boost, 3.3kw high and 1.6kw low,
• A 10 litre hot water storage unit is fitted,
• The specification includes a thermostatic hot/cold water mixer valve,
• The engine pre-heat feature facilitates engine starting,
• Power consumption is 3.0 amps on high setting, 2.2 amps on low setting.

Arguably it is too early to compare the merits of this alternative heating system against more familiar gas systems. However, it would appear to offer a number of benefits and when the diminutive size of the unit tucked away in the engine is appreciated, the space-saving advantages are immediately apparent.

Toilet provision

Virtually all motorcaravans are equipped with a toilet – which is usually an Elsan or Thetford product. In small motorcaravans there may only be space for a portable unit. However, the advent of swivel-bowl versions that use the cassette principle affords more installation opportunities when space is tight.

DIY installation

The installation of a cassette toilet is a worthy upgrade. Thetford's products are supplied with clear fitting instructions and many owners have tackled the job successfully themselves.

When contemplating this upgrade it should be

Fitting a Thetford Cassette toilet

This is a job that some experienced DIY enthusiasts will want to tackle themselves.

Sometimes it is necessary to cut and modify a shower tray as a preliminary task.

Thetford provide inner and outer templates so the cutting point can be accurately marked.

4 If cutting an aperture with a jigsaw, use plastic tape to protect the paint on the outer skin.

5 The cut-out should be treated with care because it is later inserted into the door frame.

6 Having removed insulation around the aperture, strips of wood are eased into the void.

7 A ribbon mastic sealant is recommended for weatherproofing the door frame.

8 The frame is screwed into place using stainless steel fixings.

9 Finally the cassette is slid into place, ensuring there are no obstructions.

recognised that there are different models in both standard and swivel-bowl ranges. Alternative water flushing arrangements are available and it is also important to recognise that there are both right- and left-handed versions. In other words the opening door for accessing the cassette is situated either on one side or the other.

Installation limitations sometimes arise when exterior body panels on a motorcaravan bear a curved profile. The access door supplied with a cassette toilet is intended for mounting on a flat surface – as found on most coachbuilts. Substantial modifications have to be made if this is unavailable.

Using the paper cutting templates provided, it is surprisingly easy to incise the aluminium skin

To maintain efficient blade operation, the rubber seal should be periodically cleaned with Thetford Bathroom Cleaner.

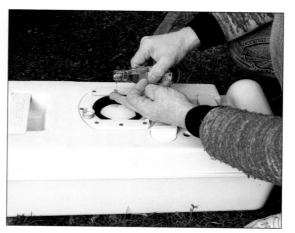

When completely dry, the seal and blade should be coated with a film of olive oil.

on a coachbuilt using a woodworking cutting knife and a steel rule. The blade is ruined, of course, but the resulting clean cut is neat – bearing in mind that the cut-out section is needed for re-mounting later within the plastic frame of the cassette access door. Alternatively an electric jigsaw fitted with a metal (or GRP) blade can be used. It has to be set to a slow speed and the body needs masking with adhesive tape to prevent the base plate of the jigsaw damaging the paintwork.

When the frame of the access door is ready for mounting, a bedding strip of mastic sealant ensures the installation is weatherproof.

To summarise, if there is space for a cassette toilet, the installation sheets certainly explain clearly the work involved. The job can be completed in a day although a DIY installation might take a weekend.

Maintenance

Motorcaravan toilets are notably robust although it is important to drain down the flushing reservoir prior to the onset of frost. Periodic cleaning is also a normal housekeeping matter and Thetford Bathroom Cleaner is an easy-to-apply combined cleaner and sanitising foam.

An important maintenance job is to lubricate the rubber seal as follows:

1. Remove the cassette.
2. Clean the rubber seal using Thetford's Bathroom Cleaner.
3. A diluted solution of warm water and washing-up fluid is an alternative approved by Thetford.
4. Work the foam into the grooves of the seal and then rinse with water.
5. Avoid using household cleaners which can damage the seal.
6. Dry the seal thoroughly.
7. Treat the seal and blade with a silicone spray or apply olive oil.

Other types of vegetable oil can damage the valve and must not be used.

The flushing water reservoir should be emptied.

All flushing water is emptied via the drain-down pipe.

Contents

Self-build projects – case histories

Although there are many fine motorcaravans on the market, a number of spirited enthusiasts prefer to build their own. The challenge proves irresistible and the reward and feeling of accomplishment on completing a major project is certainly hard to measure.

Building a motorcaravan falls within the category of achievable, though difficult, projects. There are self-built vehicles which prove beyond all doubt that some 'amateurs' are as accomplished as 'professional' builders – but alongside the personal triumphs are also the half-finished enterprises that have fallen by the wayside.

There are also examples of self-build 'motorcaravans' whose design is not exactly endearing. Converted buses or elderly ambulances are not particularly attractive. Trailer caravans bereft of wheels and mounted on the rear of a flat bed lorry similarly lack the finesse associated with the traditional image of the motorcaravan. The external appearance of a finished project is no less important than the comfort inside.

It should also be recognised that owners of these kinds of vehicles may be refused access to some sites or may have their application for membership of a club refused. These decisions are the prerogative of the site operator or club officials, whose opinion of the suitability of the vehicle may differ from that of the owner.

Without doubt, building your own motorcaravan is not an easy option; on the contrary a wide range of skills are required and it would be wrong to imagine that anyone could do all the work alone. Using expert help where necessary is strongly advised.

In this chapter, a number of practical elements are described in detail; however, the content is not aimed exclusively at readers who want to build from scratch. Owners of professionally built motorcaravans, who feel an adaptation is needed, will also benefit from the features covered here.

Different approaches

There are many levels of DIY involvement and this is partly demonstrated in the following case

histories. Perhaps the easiest approach is to work in conjunction with converters like Autocraft Motorcaravans, Nu Venture Motorhomes or Youngs, so that the project is shared. These specialists will undertake some – or all – of the work, building up a motorcaravan to customer specification on either a new or second-hand base vehicle. Help with renovation can also be discussed with some of the smaller manufacturers.

This underlines an important precept. The wise DIY builders are the ones who don't try to do it *all* themselves. It is far better during the planning stage to reflect critically on your particular strengths and weaknesses and decide which jobs need professional assistance.

If you feel you have a wide range of skills, building a motorcaravan to suit your particular requirements is certainly satisfying, but it is strongly advised that you should *not* attempt to connect up a gas supply system unless you are a qualified gas engineer – this could be a recipe for disaster. Help needed from qualified professionals might also extend to electrical installations and work concerned with safety-critical components like brake assemblies, steering components, and suspension units.

Trying to make up your own upholstery is another DIY task that can fail rather badly. Professional manufacturers commission outside specialists to make cushions and seats (this was discussed in Chapter Eight). If you are not an experienced upholsterer with access to industrial machines, it is best to limit yourself to making loose covers and curtains.

Having acknowledged the need to call for help when necessary, the next step is to compare the different types of self-build projects. Undoubtedly the easiest route is to convert a panel van. A more difficult challenge is to build an entire motorcaravan from a kit – but be warned; the word 'kit' is imprecise and the case history of the Starcraft

130

Former trailer caravans mounted behind a commercial vehicle seldom make an attractive conversion.

reported later emphasises this in no uncertain terms.

Even harder than kit projects are the motorcaravans which are self-designed and self-built from scratch. Some remarkable achievements are reported now and again, but the enormity of an undertaking like this falls beyond the scope of most people. Projects of this kind also fall beyond the scope of this manual.

Requirements

Patience, resourcefulness, space, time, money, knowledge and total determination are all pre-requisites. Skill in a number of practical areas is also necessary although it has already been emphasised that you can always 'buy-in' skilled help where necessary.

Encouraged by this, would-be builders often enquire if there are any working drawings available. Similarly, magazine readers often ask

if there's a book giving step-by-step guidance on building a motorcaravan. Needless to say, there isn't because the whole purpose of a DIY approach is to build an individual vehicle to suit individual requirements – if someone needs a step-by-step approach it probably indicates they lack the resourcefulness and general ability to complete the job in the first place.

Obviously a great deal of guidance is given in this manual, and this provides the reader intending to build his or her own motorcaravan with a fund of important information; however, the application of this knowledge ultimately has to be left to the constructor.

From the outset, it is important not to have any misapprehensions about a self-build enterprise. There are both advantages and disadvantages in this approach to ownership:

Advantages

• The final project reflects an individual's precise needs.
• The builder's flair and design skills are demonstrated.
• Details like layout can be planned from the outset.
• Decoration can reflect individual taste.
• Cost can be controlled at every stage of the build-up.
• Additions can be made at a later date if extra funds become available.
• There is great satisfaction in completing a project of this magnitude.

Disadvantages

• Sourcing components can be difficult.
• Some products, e.g. decorative 3mm ply, are not available from DIY outlets.
• Selling a DIY motorcaravan often presents problems.
• Safety elements like installing sufficient ventilation are often overlooked.

Elderly ambulances have often been converted into motorcaravans.

The less involved DIY project is to fit out a panel van.

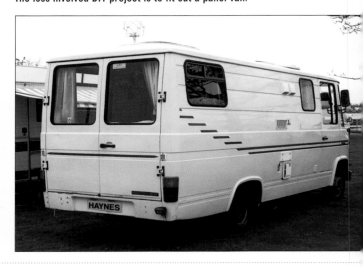

- Gross Laden Weight of the finished vehicle can all-too-easily be exceeded.
- Insuring a DIY vehicle is not always straightforward.
- New legislation is almost certain to impinge on the freedom enjoyed by self-builders.
- Access to sites and user clubs might be restricted.
- Radically altered vehicles will be subjected to new test procedures (SVA).

Administrative requirements

While a vehicle remains a van, it should be insured as such. Subsequently you need to consult an insurer about the position during and after the conversion. For example, installed equipment could be worth a large sum of money and it is important that this is covered. There may be the need to provide an Engineer's Report too, before the insurance company will extend the terms.

Equally it is a legal requirement that the Driver and Vehicle Licensing Agency (DVLA) at Swansea is informed of changes in the information recorded in section D of form V5, the Vehicle Registration Document. Changes including model/type information, engine number and even body colour have to be recorded in Section E and submitted to the Agency. From 24th March, 1997 a new registration document was phased in and form V100 (available from the Post Office) provides information on vehicle registration.

Customs and Excise used to be involved, too, because Value-Added Tax (VAT) payments had to be made on DIY motorcaravan conversions. This is no longer the case, however, because VAT is now paid on Light Commercial Vehicles at the time of the original purchase.

It is also important to be aware of the new Single Vehicle Approval (SVA) regulations which are about to affect the kit car industry. Without doubt, major motorcaravan projects – like the Starcraft and the Rancher which are covered later – will almost certainly fall within the scope of this new legislation.

The SVA system has often been described as a boosted MoT test designed for 'one-off' automotive projects. Many see it as a concession, appropriately applied in the UK whose long-standing kit car industry is unique in Europe. Strict regulations have prevented enthusiasts in other countries from embarking on projects where the resulting car, three wheeler or motorcaravan is intended for use on public roads.

Type Approval Regulations are strictly applied across Europe, but in recognition that some amateur-built projects are of a very high standard, the SVA development ensures that opportunities in this field are not brought to an abrupt halt. Details about the publication, *A Guide to Kitcars and the SVA,* are given in the Appendix address list.

Finding insurers

Whilst difficulties are often reported about insuring self-build motorcaravans, a number of specialists can often help. For instance, The Motorcaravan Insurance Agency Ltd (MIA), has offered quotations for a number of years.

Insurance Brokers who specialise in kit car schemes are usually helpful too. Adrian Flux is mentioned in the Renault Trafic case history later. Similarly, Secure Direct Insurance is mentioned in respect of the Starcraft. Other specialists advertising in kit car magazines might also be able to help.

Weight watching

One of the most important matters when preparing to commence a self-build project has nothing to do with the proposed layout. Nor for that matter is it linked to the number of beds, the choice of finish or cost calculation. The issue that should precede all these is *weight*.

Far too many self-builders proceed with constructional work, completely oblivious of the base vehicle's capacities in terms of:

- Maximum technically permissible laden mass
- Mass in running order
- Maximum user payload
- Maximum axle weights.

These terms were explained in Chapter Two and the accompanying technical tip box should be noted.

It is essential to build items like furniture and storage systems as light as possible without compromising their fitness for purpose. Ultimately, the lighter the construction, the greater the margin left for the addition of personal effects.

Sources of help

A key source of guidance about conversion work has been the NCC/SMMT Code of Practice 201: *Habitation Requirements Relating to Health & Safety for Motorcaravans.* This was published in September 1992 and it provided the definitive mechanism for deciding whether a professionally built motorcaravan could be awarded an NCC/SMMT badge. However, with effect from October 23rd, 1998, Code of Practice 201 is being replaced by a European standard and motorcaravans meeting the necessary criteria will have EN 1646 indicated on the badge.

It is obviously desirable that an amateur builder should equally observe the specifications contained in the documentation relating to BS EN 1646-1. Typical matters contained within these Habitation Standards include the strength, stability and slip-resistance of entrance steps. Bunk beds are important too, and they are required to have minimum headroom clearance, adequate mechanical strength, protection to prevent occupants from falling out, a means of safe access and so on. Further guidance on habitation standards

133

Products used in the industry, like pre-formed bathroom units, are not easily found.

Of course, some manufacturers are not so keen to supply do-it-yourselfers, so it is useful to contact specialists who buy-up 'job lots' of obsolete items – some of whom display their stock at open-air rallies. Suppliers like Magnum Mobiles and Caravan Surplus are especially well-stocked. Sinks, cookers, bathroom units, external locker doors and vehicle lamp assemblies are just a few examples from Magnum's stock-in-trade. Euro Motor Campers also publishes a detailed catalogue of accessories, and operates a supply-and-fit high-top service.

Another supplier of motorcaravan products is Caravan Accessories Kenilworth (CAK). They specialise in water products, and have huge numbers of shaped on-board tanks in stock. Hobs, cooker hoods, sink units, heaters and many other items are also listed in their catalogue. Equally their display at the National Boat, Caravan and Leisure Show, held annually at the National Exhibition Centre, demonstrates the scope of their service.

The catalogue from Autocraft Motor Caravans is equally useful. In addition to cookers, refrigerators and water tanks, there are useful – and rather unusual – layflat bedsets. In addition, toughened glass window units and a range of high-top fibre glass roofs are worth noting, too. Finally, if you want to line part of the interior with a plain-ribbed carpet as used in the industry, Autocraft can send samples in many colours.

is contained in literature published by the National Caravan Council.

Another helpful publication which is solely addressed to the amateur builder is the *Private Conversions Manual*, a 32-page guide available to members of The Motor Caravanners' Club. Equally a two-page guide, *DIY Conversion of a Motorcaravan* is available if a stamped addressed envelope is sent to the editorial office of the magazine, *Motorcaravan Motorhome Monthly*. Both of these publications are directly applicable to the task in question.

Components

Some products used in the motorcaravan industry are not always easy for the public to purchase. Items like 3mm decorative plywood, moulded plastic bathroom units and pre-made doors are very specific for this industry.

Occasionally you can buy these products by placing an order with the after-sales departments of caravan and motorcaravan manufacturers. Quantities of 3mm faced ply and hollow interior furniture doors from obsolete ranges can often be purchased in this way.

As regards fittings like hinges, catches, door pulls and drawer sliders, these are often sold at motorcaravan dealers' accessory shops – but they can be expensive and when you add up all the fittings needed for lockers, drawers and cupboards, the price may come as a surprise.

Some items suitable for use in a motorcaravan are available from DIY superstores; but check products with care – many items are only suitable for domestic use at home.

With this in mind, one of the best contacts is Woodfit, a long-established company whose mail order catalogue has been published for many years. In addition to Woodfit's prodigious array of small hardware items are the larger accessories like wire drawers, for use as blanket boxes or for vegetable storage. Retractable waste bins, roller runners, under-shelf bread boxes and revolving carousel storage systems are available too.

Several accessories from Woodfit were used in the Starcraft project, discussed later in the chapter, and many of the items in the catalogue are not available elsewhere.

General construction

Irrespective of the type of motorcaravan being built several procedures are universally followed.

Insulation

The installation of an insulating material is essential. This should have both thermal and acoustic properties. Reverberation, especially in a

A wide range of components are supplied by CAK, particularly water systems.

Self-build projects – case histories

panel van, is a problem so the amateur should follow the meticulous approach adopted by professional builders.

Glass fibre quilt should be placed over all external surfaces and tucked into recesses. Whether you install the flexible quilt used in the building industry for insulating a loft, or the more rigid glass fibre 'batts' used in brickwork cavities, is a matter of personal preference. Alternatively, 25mm polystyrene sheets such as Jablite can be used, especially on the flatter surfaces of a coachbuilt construction. The only warning is that loose polystyrene sections can move and create squeaky noises when chafing occurs against frame members, so polystyrene has to be firmly located.

If a floor is needed, sandwich construction products are available where the foam insulant is bonded to plywood. Specialists like Sheffield Insulations, whose depots are listed in the *Yellow Pages*, supplied composite material of this type for the Starcraft floor.

Sub-frame construction

A panel van has metal strengthening struts on the inside whereas a GRP shell is usually supplied with only a minimum of reinforcing struts. In both instances it is usually necessary to fix wooden battens to the inside of the shell. These provide essential fixing points for the ply panels that have to be added later and also add strength in the case of a GRP construction.

Attaching them to the metal surfaces in a

Struts and battens can be fitted into a GRP body shell using Isopon P40; paste the size of a golf ball needs three blobs of hardener the size of a garden pea to activate the chemical process.

panel van used to pose problems but modern gun-applied epoxy-based adhesives now provide remarkable adhesion. Once again there are products used in the building industry that fulfil this requirement: UniBond No More Nails, Evo-Stik Nail Free Fixing, and Everflex Gun A Nail Adhesive are examples. These are sold in cartridge form and a wire dispenser gun is needed to apply the adhesive.

Fixing timber reinforcing inside a moulded GRP shell is usually done with a polyester resin. For instance if a window opening needs strengthening, thick plywood is usually 'glassed' into the moulding. In other words, the same type of polyester resin used in the original GRP shell is mixed with a catalyst and applied around the

Professional installers like Auto-Sleepers are meticulous when fitting insulation in their conversions.

Self-build projects – case histories

• Polyester products are flammable and can damage human tissue.
• Catalysts (hardeners) can cause serious injury when coming into contact with human tissue, especially the eyes.
ALL SAFETY ADVICE IN PRODUCT INSTRUCTIONS SHOULD BE FOLLOWED.

opening. The ply is then offered up, temporarily clamped in place, coated with resin and finally covered with resin-impregnated strips of chopped strand glass mat. This lamination process integrates the ply into the structure and provides a sound fixing for the later addition of a window frame.

In some instances, however, it is easier to use a polyester paste which has been pre-mixed with a mulch of chopped glass strands. Two popular examples, used in car repair work, are Isopon P40 and U-Pol B. Sold in car accessory stores, these products are prepared on a scrap of plywood by mixing in a catalyst paste or hardener. Setting times depend on air temperature but as a guide, a blob of paste the size of a golf ball will require three blobs of hardener the size of garden peas.

The two items should be mixed thoroughly on a board (a decorator's knife is useful), then applied liberally to the strengthening wood which should then be positioned on the GRP panel. The wood will have to be wedged in position while the paste is setting; but once it starts to 'cure' it hardens rapidly and decisively. Depending on temperature and the amount of catalyst used, this only takes from 5–10 minutes. In low temperatures, more hardener may be needed to achieve this setting time.

Forming holes in panel vans

Where it is necessary to form anything from a large aperture (e.g. for a window) or a small hole (e.g. for some waste water pipe), it is essential that the structural integrity of a panel van is not compromised. In some instances professional advice should be sought.

It is also important to recognise the importance of treating any bare metal edges that become exposed when holes are formed. Professional manufacturers are especially thorough in this respect and the self-builder should be no less scrupulous in his or her approach.

Similarly, rubber grommets and protective collars are needed to shield sharp edges. This protection is especially important when electric cabling is being routed through openings.

Cut edges in a van conversion must be treated with a rust inhibitor.

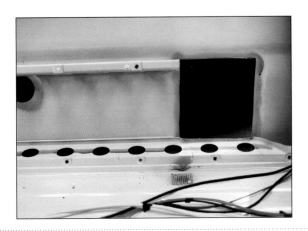

A number of specialists can supply and fit a high-top to a customer's van.

Fitting a high-top

It is not wise for an inexperienced person to indiscriminately cut away the roof of a van and replace it with a glass reinforced plastic (GRP) high-top. This can have structural implications and advice should be sought if headroom needs to be increased. A number of specialists will supply a moulded high-top, many of whom offer a fitting service as well. Rising roof structures can also be fitted by specialists such as AER Developments.

The job doesn't take long to carry out but it might still be wise to enlist professional help.

Case histories

Completely dissimilar case histories are presented in the remaining part of this chapter. A major renovation of a popular Type 2 VW is featured. All the VW Types are currently very popular and have achieved cult status, especially with young owners.

A van conversion is also featured; this is a build-up undertaken by two people who had a fervent desire to own a motorcaravan in spite of limited funds.

Finally there are reports looking closely at two GRP coachbuilts, based on kits; but as mentioned earlier, the term 'kit' is rather imprecise as the accounts illustrate.

The purpose of reporting on real build-ups is to exemplify some of the tasks that have to be tackled. Also useful to future builders are the references to some of the products used in the course of construction.

In other words, these case histories typify motorcaravan projects rather than steering readers through a set of step-by-step instructions. In any case, the Starcraft kit is currently unavailable – though examples often appear in classified advertisements. It is reported here simply because many lessons can be learnt from this particular build-up experience. Constructional work in the Starcraft is much the same in other projects.

RENAULT TRAFIC
Builders: Alison & John Freame

Notes on the base vehicle

The Trafic was launched by Renault in the early 1980s and its raking front and angular lines were distinctive. In contrast, the rear-engined VW Transporter, the Talbot Express and the Ford Transit were much squarer in appearance and lacked the French model's flair.

Minor facelifting appeared in 1990 and five years later, alternative engines were introduced; a 2.2-litre petrol unit appeared whereas the 1.7 litre version was withdrawn. Commercial users normally prefer a diesel power unit and early 2.1-litre units were later replaced by the 2.5-litre version. Currently there is also a 1.9-litre diesel.

Though never prominent, the Trafic was used by several panel van converters and a few coachbuilts appeared, too. The Machzone low profile Ecu, the Autohomes Ariane and Elddis Eclipse, and the Ranger from Holdsworth were examples.

Without doubt, the Trafic raking front was years ahead of its time. More recent models, like the Mercedes Sprinter and Volkswagen LT, now have similar sloping fronts, albeit without the sharp-edged angularity of the 'eighties'.

Perhaps the Trafic deserves a higher profile amongst motorcaravan manufacturers and there's no doubt it provides plenty of possibilities for the amateur converter. The project reported here helps to prove the point.

Project overview

This unusual project was a 'conversion' on the part of the owners as well as the vehicle. Alison and John Freame owned an elderly Elddis Shamal touring caravan but felt a motorcaravan would suit their style rather better. The problem was that having recently moved house, their available 'disposable income' was a mere £2,500.

Second-hand models falling within this limit were in a pretty poor state, so it was decided to tackle a self-build project. John possesses a wide range of practical skills and Alison is a tenacious worker, too; so they started looking for a second-hand panel van.

The challenge turned to reality when an advertisement appeared for a vegetable van in a local Lincolnshire paper. With five previous owners, the B registration, Renault Trafic Hi-Line long wheelbase, 2.1-litre diesel, had 68,000 miles recorded on a clock that had long since ceased to work. No-one was pretending that it hadn't notched up many more miles than that – least of all the garage who were asking £1,800 for it. However, diesel engines are noted for longevity and the Renault was structurally sound. The sale also included the promise of an MoT.

A new steering joint was needed to ensure the van passed the MoT, and John's offer of £1,600 was accepted. The Trafic ran well and the five-speed box was pleasingly smooth. In addition, fuel consumption was acceptable at around 26mpg – a figure normally quoted for an Elddis Eclipse coachbuilt model.

As regards conversion potential, the interior height was particularly good; even with the intended

Hard work enabled this conversion project to be completed at a remarkably low cost.

137

Lightness of the caravan fixtures was a great advantage.

addition of insulated ceiling board, it was evident that headroom of around 1.880m (6ft 2in) could be achieved.

Conversion details

The first problem arose when the cost of a new fridge, cooker, pumped water system, mains electricity supply, new side windows, roof light and so on was calculated.

John and Alison couldn't find a buyer for their trailer caravan, which didn't help matters. On the other hand it was this fact that caused John to come up with an extraordinary idea. Why not 'cannibalise' the trailer caravan, remove all the fixtures, fittings and furniture and build them into the Renault? Apart from a body leak, the 1975 Elddis Shamal 14ft caravan was in full working order so why shouldn't it be used as an inexpensive source of equipment? Of particular relevance was the fact that a caravan's furniture is light in weight. John had found the answer.

A simple sliding plywood blind was constructed for the roof-light.

Building the interior

It was soon obvious that a remarkable amount of raw material was re-usable from the caravan. For instance, the floor on the Elddis comprised 13mm (½in) ply boards with 25mm (1in) of foam bonded underneath; and in the wall voids, polystyrene block foam was just what was needed to insulate the Trafic.

Dismantling was done carefully, leaving just a traditional caravan chassis and running gear, which was then sold to a local scrap merchant who wanted to build a trailer – so a few more pounds were added to the budget.

As regards body conversion, the shell of the Renault Trafic needed little alteration. Metal struts ran across the roof to provide structural integrity and John subsequently added two full length timber battens of 36mm x 15mm (1½in x ⅝in) down the length of the interior. When fixed firmly with an epoxy adhesive, these provided anchorage points for the ceiling panels which came next. The purpose of wooden strutting was mentioned earlier in this chapter.

Openings in the roof for a skylight and cut-outs in the sides for windows were prepared using an electric jigsaw. The original windows from the caravan provided patterns for paper templates.

Reclaimed panels gave an attractive finish, with a broad frieze adding a personal touch.

John had fitted windows in vans previously and knew what was involved (at this point, it is important to express doubt about the wisdom of using the original 1975 units; prior to 1978, trailer caravan manufacturers were not obliged to fit safety glass).

On the roof, it was decided to fit a new skylight which cost £36 at a caravan dealers. Because cassette blinds are costly, John purchased some aluminium channel from a DIY Superstore. Two parallel strips mounted on either side acted as runners for a panel of 3mm faced plywood which was just as 'light-tight' as a blind.

Two more lengths of aluminium channel were fixed inside along the full length of the van at the top of the wall. This represented the intersection of wall and ceiling panels and the angled slots meant that John could enclose the edges of the boards in a neat arrangement. His experience as an interior decorator was also evident in the smart way he used a decorative wallpaper frieze to add a tasteful finish around the top.

Fitting the furniture was next. John and Alison installed the caravan's wardrobe, the bunk bed with its metal supports and brackets, the kitchen units, hob, fridge and water supply. However, the original foot pump worked irregularly so the provison of a Whale submersible unit solved the problem.

As regards the refrigerator, this has to be sealed at the back and an Electrolux Installation Manual gave John clear instructions. Details are given in this manual too, in Chapter Seven.

Bunk beds, complete with their steel support system, were taken from an Elldis 'donor' caravan.

All the kitchen appliances were taken from the elderly Elddis.

Exterior work

Funds were now low and a quotation to re-spray the exterior was excessive; so paint was purchased from an accident repair specialist and applied using high quality brushes. Whilst few coachbuilders adopt this traditional approach today, an expert can achieve notable results – given warm, wind-free weather.

The conversion was finished after nine weeks of dedicated work – helped by long summer evenings.

Insurance

The next hurdle was insurance. The moment the word 'van' was mentioned, insurance quotations seemed to rise. Typical prices were in excess of £400 with large excesses as well.

When the conversion was described as a motorcaravan, quotations were cheaper, until it transpired that this wasn't a 'professional conversion' by a known manufacturer.

Then John came across Adrian Flux & Co, whose insurance broking services are well-known to the builders of kit cars. This company recognises the particular issues involved in the ownership of specialist vehicles and insurance was arranged with Corinthian Motor Policies at Lloyds. The premium for comprehensive insurance in East Lincolnshire without a no claims discount was calculated at £180. This operated with a maximum annual mileage clause of 5,000 per annum, which was acceptable to the owners.

The Trafic in use

As always with a self-built project, 'fine tuning' was needed. In particular there were problems with the fuel injection system which took time to cure. As far as the living area was concerned, the conversion was a pleasing success. Even more impressive was the fact that the true origin of

The converted Renault Trafic produced an ideal motorcaravan for two people.

interior fixtures and fittings was scarcely discernible.

Conclusion

Understandably, John and Alison Freame are delighted with the fruits of their labours. Their project proves that it is possible to enter the world of motorcaravanning without the need for large amounts of money.

Sourcing parts in this way is certainly in keeping with re-cycling sentiments. There are several caravan breakers around the country – Franks of Luton has an accompanying shop, stocked with serviceable accessories. Items ranging from a double glazed plastic window to unusual lengths of awning zip are all on display.

Elderly trailer caravans are often tucked at the back of dealer forecourts with clearance prices on the windows. Normally there are papers to sign so

Older caravans for similar projects can often be found at the back of dealers' forecourts.

the new owner acknowledges that the goods are not deemed to be habitable. Some 'golden oldies' become site huts; others house hens. The reincarnation carried out by Alison and John Freame is a rather more noble metamorphosis.

VW WESTFALIA
Owner: Steve Rowe

Notes on the base vehicle

The VW camper has played an important role in motorcaravan history over a long period. Models from VW are categorised as follows:

• Type 1: Term used for the VW Beetle
• Type 2: Campervans – both 'split screen' and 'bay window' versions. The split screen models appeared in the 1950s.
• Type 3: The VW Variant.
• Type 4: The current front-wheel-drive transporter.
Note: The VW Variant was called the Type 3, so the 1980s Transporter was officially a Type 2S.

Over the years, many conversion specialists used these base vehicles; some retained a fixed roof, many installed an elevating roof, whereas more recent models tended to have a high-top.

In recent times, enthusiasts have ascribed 'cult status' to 'Vee Dub' campers. Young people are the keenest collectors, with surfers particularly prominent amongst the devoted owners.

Project overview

Steve Rowe is a motorcaravan journalist who drove a VW when he was a student. Ten years later he decided to revive the interest and called at BPS Campers, a well-known VW centre noted for its restoration services.

Committed customers typically inspect the large stock of dilapidated campervans, choose one that shows potential, then leave it to BPS to work a miracle. Prices are from £6,500 to £8,000 and the quality of workmanship is of a very high order.

Steve chose a 1973 Type 2 VW Westfalia Continental with a rising roof – or at least remnants of a rising roof. He realised it would take six months before the exacting work ahead would be accomplished. Steve wanted a complete refurbishment, both inside and outside, leaving him to add a few final creature comforts.

Renovation details

Barry Shotton of BPS carries out an exceedingly thorough restoration. Rusty panels are cut away and new steel sections are welded in place. Where necessary, completely new body panels, supplied by Just Kampers are fitted, many of which are still obtainable.

For the renovator there are also reclaimed parts

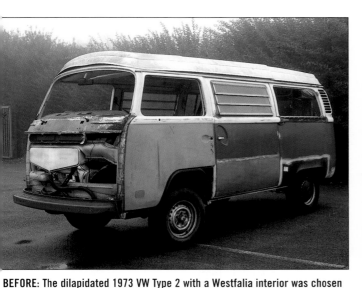

BEFORE: The dilapidated 1973 VW Type 2 with a Westfalia interior was chosen for restoration.

AFTER: The transformation achieved by BPS restoration specialists was outstanding.

– especially complete doors – that are imported from California. The kinder weather on America's west coast means that some scrapped vehicles are surprisingly free of rust.

As a further testimony to the vehicle's ongoing popularity, near-identical Type 2 air-cooled VWs are currently made in Brazil. Recognising the interest in the marque, Beetles UK has started to import them into Britain. In addition, Devon Motorcaravans has recently revived the traditional camper conversion in the spirit of the early models.

So although Steve's VW Westfalia looked grim – both below the floorpan and above – the refurbishment left nothing to chance. Even chassis sections that looked suspect were replaced, too. The accompanying illustrations show the extent of the operation and the magnificent results.

Building the interior

Moving inside, the original Westfalia furniture was refurbished without making replacements that would destroy its original character – however,

Steve had to make some important decisions with regard to this.

Some owners stick rigidly to an original design, reinstating elderly appliances and living stoically with a lack of modern conveniences. Others retain the broad character of the camper but add a few modern comforts. This latter approach seems more sensible.

Recognising the original models were not particularly warm in winter, Steve decided to have a modern heating system fitted. He also wanted a mains system installed. These tasks are described here as examples of his chosen concessions to comfort.

Fitting a mains supply

Anyone used to fitting plugs and connecting wires could consider installing a mains supply. Care at every stage is critical and the completed work must be checked by a qualified electrician. It is also best to work with a kit of components rather than trying to purchase the parts separately. This

Where necessary, complete replacement panels are used by BPS campers.

141

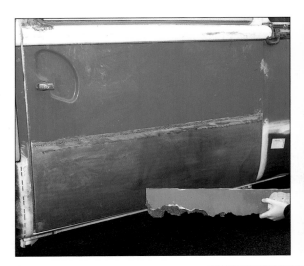

ensures you are fitting cable of the correct rating and components approved for a motorcaravan installation.

Details of the components are given in Chapter Four and kits from both W4 Accessories and Powerpart are particularly good. The Powerpart kit, for example, provides a pre-wired consumer unit, and this was fitted in the VW.

The first job was to find a location for the input socket. It would have been best to have installed a recessed socket housed in a purpose-made enclosure, but this would have spoilt the external lines and Steve wanted the socket out of sight. After a thorough search, a location below the floor was chosen which was shielded by chassis members and well away from the wheels since these throw up road dirt. Directly above the chosen location was a large ventilator which conveniently provided an entry point for the input cable.

The orange input cable needs to be as short as possible because it isn't protected by the Residual Current Device (RCD). Only cable connected *after* the RCD provides the user with the protective 'trip

switch' function of the Residual Current Device.

The input socket was duly wired-up, noting that the connections were clearly marked on its plastic casing. Inside the camper, a location for the consumer unit was selected and its casing removed to expose the fixing points. At this stage the orange input cable was disconnected, trimmed to length and reinstated.

Other wires pre-connected in a Powerpart consumer unit are:

• an earth cable covered in a yellow and green sleeve, terminated with a connecting eye.
• a white flexible 1.5mm² cable which connects up to the 13 amp sockets.

The earth has to be fixed to a chassis point and any paint or underseal must be removed to ensure a sound connection; this should be fitted with a warning 'Earth – do not remove' tag.

The white cable can then be fed to the first 13 amp socket, then the second and finally the third as shown in the installation leaflet.

An alternative is to separate the two Miniature Circuit Breakers (MCBs), which were bridged in the kit, so they can protect two entirely separate circuits. The 5 amp MCB would provide power to

One of the first jobs was to fit the input socket under the floor.

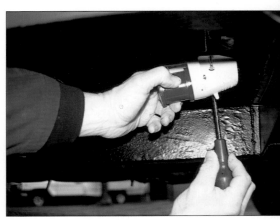

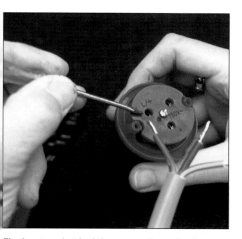

The input socket had the connections clearly marked on the plastic moulding.

The cover has to be removed to fit the consumer unit; this is pre-wired in this kit.

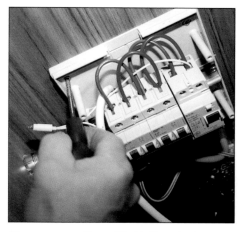

The consumer unit was fitted to the robust chipboard that formed a locker.

sockets for running a battery charger and 230v lighting e.g. a table lamp.

The 10 amp MCB would provide power for an entirely separate supply whose socket might be used for more powerful items. For instance, if you plan to use a low wattage electric kettle, it is better if this is plugged into a socket served by the 10 amp MCB.

The alternative option was considered more appropriate for the VW Westfalia.

Installing and wiring-up 13 amp sockets needs care and when the job is complete the system must be checked by a qualified electrician. There are also tester plugs shown in Chapter Four, which you insert into the 13 amp sockets to verify earth continuity and correct polarity. One of these testers is a useful purchase.

Fitting a heater

It is strongly recommended that gas appliances are fitted by a qualified gas engineer. This procedure was adopted here and a Trumatic E2400 compact

Care is needed when connecting up and installing the 13 amp sockets.

heater was chosen because it can be tucked into the smallest spaces. The photographs overleaf show how the work was carried out by the engineer and indicate the suitability of the product for small motorcaravans.

The heater is a high output device that is controlled electronically and completely enclosed. It needs an externally fitted balanced flue so that fresh air for combustion can be drawn in and waste fumes discharged. A warm air duct is coupled up to serve the living area and in the small interior of the VW there is no need for an elaborate system of outlets.

In addition there has to be a need for an internal air intake so the fan can pull in air, direct it across a heat exchanger and then return it to the living space duly heated.

The Trumatic E series heaters are controlled remotely from a small panel and are remarkably efficient. They are designed to operate while a vehicle is being driven, although this means leaving the gas cylinder on, which is not usually considered wise. An earlier Truma heater fitted in the Starcraft motorcaravan continues to give excellent service after ten years and there is every likelihood that the VW installation will achieve similar reliability.

Other installations have also been made in Steve's camper including the fitting of a leisure battery, a battery charger, and a 12v fused distribution unit. These are positioned discreetly, thereby retaining the appearance of the 1973 interior as much as possible.

Conclusion

The blend of ancient and modern results in serviceable individuality, and although a 1973 vehicle isn't exactly 'ancient', motorcaravans have advanced considerably since conversions using VW Mk2 models were carried out.

However, there is pleasure in reviving the past and Steve Rowe's VW is a fine example of its type. Renovation was completed early in 1998 and to date it has been an unreserved success.

143

Fitting a Trumatic E Series blown air heater

Preparing a gas supply is a skilful job that should be entrusted to a qualified gas engineer.

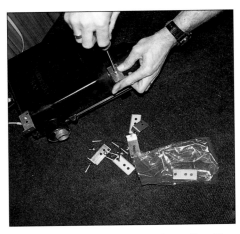

The heater has to be prepared with couplings like a balanced flue prior to installation.

The unit is mounted in a bedding box, discreetly hidden from view.

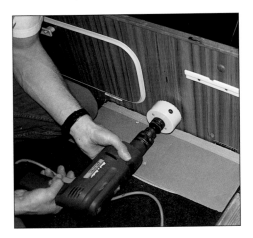

Outlets are prepared in the sides of the lockers for warm air ducting.

In the VW Camper, only a simple ducting arrangement is needed.

The remote control unit and thermostat is installed at a convenient location.

RANCHER
Builders:
John & Justin Wickersham (Ranger)
John White (Rancher)

Notes on the base vehicle

This case history is about using a kit to build a motorcaravan. The vehicle is the Rancher and a MkI or MkII Ford Escort Saloon provides the running gear including the back axle, suspension system, steering and brakes. The wiring loom and an array of smaller items are used as well.

Technically it is possible to fit an Escort 1600cc cross flow engine too, but the 2000cc Cortina ohc 'Pinto' engine and gearbox is preferred. Professionally reconditioned units are available at reasonable cost and the motorcaravan chassis can be built to suit several engine options.

It pays not to cut costs here. If you transfer a tired engine from a tired Cortina, you end up with an even wearier Rancher. Bearing in mind the finished motorcaravan will weigh around 30cwt, the engine must be suitable for the job.

As regards a 'donor car' it is best to buy an Escort with some MoT and road tax remaining. With insurance you can then drive it around to verify general condition before taking it all to bits. All re-usable parts then need cleaning and money can be recouped by trailing unwanted parts to a local scrap merchant.

After wire brushing, metal parts are then treated with a paint like Hammerite, and 'wear items' such as brake pads, suspension bushes and steering joints are replaced. An easier answer is to order reconditioned parts from a specialist such as Kit Fit. Complete assemblies from Kit Fit are 'like new' having been dipped in an acid bath, sand blasted and fitted with new rubbers, new bearings and so on. Having built several cars using both approaches, the author has found the second route is much preferred if funds permit.

Project overview

Motorcycle developments by Derek and Don Rickman have always commanded the respect of knowledgeable 'bikers'. So when the company launched a kit car called the Ranger, its extremely high qualities were instantly recognised. The Ranger was styled as an 'off-road' vehicle and used Ford Escort MkI or II parts. It is one of the easiest component cars I have built to date and the quality throughout was exceptional.

Using this as the starting point, the Rickman designers then increased the dimensions of its remarkable chassis and launched the Rancher motorcaravan designed by John White. Many elements of the Rancher were much the same as the Ranger and the large GRP shell retained features of the cab and all its front-end features. To assist with the fitting-out work, GRP modules are also designed to include kitchen furniture, wardrobe unit, overhead lockers and so on. These are 'optional' items.

This idea of using GRP furniture inside is not unusual and a similar strategy is used by Island Plastics in models like the Romahome Hytop and the St Michel.

The Rancher is a compact motorcaravan with a professional finish.

A MkII Ford Escort seems an unlikely vehicle to convert into a motorcaravan.

Most Ranchers are fitted with a Cortina 2-litre OHC engine, but several options are suitable.

Conversion details

A good instructional manual covering the mechanical elements has helped many builders produce the Ranger. The Rancher motorcaravan is no different. Once the parts from the 'donor vehicle' have been cleaned, the assembly work is remarkably easy. There have even been exceptional cases of builders whose vehicles have been ready for MoT testing after a week's assembly work. If problems are experienced, the kit manufacturer can provide guidance. In addition, Gordon Pearce who runs the Rancher Register has documented information about builders' choices of engines, suspension adaptations, interior layouts and so on.

As regards the preparatory work, the business of cutting up a car with a hacksaw, club hammer and bolster is delightfully destructive. This is the dirty phase in the project but it can still be addictive. Meanwhile, the Haynes Manual

To eliminate hours of preparation, completely refurbished assemblies are available from Kit Fit, a component specialist.

145

The complete back axle and suspension system from an Escort is used on the Rancher.

for the Ford Escort is an essential guidebook.

On the electrical front, transferring the wiring loom from an Escort to a Rancher is ridiculously easy – provided you attach identification labels to all the wires when disconnecting them in the first place.

Unusually for a kit, the Rancher has its body already fitted to the galvanised chassis. All the glass is installed, the doors are hinged, the bonnet is in place and so on. If you want pre-fitted roof level lockers inside and an overcab locker, these have to be specified when the order is placed.

Of course, not everyone will share the author's enthusiasm for transplanting automotive organs and people with neither the time nor inclination to get their hands greasy can always purchase a part-built road-legal Rancher which only needs completion inside. Several specialists offer build-up or part build-up services leaving the owner to tackle the fitting out operation.

As regards layouts, this partly depends on individual requirements. However, Ranchers are fairly compact and don't offer many variations. They are normally built to accommodate two adults and width restrictions dictate that a bed has to run along the length of the vehicle. The kitchen is normally situated at the back, just inside the rear-mounted central door. Few Ranchers include a separate shower room since this would leave little space for a wardrobe.

Building the interior

Insulating the interior shell is essential, so the approach used in the Starcraft build-up described later is recommended. If any cold surfaces are left, condensation build-up causes inconvenience.

Thereafter the procedures are left to the individual, taking account of the need for ventilation, gas drop-out holes and other safety features detailed in earlier chapters.

Exterior work

Whereas the Ranger 'off-road' style vehicle is supplied in a variety of colours, the Rancher is

Once cleaned and painted, the complete front suspension unit from the donor Escort is used for the Rancher.

An Escort steering rack and front cross member is fitted to the Rancher chassis.

Every Rancher has a layout chosen by its builder, although width requires the beds to run from front to back.

Most converters choose to build the kitchen at the rear where there's greater headroom.

manufactured in a cream colour referred to as 'flaxen'. Because colour is achieved by mixing a pigment into the resins, there is no further painting for the builder to do. Obviously it is always possible to apply an etching primer to GRP and to spray paint a different colour. However, this is a costly way to achieve individuality.

Other outside jobs include fitting door catches re-claimed from the Escort, fitting a windscreen wiper assembly, fitting headlights, a bonnet catch and so on. None of this is onerous work although fitting door catches is more easily done by someone with small fingers.

Insurance

Rickman products are well known among specialist kit car insurance brokers and finding an insurer for the Rancher is unlikely to present problems. The Owners' Club could also offer advice if required.

The Rancher in use

Provided you are looking for a compact motorcaravan, the Rancher is an excellent option. In many respects it is similar in size and style to the well-known Romahome from Island Plastics.

The Rancher's 'ladder' chassis is a remarkably strong unit built on traditional lines with heavy gauge steel. Galvanising ensures it will last for years – the body is just as tough. Glass reinforced plastic doesn't rust and the life of a Rancher would undoubtedly exceed the span of most motorcaravans.

On the road it drives extremely well. Having driven a 2-litre version around the tight lanes of the New Forest during an extended period of testing, I found its competence apparent at once. It corners as well as any tall vehicle of its type and rides the bumpy back-roads far better than its kit competitor, the Starcraft.

Several other engines can be fitted and some owners have installed diesel units like the 1.8 Turbo from a Ford P100, so there is scope here, too.

Conclusion

When the Rickman brothers retired from business, the Ranger and Rancher were bought by Lomax, a kit car specialist whose novel Citroën 2CV three-wheeler is very popular. Information on the Rancher is available from Lomax.

Compared to most 'kit vehicles', the Rancher is a very complete package. Many difficult assembly jobs have already been done prior to delivery; however, this is reflected in the price. The basic kit costs around £6,000, although by the time you have bought a new refrigerator, cooker, toilet, and soft furnishings, the total bill is unlikely to be less than £10,000.

Arguably a second-hand motorcaravan could be purchased for this sum, but building a Rancher means you have intimate knowledge of a product that could last for years. And then there's a feeling of accomplishment which more than compensates for the hard work involved.

Rear access on the Rancher offers plenty of scope when designing the layout.

147

STARCRAFT
Builder: John Wickersham

Notes on the base vehicle

Converting a Ford Cortina saloon into a motorcaravan seems rather bizarre. Nearly all Starcrafts have been built using this vehicle with the original dashboard, cab and instruments being transferred across to a new chassis. The distinguishing feature is the six-wheel configuration; a four-wheeled Starcraft based on a Ford P100 pick-up truck is seldom seen.

Most Starcrafts have a 2-litre ohv Cortina Pinto engine, although the example here was built using a 2.3-litre V6 fitted to many Cortina Ghia models.

The Starcraft Kit was remarkably inexpensive at around £2,500, but it scarcely met many people's idea of a 'kit'. It comprised little more than a steel chassis, seven pieces of glass with rubbers, six wheels (but no tyres) and a poorly finished set of glass fibre panels. The main shell had no windows, virtually no floor and no door.

In spite of this, many people with precious little mechanical background succeeded in completing these startling looking vehicles. The finish on some Starcrafts betray their builder's lack of experience; but on the other hand, a number are built to a good standard.

Tackling a build-up like this needs a lot of time. In this case history, it took the builder longer to finish the Starcraft than it took to complete his self-built four-bedroomed house!

Notwithstanding the enormity of the task, it provided sufficient pleasure and knowledge of vehicle construction to continue with three further car building projects. The Starcraft also gives continuing good service, eleven years after completion, and has been an inexpensive way to enjoy the comforts of motorcaravanning.

Project overview

Reference to the mechanical construction would be of interest to anyone seeing a pre-owned Starcraft for sale; but since the kit has currently been withdrawn from production, this element of the build-up is only briefly described.

The reason for including a case history here is

Before . . .

A Cortina 2.3 Ghia Saloon seemed an unlikely vehicle on which to base a motorcaravan.

The 2.3 litre V6 engine is ideal for a Starcraft motorcaravan although many vehicles are fitted with a 2-litre OHC unit.

Cut away and unwanted – the forward structure of the car is scrapped.

After removing its original box sections under the floorpan, the cab will be mounted on a completely new chassis..

Self-build projects – case histories

because the project exemplifies many of the tasks involved in fitting-out any basic shell. The report also refers to a number of products that motorcaravan builders might find useful in other projects.

As a point of reference the Starcraft is equipped with:

- an Electrolux AES fridge,
- a Goldstar compact microwave oven,
- a Rinnai instantaneous water heater,
- a Whale water system with Evenflow pump,
- a Carver/Truma E1800 blown air heater,
- Speedograph Richfield cab seats,
- Caralux upholstery,
- a Plug-In-Systems Power Kestrel power supply unit,
- a Power Box inverter from Power Electronics (PEL),
- a washroom fitted with a Thetford Porta Potti,
- a tailor-made roof rack by Hornchurch Motorcaravans,
- a tow bar designed by Watling Engineers,
- a bespoke exhaust system by Custom Chrome.

Conversion details

Buying a family saloon car from a vicar and cutting it into sections with a jigsaw in the hope of turning it

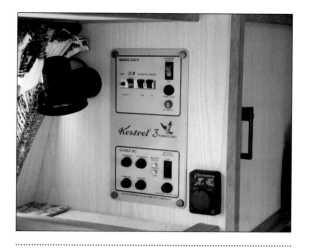

A Plug-In-Systems combined mains and 12v fused distribution unit controls all the electrical circuits.

into a motorcaravan was certainly an act of faith. The accompanying illustrations show quite clearly that this kit called for considerable commitment.

Even if the builder possessed little previous experience repairing cars, a burning ambition to meet a challenge was the driving force behind the project. Several crises appeared from the outset, but an early lesson showed that when advice was sought, answers were often just around the corner.

After . . .

A GRP shell is lifted on to the new chassis and the forward section will rest on the Cortina cab.

With the cab and engine installed on the new chassis, it is possible to drive the vehicle, albeit on private roads.

Windows, a door, and a complete floor had to be constructed before the living area could be fitted out.

Over a thousand hours later, the finished Starcraft looks unlike a converted Cortina.

149

A Power Box inverter mounted under the glove box draws from the leisure battery and provides a mains supply.

Equally it brought home the fact that you should never try to do everything yourself; enlisting the help of an expert in a particular field is sometimes the best way to overcome a problem.

After around 540 hours, spread out over almost a year, an empty Starcraft passed its MoT.

Exterior building work

Much of the work encountered would need to be done on any motorcaravan. Window installation is a case in point.

Fitting windows

Fitting windows confronts most converters. If the installation is in a panel van, the work might be best undertaken by a specialist. A number of window manufacturers will supply and fit their products.

Cutting holes in panels – irrespective of material – leads to an overall weakening of the structure, and whereas it is possible to add strengthening laminations around an aperture cut in a GRP shell, the procedure with steel panels is less straightforward.

Fitting windows on the Starcraft was certainly time-consuming – it was also messy. The large rear window took a full day to complete because the GRP around the aperture was too flexible. After repeated failure, fresh laminations were built up. In addition, black sealant injected into the rubber surrounds later oozed everywhere.

Careful measurement of the rubber surround showed that the cut-out for a window had to be 7mm larger all round than the section of glass supplied. Accuracy is critical and if an aperture is cut too large, problems lie ahead.

The glass was laid on some brown paper and a small piece of wood, 7mm wide, was moved around the perimeter in register with the pencil that was used to mark the cutting line. After the paper template had been cut out carefully it was taped to the Starcraft's body and a final cutting line marked on the glass fibre. Accuracy here is critical.

To cut through GRP, a jigsaw will achieve the task as long as it is set to a slow speed and fitted with a blade designed to cut plastic. If the saw operates at high speed, heat is generated and the

teeth on the blade will soon be dulled.

Fitting the surround was done by hand, and black sealant injected with a cartridge gun. The glass was then carefully eased into the groove in the rubber. Once located, a locking strip was fed into a further groove to tighten the grip on the glass. This strip was inserted using wire from an old coat hanger, but it took so long that it would have been sensible to have purchased the proper fitting tool from a rubber extrusion specialist like Woolies.

Installing high level ventilators

Roof ventilation is another universal requirement on a motorcaravan – especially if it stands parked for an extended period. Ventilation helps to prevent a build-up of damp and releases excessive temperatures on sunny days.

Elevating roof lights are often preferred and most types now provide a measure of ventilation, even when completely lowered. However, there is also the GY20 domed ventilator from Electrolux which provides constant ventilation without having moving parts.

On the Starcraft, it was decided to fit both – together with an externally vented cooker hood. At the forward end of the roof, a Fiamma double-glazed ventilator with an electrically operated fan was installed. To the rear, the GY20 was chosen. The principle of installation was the same, even though the apertures were of a different size. One unusual detail of a GY20 ventilator is the aerodynamic shape of its dome. Movement of air across the top creates a lift effect, thereby drawing air from the interior.

Installing the ventilator involved:
• Creating safe access on to the roof
• Marking out a cutting line
• Drilling pilot holes from the outside
• Making a cut through the GRP
• Trimming the aperture with a wood rasp
• Preparing spacer inserts for the void between the roof and the ceiling ply
• Applying Carafax ribbon sealant on the roof around the aperture
• Fitting the inner and outer sections of the GY20.

Roof rack and ladder design

Although a number of standard racks and ladders are available from manufacturers like Fiamma, these certainly wouldn't have matched the particular shape of the Starcraft, so a custom-made product was needed. Some self-builders would build a rack themselves, but the author's experience of welding thin gauge tubing was limited, and since Hornchurch Motorcaravans are noted for manufacturing bespoke racks, carriers and ladders, it was felt that this was the best way forward.

After explaining what was needed, and booking an apppointment, the product was skilfully made. The shape of the vehicle was sympathetically reflected in the final construction.

Self-build projects – case histories

Working at slow speed and with a blade for cutting plastic, a jigsaw prepares the aperture.

A barbed wood rasp is ideal for trimming both the GRP and the timber spacers fitted in the void.

An inner collar fits on the ceiling inside; this is screwed tightly to the assembly mounted on the roof.

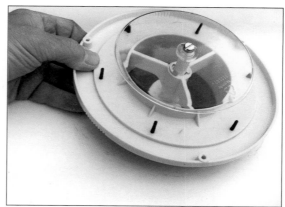

The outer cover prevents rainwater from entering the interior.

The protective dome is fitted last, using three stainless steel screws.

Rear bumper and towing bracket

Changing legislation will make it increasingly difficult for small-scale manufacturers whose work is the fabrication of towing brackets. However, there is a continuing need for unusual vehicles to be fitted up for towing and Watling Engineers has been involved in this work for many years.

It is also important to emphasise that finding the appropriate pick-up points on a chassis is critical for safety. This work should not be tackled by anyone without the appropriate engineering background; so Watling Engineers undertook the design and construction of both the bracket and rear bumper although the author carried out all the wiring work for the 12N and 12S sockets. Further information on the electrical provision needed for towing is given in Chapter Three of *The Caravan Manual* published by Haynes.

Building the interior

As mentioned earlier in the chapter, insulating an interior is most important. Using the Starcraft in a part-finished state was quite revealing; condensation running down some uninsulated sections of the GRP shell damaged several books. Everything has to be insulated and the single-glazed windows are protected at night with Silver Screens, the made-to-measure insulating panels. Only when the walls are insulated and lined is it advisable to construct fixed items of furniture.

Taking the ceiling, for example, strutting was fixed using U-Pol B polyester compound. Frames were prepared to provide a fixing point for screws that would later secure lighting units, roof ventilators and other fittings. All wiring was

151

Roof racks and access ladders can be designed and made to order at Hornchurch Motorcaravans.

On any GRP shell, struts have to be fitted throughout the interior to provide fixing points for the lining material.

installed in the voids and either rigid polystyrene or glass fibre quilt insulation was fitted into each section.

The ceiling was then lined with 3mm decorative ply, purchased directly from a caravan manufacturer's after-sales department. Some parts of the panels were held with brass screws (cover strips of prepared wood were added later to hide the heads); large sections were held in place using a heavy duty adhesive. Panels were located then held in place with T-shaped struts wedged against the floor – copying the technique used when plaster-boarding a ceiling.

Another important preparatory task was to fit vertical sections of 9mm (⅜in) plywood as support bulkheads. These provide support near the door and at the front near the junction with the cab. By 'fibre-glassing' these panels to the sides of the shell, floor and ceiling, support is achieved under the feet of the roof rack. This bracing function of the bulkhead panels gives suffcient strength to allow anyone to stand on the rack when attaching canoes, skis or similar loads.

Even after finishing the lining work, the interior dimensions of a Starcraft are greater than a Rancher. In particular the interior width is sufficient to consider mounting a double bed crossways. Advantage was taken of this and the resulting bed, when made up, offered adequate size for anyone up to 1.830m (6ft) tall. There was also additional room over the cab to provide a bunk for two small children.

Fitting out a shell like this was reminiscent of fitting out a boat. Multiple angles caused by complex tapers provided a joinery challenge. Patience and a precision saw bench proved essential.

Many furniture items were made using a framework of teak that was cut and planed from sawn timbers. Teak is strong, though heavy, but it complemented the lightness of 3mm faced ply. Light cupboard fronts were modified from obsolete items bought from a caravan manufacturer and weight was diligently watched.

Heavy items, like a drawer intended for tins of food and drink, was located at low level and set on special runners purchased from Woodfit. This runs like a filing cabinet drawer and is almost as large.

A crockery cupboard was made too, ensuring that the dividers for holding plates and saucers prevented each unit from touching each other in transit. Clinking crockery is an annoying feature in a motorcaravan. Equally, a special shelf was made to house a removable microwave oven, which can be removed for storage and used at home when the Starcraft is parked for an extended period.

Single-glazed windows in a motorcaravan cab can be fitted with a made-to-measure Silver Screens insulating cover.

Reading lamps bought from a motorcaravan accessory shop provide a good output on the 12v system.

Below the Mini Kitchen from Optimus, a pull-forward flap provides instant access to a rectangular waste bin. Unlike professionally built motorcaravans, the Starcraft does have provision for spent tins, tea bags and other refuse.

An unusual feature in the Mini Kitchen is the use of a domestic size waste outlet. This is coupled up to PVCu domestic waste and when the plug is pulled, water discharges at a rate seldom seen in a professionally built motorcaravan. Ridged, flexible hose gives a disappointing flow rate, but professional builders persist in using it. Incidentally Optimus is no longer producing the Mini Kitchen but very similar units are available from Alde International (UK).

Finally, the upholstery work was a shared exercise, by drawing together Speedograph Richfield with Caralux. The former is a specialist in vehicle seating; the latter provides a bespoke upholstery service.

To ensure there was continuity in the material used in the cab with materials used in the living area, the two specialists provided each other with complementary fabrics. These were used as panels or edging for seat squabs, mattresses, seat backs and cab door linings – so there is visual continuity of fabrics from the cab right through to the living area.

Insurance

There shouldn't be a problem insuring the Starcraft. Secure Direct Insurance (formerly Snowball Insurance) has dealt with specialist vehicles for many years, and the Starcraft Owners' Club can also provide advice about other insurers.

The Starcraft in use

After around 50,000 miles and eleven years of use, the following points are offered:

For:
• This is an excellent vehicle for fast motorway cruising.
• There is good internal space and pleasing headroom in the kitchen area.
• The six-wheeled Starcraft is extremely stable in side winds.
• An outlay of £5,250 in 1987 has represented remarkable value for money.

Against:
• Fitting out this, or any similar shaped interior is not easy; this is why so many mass-produced models are prosaically slab-sided.
• The six-wheeled Starcraft gives a poor ride on bumpy and twisty lanes.

Conclusion

It took over 1,000 hours to build the Starcraft, and over a year on the road to get the rear suspension behaving properly; but many lessons were learnt and this opened the door to motorcaravanning.

The idea of using a powerful car as the base for a motorcaravan is unusual but not unprecedented. One project has been built using the cab and engine from a front-wheel-drive Audi saloon. Another builder integrated an Adria twin-axle caravan with a Vauxhall Cavalier. These mixed marriages have much to commend them. Commercial vehicles are the normal base on which to build a motorcaravan, but there is great merit in using a car. On the road, driving performance can be especially agreeable.

Just as this book was being completed, one of the first reports on the Nu Venture Rio built on a Fiat Scudo emphasised how pleasant it was to drive a conversion that felt like driving a car. The higher sitting position in more common base vehicles may be comfortable but it cannot disguise a van's commercial origin.

Appendix A

Standards and regulations

For the purpose of definition, the European Directive for Whole Vehicle Type Approval contains the following statement:

'...a motorcaravan is a Special Purpose M1 Category Vehicle constructed to include at least the following equipment: Seats and table, Sleeping accommodation which may be converted from the seats, Cooking facilities, Storage facilities. The equipment shall be rigidly fixed to the living compartment; however, the table may be designed to be easily removable.'

Legislation and codes of practice applicable to motorcaravans are currently undergoing radical amendments. Whilst the information here is accurate at the time of writing, continuing changes are certain to take place.

Issues relating to motorcaravans include:

a) The **vehicular** element, i.e. the base vehicle,
b) The **habitation** element, i.e. the living quarters,
c) Subsidiary **items of equipment**, e.g. towing brackets.

The base vehicle

Of the many matters that relate to road-going vehicles, the implementation of **European Whole Vehicle Type Approval (EWVTA)** is a critical one. The rationale behind EWVTA includes the following:

1. European Member States are anxious to create a market of free trade. In consequence if a vehicle is deemed safe and roadworthy in one Member Country, it should be possible to sell it in another Member Country *without any need to subject it to further testing*. This would be achievable if a single European testing programme is conducted by *all* Member States, thereby bringing to an end a situation where different countries carry out tests of their own.
2. Rather than test *every* vehicle leaving a production line, it is more practicable to scrutinise *one* example of a particular type of vehicle. If it can then be verified that a manufacturer has the production facility to produce exact replicas of the sample tested, the approval process is a manageable procedure. This testing strategy is called 'Type Approval'.

From 1st January, 1998, manufacturers of passenger cars have had to meet this requirement – contained in Directive 92\53\EC.

Whereas the establishment of a European Type Approval test is possible in respect of cars, serious difficulties arise in respect of motorcaravans. To begin with, a motorcaravan isn't the work of a single manufacturer – the finished product embodies the work of two or even more manufacturers. For instance there is the manufacturer of the base vehicle; then there is the manufacturer who builds the living quarters. Some motorcaravans are also built on a special chassis like the AL-KO Kober AMC product. In this instance, a third manufacturer is involved.

Clearly a motorcaravan is not like a car, and from a technical viewpoint it is described as a multi-stage built product. This carries the problem of a number of liability elements e.g. the manufacturer of the living quarters should not carry a responsibility for the integrity of the braking mechanisms manufactured by someone else – and vice versa.

On account of this problem, discussions are currently taking place to see how tests can be devised and carried out on a multi-stage product. Quite obviously a motorcaravan cannot be treated like a car, so the requirements contained in the new Directive 92\53\EC have been temporarily deferred until 1st January, 2000.

Suffice it to say, the problems of multi-stage construction are not unique to motorcaravans. Ambulances, hearses and armoured vehicles are also built in stages; equally they are built in relatively small volumes and by specialist converters. Moreover, there is no doubt that many multi-stage builders would go out of business if it became mandatory for their products to comply with Directive 92\53\EC as currently written.

Similar difficulties have been faced by manufacturers of kit car packages. At least three self-built motorcaravan kits have been available in the last few years; the Ranger described in Chapter Eleven is one of them. This opportunity to self-build a car or motorcaravan from scratch is unique to Britain and strict legislation has meant there are no kit car manufacturers in other European Member States. Without doubt, it would be impossible for self-build car constructors or the manufacturers of their components to comply with Directive 92\53\EC on the grounds of costs. If there was no alternative legislation, this thriving, though small, industry would die overnight.

In recognition of this, a special **Single Vehicle Approval (SVA)** scheme has been prepared in Great Britain and this approval mechanism extends to motorcaravan construction as well. The scheme means that a 'one-off' vehicle can be subjected to an exacting examination – described by the Press as a 'beefed up MoT'.

It was intended to have the SVA scheme in place on 1st January, 1998. However, clarification about 'what' is tested, 'by whom' and for 'how much' was not finalised in time and it was deferred until 1st August 1998.

A publication which clarifies what is involved in the SVA test is noted in Chapter Eleven. From information available at the time of writing, it is anticipated that the cost of the test is likely to be in the region of £500 to £600. This is a small price to pay to ensure a vehicle is safe on the road, especially bearing in mind that kit builders are seldom qualified automotive engineers. Furthermore, the introduction of the SVA scheme ensures continuance of an aspect of automobile development which has led to some notable pioneering achievements in Britain. Designers and builders of custom motorcaravans are one of the likely beneficiaries.

A further possibility that might help small volume motorcaravan manufacturers is the introduction of a **National Small Series Approval Scheme**. Discussions are taking place about a less onerous testing procedure as an alternative to full Type Approval. On the other hand, there is a worry that schemes unique to individual nations could thwart the politicians' declared objectives of creating an open market working within a universal legislative framework.

Yet another facet of current measures is an obligation being placed on manufacturers to give guidance about material recycling in readiness for the time when products reach the end of their working life. Ironically the unique kit car industry in Britain has re-used components from moribund motors for many years, albeit in a rather special way. Nevertheless, this new directive will have a serious impact on motorcaravan manufacturing although for the time being at least, *some* relaxation of the **EU Draft Directive COM (97)358 on End of Life Vehicles** has been agreed.

Habitation elements

For some years, the construction of the living quarters in a motorcaravan has been covered by British Standards; these are now in the process of being superseded by new European Standards.

Society of Motor Manufacturers and Traders (SMMT) and the National Caravan Council (NCC) Badge

In 1989, the SMMT introduced *The Motorcaravan Code of Practice* – later replaced by the *SMMT/NCC Habitation Code of Practice 201* which took effect in September, 1992. This Code is in operation until 23rd October 1998, after which it will be superseded by EN 1646.

To establish if a motorcaravan meets the standard, a sample model submitted by a manufacturer has to be scrutinised by NCC Certification Engineers. If it complies with all requirements, the manufacturer is thereafter permitted to affix the SMMT/NCC badge of approval to all identical models.

Since 1989, motorcaravans from many large manufacturers have been submitted for approval and accorded this mark of accreditation. However, compliance with COP 201 (and subsequently EN 1646) is not a legal requirement and a significant number of motorcaravans are not 'badged' and may not be compliant with the standards. Some are products from well-respected – but often smaller manufacturers – some of whom complete their conversions to exacting standards.

With the development of a larger European market, the need to create European Standards in respect of the living accommodation was recognised in the early 1990s. Equally, where a manufacturer wishes to market British-built motorcaravans throughout Europe, compliance with EN1646 has to be verified by a Certification Body which has gained the approval of the United Kingdom Accreditation Service (UKAS). Accordingly, the NCC is currently working closely with UKAS so that the Badge Scheme can achieve formal recognition as the instrument for verifying compliance.

In the past, the inspection and certification process has been drawn up using British Standards. However, in anticipation of the need to comply with European Norms (ENs), the NCC and SMMT modelled their post 1992 criteria on draft European Standard 1646-1. The drafts for this standard were finally approved in 1998 and since 1st September, 1998, all motorcaravans meeting the criteria bear a revised SMMT/NCC badge. Instead of specifying Code of Practice 201, this is replaced by EN 1646.

A summary of the European Standards now in force are as follows:

EN 1646-1 Leisure Accommodation Vehicles – Motor Caravans – Pt 1 Habitation Requirements.
EN 1646-2 Leisure Accommodation Vehicles – Motor Caravans – Pt 2 Payloads.
EN 721 Leisure Accommodation Vehicles – Safety Ventilation Requirements replacing BS 5601 Pt 1.
EN 1648 – 2 (12v DC installations in motorcaravans) It is the intention of the British Standards Institution (BSI) to publish these in August 1998 and they will replace current BS documents.
EN 1646 – 1 & 2 will replace NCC/SMMT Code of Practice 201.

A further replacement intended for publication in 1999 concerns LPG installation in leisure accommodation vehicles. It is proposed that EN 1949 (LPG installations) will replace BS 5482 part 2.

With regard to constructional elements embraced in EN 1646-1 specified standards include: the rigidity of entry steps, door dimensions, warning notices on childproof locks, bunk and bed detailing, waste water tank capacities, thermal insulation, ventilation, and emergency windows. Fuller descriptions are given in a booklet, 'European Standard for Caravans' which embraces Motorcaravans and Caravan Holiday Homes within its title.

NOTE: *Copies of the booklet,* European Standards for Caravans, *issued August 1998 and compiled by John Lally are available from* Caravan Business Magazine, *7 Marennes Crescent, Brightlingsea, Essex, CO7 0RX.*

Towing brackets

New rulings on the design of towing brackets were intended to take effect from 1st January, 1998. However, the Government's plans were then deferred to late Spring; then they were deferred again and finally put in place on 1st August, 1998.

These rulings are contained in European Directive 94/20/EC and apply to all new light passenger vehicles which carry a European Whole Vehicle Type Approval (EWVTA) Certificate of Conformity and which were first registered on or after 1st August, 1998. This Directive has now been embraced as an amendment within the Road Vehicles (Construction and Use) Regulations 1986. So compliance with the Directive is mandatory and it specifies that only Type Approved towbars can be fitted to the vehicles described above. In the event there are a number of towbars on the market which do not comply.

However, the key point about this directive is that it does not apply to commercial vehicles – which is an important element for almost all motorcaravans. On the other hand, it seems unlikely that motorcaravan base vehicles will remain ever-exempt from requirements of this kind. Ongoing discussions will undoubtedly address this issue.

At least for the time being, fitting only a Type Approved towbar is not an obligation as far as motorcaravanners are concerned. Rather more important is finding a towbar which can be fitted correctly and the problem of underfloor tanks and similar accessories was highlighted in Chapter Nine.

155

Contact addresses

The information given here is to assist readers and both the address and telephone number was correct as at 1st September 1998. In the event of difficulties, details of suppliers and manufacturers are reported in motorcaravan magazines.

Adroit Services,
106 Grosvenor Road,
Rugby,
Warwickshire CV21 3LB
Tel: 01788 333058
(Cruise 2000 Electronic Cruise Control kit)

AER Developments,
10 Westgate,
Ruskington,
Sleaford,
Lincolnshire NG34 9ES
Tel: 01526 833569
(Elevating (rising) roof suppliers/installers)

Airflow (UK) Ltd,
Crown House,
Faraday Road,
Newbury,
Berkshire RG14 2AB
Tel: 01635 569569
(Airflow battery chargers)

AirMuscle Ltd,
12 Orchard Close,
Cranfield,
Bedfordshire MK43 08X
Tel: 01234 750791
(Flexator leveller)

Alde International (UK) Ltd,
Sandfield Close,
Moulton Park,
Northampton NN3 6AB
Tel: 01604 494193
(Central heating systems, Camco antifreeze, Gas leak detector, kitchen systems)

Amber Plastics Ltd,
Broombank Road,
Chesterfield Industrial Estate,
Sheepbridge,
Chesterfield S41 9QJ
Tel: 01246 453544
(Inboard fixed tanks)

AL-KO Kober Ltd,
Queensway,
Royal Leamington Spa,
Warwickshire CV31 3JP
Tel: 01926 466500
(AMC conversions)

Apache Awnings,
C.G.I. Camping,
P.O. Box 373,
Newcastle-under-Lyme,
Staffordshire ST5 3TD
Tel: 01782713099

Apollo Chemicals Ltd,
Sandy Way,
Amington Industrial Estate,
Tamworth,
Staffordshire B77 4DS
Tel: 01827 54281
(Adhesives for repairing delaminated composite panels)

Apollo Motorhomes,
AG Motors,
Cross Street,
Heywood,
Lancashire OL10 2EW
Tel: 01706 628057
(Manufacturer of motorhomes and dismountables)

Assembled Supplies (Electrical) Ltd,
Albany Road,
East Gateshead Industrial Estate,
Tyne and Wear NE8 3AT
Tel: 0191 477 3518
(Non-intrusive water level monitoring system)

Autocruise CH,
Rowms Lane,
Swinton,
Mexborough,
South Yorkshire S64 8AA.
Tel: 01709 571411
(Formerly Cockburn Holdsworth. Manufacturer of coachbuilt models)

Autocraft Motor Caravans,
Fan Road Industrial Estate,
Fan Road,
Staveley,
Chesterfield,
Derbyshire S43 3PT
Tel: 01246 471199
(Motorcaravan conversions, renovation and accessory sales)

Autogas 2000 Ltd *(formerly Tartarini UK Ltd),*
Carlton Miniott,
Thirsk,
North Yorkshire YO7 4NJ
Tel: 01845 523213
(Caratank LPG bulk storage tanks)

Autohomes Motorcaravans – *see Elddis*

Auto Glym,
Works Road,
Letchworth,
Herts SG6 1LU
Tel: 01462-677766
(Interior shampoo and other cleaning products)

Auto-Sleepers
Orchard Works,
Willersey,
Broadway,
Worcestershir WR12 7QF.
Tel: 01386 853338
(Manufacturers of van and coachbuilt conversions)

Auto-Trail,
Unit 1,
Manby Road By-pass,
Immingham,
NE Lincs DN40 2DW.
Tel: 01469 577944
(Manufacturers of van and coachbuilt conversions)

Autovan Services Ltd,
32 Canford Bottom,
Wimborne,
Dorset BH21 2HD
Tel: 01202 848414
(Major body repair and rebuilding work)

Awning World,
Dave Barron Caravans,
Chapel Lane,
Coppull,
Chorley,
Lancashire PR7 4NE
Tel: 01257 793008
(Display and sale of awnings)

Bailey & White Ltd,
2 Corn Kiln Close,
Cogenhoe,
Northampton NN7 1NX
Tel: 01604-890686
(Centinel Clutch Claw and Posts)

Bakers of Cheltenham,
The Quadrangle,
Imperial Square,
Cheltenham,
Gloucestershire GL50 1PZ
Tel: 01242 528844
(Indoor storage specialist, motorcaravan insurance)

A. Baldassarre,
Upholsterer and Coachtrimmer,
103, Coventry Road,
Queens Park,
Bedford MK40 4ES

Tel: 01234 359277
(All types of upholstery work and soft furnishings, foam supplied to order. Edge finishing of removable carpet pieces)

Ashley Banks Ltd,
5 King Street,
Langtoft,
Peterborough PE6 9NF
Tel: 01778 560651
(Suspension unit supplier)

BCA Leisure Ltd,
Unit 7E,
Westfield Mill,
Mytholmroyd,
Hebden Bridge,
West Yorkshire HX7 8SH
Tel: 01422-885266
(Manufacturers of Powerpart mains kits)

Beetles UK Ltd,
The Stables,
Tan House Lane,
Rangeworthy,
South Gloucestershire BS37 7LP
Tel: 01454 228999
(Type 2 VW Brazilian imports)

Belling Appliances,
Talbot Road,
Mexborough,
South Yorkshire S64 8AJ
Tel: 01709 579902
(Belling cookers, hobs and water heaters)

Bessacarr Motorhomes – *see Swift*

Bilbo's Trading Co.,
Eastbourne Road (A22),
South Godstone,
Surrey RH9 8JQ
Tel: 01342 892499
(Complete and partial conversion on new/used Volkswagens)

Blue Diamond Products,
Unit 13,
Bottoms Mill,
Rouse Mill Lane,
Batley,
Yorkshire WF17 5QB
Tel: 01924 420048
(Awning spares and accessories)

BPS Campers,
Portsmouth Road,
Bramshott Chase,

Hindhead,
Surrey GU26 6DE
Tel: 01428 608100
(VW camper renovation and sales)

British Car Auctions Ltd,
Sales & Marketing Department,
Expedier House,
Portsmouth Road,
Hindhead,
Surrey GU26 6TJ
Tel: 01428 607440
(Motorcaravan auctions)

Broadview Blinds, Ltd,
57 Hatchpond Road,
Nuffield Estate,
Poole BH17 OJZ
Tel: 01202-679012
(Omnistor roller blinds)

Brownhills Motorcaravan & Leisure Centre,
A1/A46 Junction,
Newark,
Nottinghamshire NG24 2EA
Tel: 01636 704201
(Supply and fitting of fresh and waste water couplings for American RVs; Fleetwood RVs)

Buccaneer,
Full Sutton,
York YO4 1HS.
Tel: 01759 372325
(Luxury coachbulit motorhomes on Fiat AL KO chassis)

Bulldog Security Products Ltd,
Units 2, 3, & 4,
Stretton Road,
Much Wenlock,
Shropshire TF13 6DH
Tel: 01952-728171/3
(Bulldog security devices and posts)

A.B. Butt Ltd,
Frog Island,
Leicester LE3 5AZ
Tel: 0116 251 3344
(Solar System Supplies)

C.A.K. Tanks,
Caravan Accessories (Kenilworth) Ltd,
10 Princes Drive,
Kenilworth,
Warwickshire CV8 2FD
Tel: 01926 854271
(Inboard fixed tanks and water accessories)

Calira Apparatebau,
Trautmann KG,
Lerchenfeldstr. 9,
87600 Kaufbeuren,
Germany,
Tel: 08341/9764 0
(LED water level gauges)

Calor Gas Ltd,
Athena Drive,
Tachbrook Park,
Warwick CV34 6RL
Tel: 0800 626626
(Supplier of butane, propane and LPG appliances)

The Camping & Caravanning Club,
Greenfields House,
Westwood Way,
Coventry CV4 8JH
Tel: 01203 694995

The Caravan Club
East Grinstead House,
East Grinstead,
West Sussex RH19 1UA
Tel: 01342 326944

E.E. Calver Ltd,
Woodlands Park,
Bedford Road,
Clapham,
Bedford MK41 6EJ
Tel: 01234 359584
(Indoor motorcaravan storage)

Camco Products,
Alde International UK Ltd,
Moulton,
Northampton NN3 6AB
Tel: 01604 494193
(Camco awning cleaner)

Campingaz
Coleman UK Inc.,
Parish Wharf Estate,
Harbour Road,
Portishead,
Bristol BS20 9DA
Tel: 01275 845024
(Supplier of Campingaz butane and LPG appliances)

Camping International Superstore,
Clock Tower House,
Watling Street,
Gillingham,
Kent ME5 7HS
Tel: 01634 577326
(Display and sale of awnings)

Caralux Upholstery,
Amber Buildings,
Meadow Lane,
Alfreton,
Derbyshire DE55 7EZ
Tel: 01773 831242
(Spring interior mattresses, refurbishment services, new foam, composite bonded foam to specification, fabric samples)

Carafax Ltd,
Rotterdam Road,
Sutton Fields Industrial Estate,
Hull HU7 0XD
Tel: 01482 825941
(Caraseal ribbon and cartridge sealants)

Car-A-Tow Ltd,
Unit 1,
565 Blandford Road,
Hamworthy,
Poole,
Dorset BH16 5BW
Tel: 01202 632488
(Car towing frames; solar panels)

Caravan Accessories (Kenilworth) Ltd,
10 Princes Drive,

Kenilworth,
Warwickshire CV8 2FD
Tel: 01926 854271
(Trav L Cool water-evaporative air conditioners, ventilators, cabinet stays and furniture hardware)

The Caravan Seat Cover Centre,
Kings Road,
Brislington,
Bristol BS4 3HH
Tel: 0117-9770797
(Stretch covers, new foam, washable, non-shrink curtains to match covers)

Carver plc,
Engine Lane,
Coppice Side Industrial Estate,
Brownhills,
Walsall,
West Midlands WS8 7ES
Tel: 01543 452122
(Space heating and water heating systems; Carver semi-rigid pipework system; waterline connection and all plumbing accessories)

Classic Leisure Lighting,
Fernwood House,
5, Fernwood Road,
West Midlands, B73 5BG
Tel: 0121 3828093
(Inverter operated lamps)

Compass and Herald Motorhomes,
Explorer Group,
Riverside Industrial Park,
Langley Park,
Durham DH7 9TT
Tel: 01913 730899

Crossley Coachcraft,
Unit 33A, Comet Road,
Moss Side Industrial Estate,
Leyland,
Lancashire PR5 3QN
Tel: 01772 623423
(Major body repair and rebuilding work)

Custom Chrome Ltd,
Seymour Road,
Attleborough,
Nuneaton,
Warwickshire CV11 4JD
Tel: 01203 387808
(Custom exhausts for special vehicles)

Customer Enquiries (Vehicles),
DVLA,
Swansea SA99 1BL
Tel: 01792 772134
(Guidance on vehicle registration)

W. David & Sons Ltd,
Denington Industrial Estate,
Wellingborough,
Northamptonshire NN8 2QP
Tel: 01933 227186
(Isopon resin and filler paste)

Design Developments,
Mulberry House,
Mulberry Lane,

Cosham,
Portsmouth,
Hampshire PO6 2QU
Tel: 01705 37977
(Barry Stimson design consultant and motorcaravan manufacturer)

Devon Motorcaravans,
Mainsforth Road,
Ferryhill,
County Durham DL17 9DE
Tel: 01740 655700
(Manufacturer of panel van conversions; accident repairs)

Driftgate 2000 Ltd,
Little End Road,
Eaton Socon,
Cambridgeshire PE19 3JH
Tel: 01480-470400
(Manufacturers of XCell Mains inverters)

Drivelodge Motorhomes,
Unit A,
Airedale Trading Park,
Crosshills,
Keighley,
Yorkshire BD20 7DS
Tel: 01535 637777
(Manufacturer of panel van conversions)

Driverite Ltd,
Unit 10,
Parkmore Industrial Estate,
Long Mile Road,
Dublin 12,
Ireland.
Tel: 00353 1 450 7833
(Air Suspension Manufacturer)

Dudleys American Motorhomes,
A415 Abingdon Road,
Ducklington,
Witney,
Oxon OX8 7XA.
Tel: 01993 703774/774040
(Importers of Coachmen, Safari, Trail Wagon and Winnebago American motorhomes)

Elddis,
Delves Lane,
Consett,
Co Durham DH8 7LG.
Tel: 01207 503477
(Manufacturer of Autohomes van conversions and coachbuilts and Elddis coachbuilts)

Elecsol Europe Ltd,
47 First Avenue,
Deeside Industrial Park,
Deeside,
Flintshire CH5 2LG
Tel: 0800 163298
(Elecsol batteries)

Electrical Contractors Association (ECA),
3 Buenavista Gardens,
Glenholt,
Plymouth
Tel: 01752 700981

Electrolux Leisure Appliances,
PO Box 88,
Oakley Road,
Luton,
Bedfordshire LU4 9QQ
Tel: 01582-494111
(Trimline roller blinds, air conditioners and refrigerators)

Euro Motor Campers Ltd,
Lamb Inn Road,
Racca Green,
Knottingley,
West Yorkshire WF11 8AU
Tel: 01977 676028
(High-top supplier and fitter; accessory specialist)

Europa Specialist Spares,
Fauld Industrial Park,
Tutbury,
Burton upon Trent,
Staffordshire DE13 9HR
Tel: 01283 815609
(Vehicle trims, light clusters, and all specialist vehicle parts)

Eurovent UK,
17 Wentworth Drive,
Nuneaton,
Warwickshire CV11 6LZ
Tel: 01203 329033
(Eurovent Awnings)

Exide Leisure Batteries Ltd,
Gate No. 3,
Pontyfelin Industrial Estate,
New Road,
Pontypool NP4 5DG
Tel: 01495 750075
(Exide Leisure Batteries)

Fiamma water pumps and water tanks
Contact your motorcaravan dealers for Fiamma products.

Flavel Leisure,
Clarence Street,
Leamington Spa,
Warwickshire CV31 2AD
Tel: 01926 427027
(Flavel cookers and hobs)

Adrian Flux Insurance,
126 London Road,
Kings Lynn,
Norfolk PE30 5ES
Tel: 01553 777888
(Insurance of kit cars and conversions)

Foam for Comfort Ltd,
Unit 2,
Wyther Lane Trading Estate,
Wyther Lane,
Kirkstall,
Leeds LS5 3BT
Tel: 0113-274 8100
(New foam, composite bonded foam to specification, stretch covers, upholstered covers)

Franks Caravan Spares,
16/27 Wigmore Street,
Stopsley,
Luton,
Bedfordshire LU2 8AA.

Tel: 01582 732168
(Caravan breakers and sales)

Gardner of Wakefield Ltd,
76 Wakefield Road,
Flushdyke,
Ossett,
West Yorkshire W5 9JX
Tel: 01924 265367
(Portable showers and water container protective covers)

Gibson Insurance
170 Green Street,
Enfield,
Middlesex EN3 7LB
Tel: 0181 805 7490
(Motorcaravan insurance)

Grade UK Ltd,
3 Central Court,
Finch Close,
Lenton Lane Industrial Estate,
Nottingham NG7 2NN
Tel: 0115 986 7151
(Gaslow Detectors; Status TV aerials and accessories)

Grayston Engineering Ltd,
115 Roebuck Road,
Chessington,
Surrey KT9 1JZ
Tel: 0181 9741122
(Spring assister kits)

Hella Ltd,
Wildmere Industrial Estate,
Banbury,
Oxfordshire OX16 7JU
Tel: 01295 272233
(Hella Towing electrical Eequipment)

Herald Motorhomes – *see Compass*

Richard Holdsworth,
PO Box 2603,
Reading,
Berkshire RG4 6FG
Tel: 0118 9695919
(Importer of La Strada panel van conversions built by Baumgartner-Reisemobile of Germany)

Hope Technical Developments Ltd,
High Street,
Ascot,
Berkshire SL5 7HP
Tel: 01344 624855
(Motorcycle racks and towing brackets)

Hornchurch Motor Caravan Centre,
5–7 Broadway Parade,
Elm Avenue,
Hornchurch,
Essex RM12 4RS
Tel: 01708 444791/443782
(Custom-made roof racks, cycle racks, motorcycle racks and ladders)

Indespension Ltd,
Belmont Road,
Bolton,
Lancashire BL1 7AQ

Tel: 0800 720720
(The Indespension Towing Manual)

Index Marine,
Clump Farm Industrial Estate,
Blandford,
Dorset DT11 7TE
Tel: 01258 452398
(TV coaxial cable external couplings)

Island Plastics,
Prospect Road,
Cowes,
Isle of Wight PO31 7AD
Tel: 01983 292451
(Manufacturer of Citroën Romahome and Renault St Michel motorcaravans)

J & M Designs,
'Broadgates',
Bank Street,
Cleckheaton,
West Yorkshire BD19 5EP
Tel: 01274-872151
(Hacienda Awnings and Silver Screens insulated window covers)

Johns Cross Conversions,
Unit 3,
Rutherford Business Park,
Marley Lane,
Battle,
East Sussex TN33 OHZ
Tel: 01424 774414
(Manufacturer of Daihatsu-based micro coachbuilt and other conversions)

Jo-Jo UK Ltd,
7 Morris Close,
Park Farm Industrial Estate,
Wellingborough,
Northamptonshire NN8 6XF
Tel: 01933 675333
(Pocket-sized tyre inflators)

Just Kampers,
77 Lynchford Road,
Farnborough,
Hampshire,
GU14 6EJ
Tel: 01252 371331
(VW Camper and Transporter parts 1968–1992)

KCI Ltd (S.V.A. Guide),
Norfolk Lodge,
Balcombe Road,
Crawley,
West Sussex RH10 3NJ
(Guide to Single Vehicle Approval regulations; A Guide to Kit Cars and the SVA)

Kenlowe Ltd,
Burchetts Green,
Maidenhead,
Berkshire SL6 6QU
Tel: 01628 823303
(PROwatt Inverters; radiator cooling fans and automatic transmission oil coolers)

Kit Fit,
Redmay Industrial Estate,

Church Lane,
South Scarle,
Newark,
Nottinghamshire NG23 7JP
Tel: 01636 893453
(Supplier of refurbished car components)

LabCraft Ltd,
Bilton Road,
Waterhouse Lane,
Chelmsford,
Essex CM1 2UP
Tel: 01245 359888
(TP2 battery box, lighting units)

Leisure Accessories Ltd,
Britannia Works,
Hurricane Way,
Airport Industrial Estate,
Norwich NR6 6EY
Tel: 01603 414551
(Qest Plumbing and Shurflo Pumps)

Lomax Motor Company Ltd,
Endurance Works,
Maypole Fields,
Cradley,
Halesowen,
West Midlands B63 2QB
Tel: 01384 410910
(Supplier of Rickman Rancher Kits)

Lowdham Leisureworld,
Lowdham Road (A6097),
Gunthorpe,
Nottingham NG14 7ES
Tel: 0114 9663838
(Importers of Laika coachbuilts from Italy)

Lunar,
Sherdley Road,
Lostock Hall,
Preston,
Lancashire PR5 5JF
Tel: 01772 337628
(Manufacturer of coachbuilt motorhomes)

Machzone,
Unit 1,
Eagle Terrace,
Cleveland Street,
Hulll HU8 7BJ
Tel: 01482 212208
(Manufacturer of coachbuilt and A-class motorhomes; coachbuilt body shells supplied)

Madisons,
Blackpool Road,
Clifton,
Preston,
Lancashire PR4 OXN
Tel: 01772 684619
(Importers of Hyme and Niesmann+Bischoff models from Germany; suppliers of the Super Nova luxury coach from Ultra-Mobile)

Marlec Engineering Ltd,
Rutland House,
Trevithick Road,
Corby,
Northamptonshire NN17 5XY

Tel: 01536 201588
(Wind and Solar systems)

Magnum Mobiles and Caravan Surplus,
Unit 9A,
Cosalt Industrial Estate,
Convamore Road,
Grimsby DN32 9JL
Tel: 01472 353520
(Caravan/Motorcaravan Surplus Stock)

Marquis Motorhome Centre,
Winchester Road,
Lower Upham,
Southampton SO32 1HA
Tel 01489 860666
(Hire and buy scheme)

Maxview,
Common Lane,
Setchey,
King's Lynn,
Norfolk PE33 0AT
Tel: 01553 810376
(Maxview TV aerials)

Merlin Equipment,
Unit 1, Hithercroft Court,
Lupton Road,
Wallingford,
Oxfordshire OX10 9BT
Tel: 01491 824333
(PROwatt Inverters)

Mer Products Ltd,
Whitehead House,
120 Beddington Lane,
Croydon,
Surrey CRO 4TD
Tel: 0181 401 0002
(Distributor of Mer Car Care products)

Morco Products Ltd,
59 Beverley Road,
Hull HU3 1XW
Tel: 01482 325456
(Instantaneous Water Heaters)

Motorcaravan Insurance Agency,
34 New Street,
St. Neots,
Huntingdon,
Cambridgeshire PE19 1NQ
Tel: 01480 218273
(Insurance of private conversions)

The Motor Caravanners' Club,
22 Evelyn Close,
Twickenham,
Middlesex TW2 7BN
Tel: 0181 8933883

The Motor Caravan Information Service,
Maxwelton House,
Boltro Road,
Haywards Heath,
West Sussex RH16 1BJ
Tel: 01444 453399

Munster Simms Engineering Ltd,
Old Belfast Road,
Bangor BT19 1LT
Northern Ireland.
Tel: 01247 270531

(Whale semi-rigid pipework system, Aqua source connection and all plumbing accessories)

Murvi Motor Caravans
4 East Way,
Lee Mill Industrial Estate,
Ivybridge,
Devon PL21 9PE
Tel: 01752 892200
(Manufacturer of panel van conversions and business/leisure vehicles)

The National Caravan Council,
Catherine House,
Victoria Road,
Aldershot,
Hampshire GU11 1SS
Tel: 01252 318251

National Inspection Council for Electrical Installation Contracting,
(NICEIC)
Vintage House,
36–37 Albert Embankment,
London SE1 7UJ
Tel: 0171 582 7746
(Certification to confirm a caravan is correctly wired for mains electricity)

Niche Marketing,
Park House,
Park Lane,
Manby,
Lincolnshire LN11 8UF
Tel: 01507 327172
(Importers of Adventure RV Mfg dismountable and fifth wheel models from USA)

NR Components (Todmorden) Ltd,
Der Street,
Todmorden,
Lancashire OL14 5QY
Tel: 01706-815821
(NR Awnings)

Nu Venture Motorhomes,
Unit 2,
Seven Stars Road,
Wigan,
Lancashire WN3 5AT
Tel: 01942 494090
(Motorcaravan conversions on new or second-hand vehicles)

On Two Wheels,
Phoenix Way,
Garngoch Industrial Estate,
Gorseinon,
Swansea SA4 1GZ
Tel: 01792 224470
(Distributor of Crystal Glo Acrylic Wash and Polishes)

Peter Miller Leisure,
4 Laburnham Avenue,
Mildenhall,
Bury St. Edmunds,
Suffolk IP28 7PL
Tel: 01638 716206
(GLOBE satellite aerial, mast system, 12v receivers in both analogue and digital systems)

Perkson Ltd,
PO Box 8,

The Hayes,
Lye,
Stourbridge,
West Midlands DY9 8NS
Tel: 01384 424984
(Keep-It security devices and posts)

PGR Products Ltd,
16 Crofton Road,
Lincoln,
Lincolnshire LN3 4NL
Tel: 01522 534538
(Sectional TV mast, wheel clamps)

Phoenix Power & Equipment Ltd,
14–30 Middleton Street,
Beeston,
Nottingham NG9 1BB
Tel: 0115 9436156
(Generator specialist)

Pilote UK,
PO Box 38,
Wednesbury,
West Midlands WS10 8UL
(Coachbuilt and A-class motorhomes from France)

CEC Plug-In-Systems,
Grange Park Lane,
Willerby,
Hull HU10 6EQ
Tel: 01482 652523
(Low voltage control components, water level sensors and gauges, IDM2 electronic alarm)

P.E.L.,
Unit 2, Rectory Farm Business Park,
Meppershall Road,
Upper Stondon,
Bedfordshire SG16 6LJ
Tel: 01462 851454
(Manufacturers of power box Inverters)

Pyramid Products Ltd,
Unit 1,
Victoria Street,
Mansfield,
Nottinghamshire NG18 5RR
Tel: 01623-421277
(Patriot wheel clamp and accessories)

Rancher Owners' Club
Rancher Register,
Gazebo,
Newton Lane,
Whiteparish,
Salisbury,
Wiltshire SP5 2QQ

Reinforced Constructions,
Unit 2 & 2A,
Beaumont Street,
Oadby,
Leicester LE2 4DB
Tel: 0116 2718391
(Bak-Paka rear mount storage boxes)

Remis UK,
1 Manor Close,
Great Harrowden,
Wellingborough,
Northamptonshire NN9 5AG
(Remis blinds and flyscreens)

RT Marshall,
Woodside Industrial Estate,
Bayton,
Kidderminster,
Worcestershire DY14 9NE
Tel: 01299 832533
(Motorcaravan satellite TV systems)

Ryder Towing Equipment Ltd,
Mancunian Way,
Ardwick,
Manchester M12 6HW
Tel: 0161 2735619
(Electrical towing equipment & 'The Practical Guide to Towbar Electrics')

Safe and Secure Products Ltd,
Chestnut House,
Chesley Hill,
Wick,
Bristol BS30 5NE
Tel: 0117-937 4737
(SAS security devices and posts)

Secure Direct,
43/44 High Street,
Pelsall,
Walsall WS3 4LT
Tel: 01922 686100
(Insurance of kit cars and conversions)

SF Detection Ltd,
Hatch Pond House,
4 Stinsford Road,
Nuffield Industrial Estate,
Poole,
Dorset BH17 0RZ
Tel: 01202 665330
(SF330 Carbon monoxide detector)

Sika Ltd,
Watchmead,
Welwyn Garden City,
Hertfordshire AL7 1BQ
Tel: 01707 394444
(Sikaflex Cartridge Sealants)

The Society of Motor Manufacturers and Traders,
Trade Sections Department,
Forbes House,
Halkin Street,
London SW1X 7DS
Tel: 0171 2357000
(Information on the Motorcaravan Annual Habitation Service Check)

Sold Secure Trust,*
Block 36,
Police Headquarters,
Ponteland,
Newcastle-upon-Tyne NE20 0BL
Tel: 01661 868446
(Sold Secure product list)
* Service may be temporarily suspended pending trust reorganisation

Somar Transtec,
Unit 33,
Northwick Business Centre,
Blockley,
Gloucestershire GL56 9RF
Tel: 01386 700127
(Power assisted steering specialists)

Speedograph Richfield Ltd,
104 Rolleston Drive,
Arnold,
Nottingham NG5 7JR
Tel: 0115 926 4235
(Cab seating and re-upholstery service)

Stain Devils Information Service,
107-111 Fleet Street,
London EC4A 2AB
Tel: 0171 353 4499
(Guidance on stain removal)

Starcraft Owners' & Social Club,
Mr M. Clarke
2 Rose Cottage,
Power Station Road,
Stourport-on-Severn,
Worcestershire DY13 9PF
Tel: 01299 826529

Stoves plc,
Stoney Lane,
Prescot,
Merseyside L35 2XW
Tel: 0151 426 6551
(Stoves, cookers and hobs)

Superpitch,
Conduit Road,
Conduit Industrial Estate,
Norton Canes,
Cannock,
Staffordshire WS11 3TJ
Tel: 01543 270987
(Superpitch motorcaravan conversion accessories)

Swift and Bessacarr Motorhomes,
The Swift Group,
Dunswell Road,
Cottingham,
Hull HU16 4JX
Tel: 01482 847332
(Manufacturers of high to and coachbuilt motorhomes)

SVO,
Redman Road,
Porte Marsh Industrial Estate,
Calne,
Wiltshire SN11 9PR
Tel: 01249 815141
(Power assisted steering installations)

Symonspeed Ltd,
Cleveland Garage,
1 Cleveland Road,
Torquay,
Devon TQ2 5BD
Tel: 01803 214620
(Air suspension specialist)

TB Turbo Ltd,
Turbo House,
Port Royal Avenue
Off Willow Lane,
Lancaster LA1 5QP
Tel: 01524 67157
(Turbo charging conversion and Intercoolers)

TEK Seating Ltd,
Unit 28-32,
Pate Road,
Leicester Road Industrial Estate,
Melton Mowbray,
Leicestershire LE13 0RG
Tel: 01664 480689
(Cab seating)

Tockfield Ltd,
Pitt Lane,
Shirland,
Nr. Alfreton,
Derbyshire DE55 6AT
Tel: 01773 834968
(Spring interior mattresses, refurbishment services, new foam, composite bonded foam, fabric samples)

Tracker Network (UK) Ltd,
106 Oxford Road,
Uxbridge,
Middlesex UB8 1NA
Tel: 01895 234567
(Tracker stolen vehicle recovery system)

Travelworld American Motorhomes,
Stafford Road,
Wolverhampton WV10 6HL
Tel: 01902 420724
(Importers of Gulf Stream Coach and Monaco American motorhomes)

Truma UK,
Truma House,
Rolleston Trading Estate,
Hawkins Lane,
Burton-upon-Trent,
Staffordshire DE14 1PT
Tel: 01283 511883
(Space heating and water heating systems; Atwood spares)

Trylon Ltd,
Thrift Street,
Wollaston,
Northamptonshire NN29 7QJ
Tel: 01933 664275
(Supplier of products and guidance on laminated glass fibre techniques)

Unique Furnishings Ltd,
Station Road,
Castle Donington,
Derbyshire DE74 2NJ
Tel: 01332 814144
(Upholstered covers, new foam, spring interiors, curtains and soft furnishings)

Ultimate Design,
37 Pytchley Road,
Kettering,
Northamptonshire NN15 6ND
Tel: 01536 514400
(Cruise control kits; security systems)

Van Bitz,
Cornish Farm,
Shoreditch,
Taunton,
Somerset TA3 7BS
Tel: 01823-321992
(Strikeback motorcaravan security systems)

VanGuard Security,
36 King Harold Road,
Colchester,
Essex CO3 4SE
Tel: 01206 768356
(VanGuard Battery Mate)

Van Window Specialists,
Unit 4,
Riverside Works,
Methley Road,
Castleford,
West Yorkshire
Tel: 01977 552929
(Made to measure windows, supply and fit)

Vehicle & Marine Window Co.,
Victoria Street,
Birmingham B9 5AA
Tel: 0121 772 6307
(Window manufacturers, fitters and suppliers)

W4 Ltd,
Unit B,
Ford Lane Industrial Estate,
Arundel,
West Sussex BN18 0DF
Tel: 01243 553355
(Suppliers of 230v kits, double-pole switched sockets, and socket testers, ribbon sealants)

Watling Engineers Ltd,
88 Park Street Village,
nr. St. Albans,
Hertfordshire AL2 2LR
Tel: 01727 873661
(Specially designed towing brackets)

Westcroft American Motorhomes
Cannock Road,
Westcroft,
Wolverhampton WV10 8QU
Tel: 01902 731324
(Importers of Allegro, Cobra, Damon and Rockwood American motorhomes)

Whale – *see Munster Simms*

Welland Holiday Hire & Sales,
Postland Road,
Crowborough,
Peterborough PE6 0JB,
Tel: 01733 210560
(Display and sale of awnings)

Witter Towbars,
18 Canal Side,
Chester CH1 3LL
Tel: 01244 341166
(Towbar systems and cycle carriers)

Woodfit Ltd,
Kem Mill,
Whittle-le-Woods,
Chorley,
Lancashire PR6 7EA
Tel: 01257 266421
(Hinges, fittings, hardware, wire storage baskets and catches)

Woolies,
off Blenheim Way,
Northfields Industrial Estate,
Market Deeping,
Peterborough PE6 8LD
Tel: 01778 347347
(Trim, accessories and window rubbers)

Young Conversions,
Unit 47,
Barton Road,
Water Eaton,
Bletchley,
Milton Keynes,
Buckinghamshire MK2 3BD
Tel: 01908 639936
(Full or part conversions on any base vehicle; specialists in one-off designs to customer specification)

ZIG Electronics,
Phoenix Works,
Thrupp,
Stroud,
Gloucestershire GL5 2BU
Tel: 01453 731700 01527 556
(Low voltage control components, chargers, water level sensors and gauges)

Index

Acknowledgements

This manual touches on many technical subjects and to ensure accuracy in words and illustrations, a large number of specialists proof-read either the entire manuscript or particular specialist sections.

The author and publishers would like to thank the following:

Stuart Craig (Editor, *Which Motorcaravan*)
Peter Frost (The Camping & Caravanning Club)
Nick Harding (Freelance motorcaravan writer)
John Hunt (Consultant Editor, *Motorcaravan Motorhome Monthly*)
Mike Jago (Editor, *Motorcaravan Motorhome Monthly*)
John Parsons (The Caravan Club)
Colin Reay (The Motor Caravanners' Club)
David Whitehead (formerly of the National Caravan Council)

Specialist Sections
Gordon Carson (Whale Products)
John Corbett (Carver Products)
Hugh Lamberton (Electrolux Products)
Peter Lievers (Truma Products)
Richard Miller-Mead (AL-KO Kober Products)
Steve Rowe (Motor Caravan Magazine)
Peter Swanborough (Plug-In-Systems)
Michael Williams (AutoGlym)

Photographs and Illustrations
Front cover shot supplied by Bessacarr Motorhomes, East Yorkshire.
(Bessacarr Motorhomes is a member of the Swift Group)
Auto-Trail Ltd.
Geoff Denney (Geoff Denney Associates)
Barry Stimson (Design Developments)
Janette Lavery (Practical Caravan)
Gary Martin (Editor, *Motor Caravan Magazine*)
Steve Rowe (*Motor Caravan Magazine*)

Additional Assistance
Anthony and Charles Trevelyan (Auto-Sleepers)
Michael Leete (Electrolux)